"A Proper Player"

A Tribute to
John Sheridan

By E. J. Huntley

Published by youbooks.co.uk

Printed by Pickards.org.uk,
11 Riverside Park, Sheaf Gardens, Sheffield S2 4BB
Telephone 0114 275 7222 or 275 7444
Facsimile 0114 275 8866

Published by
youbooks.co.uk

Front Cover:
An illustration by Gary Mackender of
John Sheridan in his Sheffield Wednesday playing days,

Back Cover:
An electronic painting by Gary Mackender of
John Sheridan, the Chesterfield manager.

Introduction

John Sheridan was without doubt one of the most gifted ball-playing midfielders of his generation. At all the clubs he represented he was the man that made the side tick.

Sheridan was like a chess player; forever several moves ahead of the game. He was particularly adept at finding space. In fact his movement was impeccable, always making himself available to receive the ball, and when he received it he always had enough time to control it, look up and invariably make a telling pass, long or short with unerring precision, without any other opposition player getting near him. His instinctive awareness of the position of players around him and economical use of a football was such that he rarely gave the ball away, while his vision and quick-thinking split countless defences to create innumerable chances for his grateful team-mates over the course of his twenty-two year professional career. Blessed with a powerful shot, Sheridan also scored over one hundred League and Cup goals himself, with spectacular free-kicks being a particular speciality.

The teams he played for were always better with him in it. At Leeds he was the one beacon of light that shone in their colours throughout their long hibernation in the old Second Division during the 1980s under first Eddie Gray (who gave him his debut aged eighteen) and then Billy Bremner. In 1987 he helped the club to within minutes of both an FA Cup Final and a return to the top flight and was also Leeds top scorer in the League for two consecutive seasons from midfield.

Although Sheridan was allowed to leave Elland Road at the end of Howard Wilkinson's first season in charge this was never a reflection on Sheridan's ability. Wilkinson was a self-confessed disciple of a more physical and direct style of play and a player of Sheridan's flamboyant gifts was simply not his sort of player. The fact that Wilkinson replaced Sheridan with Wimbledon hard-man Vinnie Jones really says it all.

Sheridan left Leeds United after over two-hundred and fifty games and over fifty goals and headed to Nottingham Forest where he endured a nightmare three months playing, or rather not playing, for Brian Clough. Salvation arrived in the form of Sheffield Wednesday boss Ron Atkinson who spent £500,000 to bring Sheridan to Hillsborough, arguably the best money the South Yorkshire club ever spent.

Although Sheridan was unable to prevent Wednesday's relegation from the old First Division (on goal difference) at the end of his first season with the club, the Owls would bounce straight back the following season, with Sheridan the key man. Sheridan was the only man to play in every League game during Wednesday's 1990-91 promotion campaign and of course it was his half volleyed winner that secured Wednesday's League Cup triumph against Alex Ferguson's Manchester United that same year – the Owls' only major trophy of the last seventy-six years and counting.

His great form continued when the Owls returned to the top flight in 1991-92 under Trevor Francis as the Owls finished third in Division One, just seven points behind Champions Leeds, and qualified for Europe. The following season he played his part in guiding Wednesday to both domestic finals where they were unfortunate to lose on both occasions to Arsenal.

It was at Hillsborough that Sheridan played the best football of his career and he would perform stylishly for Wednesday until 1996 when David Pleat (who had replaced Francis and inexplicably tried to offload the remaining stalwarts of the previous regime), mindlessly first mothballed him in the reserves, loaned him out to Birmingham (for whom he played in the League Cup Semi-Final against Leeds United) and then finally allowed him to leave the South Yorksire club, releasing him far too early in the unanimous view of the Hillsborough faithful. It is surely no coincidence that Sheridan's departure coincided with Wednesday's slalom down the Leagues.

Sheridan moved to Bolton Wanderers where he helped Colin Todd's men win the First Division Championship by a record margin in 1997. Although a knee injury that would plague the rest of his career kept him out of much of his second season with the Wanderers his eventual return to their side almost, though not quite, kept them in the Premiership (they would go down on goal difference).

After a brief spell in the Conference with Doncaster Rovers, Sheridan pitched up at Oldham Athletic, ostensibly to help his old friend and former Leeds team-mate Andy Ritchie, on a short term basis. Instead Sheridan ended up playing over 150 games for the Latics to prolong his career for a further six years before his damaged knee finally forced him to hang up his boots first in 2003 and then, following an unexpected comeback, again in 2004.

He then turned to coaching, learning his trade in Oldham's Youth and Reserve teams before finally taking over as their First Team manager in 2006, and led his team to the League One play-offs in his first season in charge before a run of poor results cost him his job in March 2009. His spell out of the game, however, lasted barely three months when he was appointed manager of Chesterfield in June.

But for several serious injuries – a broken leg for Leeds in 1983, knee and then groin problems that interrupted his Wednesday career between 1992 and 1994 and further knee problems in 1997-98 whilst playing for Bolton – he would have undoubtedly have played more games. Despite these setbacks he would still finish his career having played over seven-hundred League and Cup games, scoring over one hundred goals.

In addition to his success and longevity at club level he also played thirty-four times for the Republic of Ireland, appearing in the Quarter-Finals against hosts Italy in the 1990 World Cup and starting all four of Ireland's games at the 1994 tournament in USA.

Sheridan's was a career that most players would only dream about, and it says a great deal about his ability and popularity wherever he played that he was always given a hero's welcome whenever he returned to one of his former clubs either as a player or as a manager.

Never was this better illustrated than when he returned to Hillsborough in 2003. It was his first League game after re-registering as an Oldham player to solve a massive player shortage. Sheridan was approaching his 39th birthday, had only one good knee (which had already caused his first retirement), hadn't played a game for twelve months and hadn't trained in five months. Even then he still passed Wednesday off the park and it says much for his impact at Sheffield Wednesday that when he scored a penalty after only three minutes his goal was applauded by both sets of supporters and at the end of the game he was given an ovation from all four sides of the ground.

Most professional footballers struggle to become bona fide legends at one club let alone two, let alone three. John Sheridan the player is revered to this day by fans of Leeds United, Sheffield Wednesday and Oldham Athletic and, having recently guided Chesterfield to the Division Two title, Sheridan might even become a legend at a fourth club, this time as a manager, if he hasn't already.

This is a tribute to his career.

Chapter One

John Joseph Sheridan was born 1st October, 1964, the eldest of six brothers to Dublin-born parents, Patrick and Dinah. He attended St Mary's School in Manchester and grew up in Stretford.

Sheridan wanted to be a footballer from a very early age and was selected for his Under-11 school side at the age of seven.

Despite growing up underneath the shadow of Old Trafford, Sheridan supported Manchester City as a boy and dreamed of emulating their midfield fulcrum, Colin Bell.

Sheridan did actually play for City's junior sides from the age of eleven and sixteen (signing schoolboy forms with the club when he was fourteen) and attended training sessions at the club's facilities in Cheadle alongside future City stars Andy May and Steve Kinsey.

Although he would later make his name as a ball-playing midfield schemer, Sheridan actually started out as a striker. "I played centre forward in my younger days," Sheridan explained, "and strange as it sounds my legs went when I was fourteen and I reverted to midfield."

Despite being abundantly blessed with talent, Sheridan would later admit that he did not always take things as seriously as he might have done whilst at City.

"I think the coaching staff thought I had the talent to make the grade but my attitude was all wrong as a kid," he later reflected. "I was more interested in hanging around with my mates than preparing myself for a career in soccer so, looking back, it was probably no surprise that City didn't take me on as an apprentice."

"I suppose they might have taken me on if I'd shown the right attitude. But I have no regrets. It was a lesson learned. I kept missing training and you can't expect to win favour if you do things like that. My advice to kids is that you've got to have the right approach to the game."

After being released by City Sheridan began playing for local amateur side, Stretford Victoria on Sundays and it was then that fate and good fortune intervened.

John's younger brother Darren, who was then an apprentice at Leeds (he had signed schoolboy forms in January), put his elder sibling's name forward for a trial. A scout was duly despatched to watch Stretford Victoria, Sheridan scored a hat-trick and the next thing he knew he was at Elland Road, sharing digs with fellow youth teamers Denis Irwin, Tommy Wright and Scott Sellars.

On 6th March 1982, Sheridan made his first appearance in a Leeds shirt when he lined up for the Juniors in a 3-2 win against Hartlepool and a fortnight later he scored in a 2-0 win against Darlington.

Sheridan had performed well in the two games, so well in fact that he was immediately offered a year's contract as an apprentice: "I bit their hands off," Sheridan recalled. "Allan Clarke was manager and Martin Wilkinson was his assistant and Martin, in particular, was great for me. It was a matter for me of buckling down. I always had the ability, but ability alone doesn't always get you very far. I was helped along in that regard by Keith Mincher, the youth team manager, and I blossomed from there."

After only two games for the Juniors, Sheridan was promoted to the Reserve side and ironically made his Central League debut against Sheffield Wednesday on 24th March. Despite the presence of another future international, David Seaman in their goal, Leeds were beaten 3-0.

Sheridan continued to play for both the Juniors and the Reserves for the rest of the season and it wasn't long before his displays had attracted the attention of the selectors of the Republic of Ireland (for whom he was eligible to play via parental qualification), earning his first clutch of Irish Youth caps.

Even though Sheridan had been born in Manchester there was never any question of him playing for the country of his birth. "I have always classed myself as Irish," Sheridan explained many years later, "all my family and relatives are from there."

*****

Although Sheridan had made enormous strides during these early stages of his career the club he had joined had been on a long inexorable slide downwards prior to his arrival culminating in their relegation at the end of the 1981-82 season.

The greats of the Revie era had drifted away one by one and in most cases had never been adequately replaced. Manager Allan Clarke by common consent had spent money unwisely in the transfer market but even then Leeds could still boast virtually an entire team of internationals such as Brian Greenhoff, Frank Worthington, Peter Barnes, Trevor Cherry (England), Derek Parlane, Arthur Graham, Kenny Burns, Frank and Eddie Gray (Scotland), and Brian Flynn (Wales) and England Under-21 international keeper John Lukic.

Despite this wealth of experience, Leeds were hovering just above the relegation zone in the First Division when Sheridan arrived in March 1982. Even so it seemed almost unthinkable that the mighty Leeds would actually lose their top flight status. Leeds were goal shy, yes, but Elland Road remained virtually impregnable. In fact, when they lost at home to Ipswich in February it was the first time Clarke's men had been beaten at home for eleven months.

Following the Ipswich defeat Leeds could only win four of their next twenty games and yet despite this they still went into their last fixture of the 1981-82 season – away at West Bromwich Albion – with their fate still in their own hands. Unfortunately the Baggies' 2-0 win (in a game that was marred by rioting Leeds fans) meant it was they who stayed up with 44 points. Leeds were now on 42 and could still have escaped the drop had the Baggies then beaten Stoke in their final fixture. Instead Stoke romped home 3-0 winners and Leeds were duly relegated to the second tier of English football for the first time since 1964. The man who had bought Sheridan to the club was relieved of his duties, though not before signing the young Mancunian on full professional terms.

Instead of a more established managerial replacement for Clarke, the club turned to Eddie Gray, much to the Scot's surprise. With the club in the direst of financial straits, Gray was the cheapest option; since he was already on the playing staff – appointing him in a dual capacity would only involve the club forking out an extra £5000.

Gray's 'to do' list was short: get Leeds back into the top flight as soon as possible and, since the club were reportedly £2million in debt and facing a certain decline in revenue as a result of their relegation, slash the wage bill.

On the face of it, Gray's two-fold brief appeared mutually incompatible. How was the manager supposed to field a side, let alone mount a credible promotion charge, if he sold his so-called star or at least most experienced (and therefore highest-earning) players? And if the club needed the money to finance their debts how was he supposed to replace the players he would have to let go?

The reality was somewhat different, however. Although the likes of Trevor Cherry, Frank Worthington, Peter Barnes and Brian Flynn had all been superlative players in their day, and, in the case of Cherry and Flynn, excellent Leeds servants. Without wishing to be brutally unkind, their best days were now behind them, and in addition these were among the players who had not only taken the club down, but, unmotivated by Second Division football, also wanted away. By all accounts morale was dangerously low at Elland Road as the club faced up to life in Division Two, with cliques having formed and many of the players openly bickering amongst each other.

By December, virtually all the deadwood and more besides had been cleared out. Greenhoff had been given a free transfer in the summer and pitched up as player-coach at Rochdale, winger Carl Harris was sold to Charlton for £100,000, Derek Parlane and Peter Barnes were shipped out on loan (to Hong Kong side Bulova and Spanish side Real Betis respectively), Flynn joined Burnley (for £60,000) in November, Worthington joined Sunderland (for £50,000) and club captain Cherry left to take up the player-manager's role at Bradford City for £10,000 (one League appearance for Leeds shy of four-hundred).

Despite being shorn of over half of his squad and without funds available to buy replacements, Gray was fortunate on two counts. Firstly, a nucleus of experienced players remained such as John Lukic, the manager's younger brother Frank, Kenny Burns, Paul Hart, Arthur Graham and the manager himself and secondly Leeds' reserve and youth team was stocked with the sort of talent that most clubs would have given their high teeth for: alongside Sheridan, Wright, Irwin and Sellars there was also Neil Aspin, Terry Phelan and future England keeper David Seaman (although the latter was allowed to join Peterborough in August for £4,000 because the manager saw John Lukic as his first choice keeper and didn't wish to stand in the way of Seaman's desire for first team football).

Despite these positives, Leeds were clearly in a transitional phase and it would take time for Gray to fashion the materials at his disposal into credible genuine promotion candidates. Time was something the new manager didn't really have. As it remains to this day, the second tier of English football is a notoriously hard division to get out of, particularly for teams relegated from the top flight. Leeds would be handicapped by teams visiting Elland Road desperate to put one over on such an iconic team. What Leeds really needed was a settled team with bags of experience and no small amount of muscle in key areas: a proven goal scorer and a manager with knowledge of what was required to get out of the second tier. Probably more than anything what Leeds needed was an esprit de corps, a squad of players who not only wanted to play for the team (rather than themselves) but were also prepared to roll up their sleeves and pull in the same direction throughout the long season. The sad fact of the matter is that Leeds appeared to have none of these vital ingredients as the manager himself would later concede: "In striving to achieve what Leeds expected, or hoped for, I was in a no-win situation. I had virtually no chance. It was very naive of me to ever think otherwise."

Having impressed in the youth and reserve sides during his short time at the club Sheridan was invited to train with the First Team at the start of the new season.

"Sheridan, Wright, Irwin and Sellars shared the same digs and were the closest of friends," Eddie Gray explained. "Sheridan, the oldest of the group, seemed to like to get lost in a crowd. He was very quiet, and although he had signed a full professional contract by the time I became manager, he spent all his time with his youth-team pals. Jimmy Lumsden and I had received good reports about him from our youth team coach, Keith Mincher, and we all agreed that, in order to bring him out of his shell, he might benefit from training with the first team squad."

Leeds started the season fairly well losing only two of their first fifteen League matches but off the field their problems, which were already considerable in financial terms, were mounting yet further. The club's notorious hooligan element returned with a vengeance and for a while it looked like they would never go away.

Despite the warnings dished out by the FA following the trouble at the Hawthorns in May, on the opening day of the season trouble involving Leeds fans again flared up, causing £6,000 worth of damage to Grimsby's Blundell Park ground.

The club's directors attempted to deal with the problem 'in-house' by urging the thugs to consider the fact that the club were operating under such dire financial straits that any heavy fine or ground closure imposed by the FA could literally force the club out of existence.

Lamentably the warnings went unheeded and there were clashes with Chelsea fans on 9th October and when Newcastle visited later that month some of their players, among them Kevin Keegan, were sickeningly pelted with ball-bearings by mindless thugs.

It was as a result of the latter incident that the FA's disciplinary committee ordered, as punishment, the closure of the terraced areas for Leeds' home games against Queen's Park Rangers and Shrewsbury.

Thankfully, aside from one further spot of trouble at Derby County's Baseball Ground in December (after which both clubs were found guilty of "failing to exercise proper control over their supporters") the rest of the season passed without further disturbance.

Nevertheless it was against this backdrop that John Sheridan, aged then only eighteen, would make his Leeds debut against Middlesbrough at Elland Road on 20th November 1982.

Sheridan had impressed following his elevation to the first team squad and his manager was in no doubt that the young midfielder was more than capable of making the step up: "From [the point we brought him into the squad]," Gray elaborated, "we realised our impression of John as a shy, retiring lad was wrong. A tremendous passer of the ball, he showed a touch of arrogance in his play even at that age... He was as strong mentally as any teenager I have worked with."

Called into the squad the day before the match due an injury to Brian Flynn and doubts over the fitness of Eddie Gray, John only heard he was definitely playing on the Saturday morning.

Although the match ended goalless, Sheridan (who admitted he had been "nervous as a kitten" prior to the match) acquitted himself well on his debut, so well in fact that he won the man of the match award from the match day sponsors.

His manager was bowled over by Sheridan's maturity and poise and it was clear that he and Leeds had at last unearthed someone to fulfil the role of ball-playing midfield schemer that they had been so sorely lacking since Tony Currie left the club in 1979. "After we had brought him into the first team," Eddie Gray would later remark, "there was no way we could leave him out of it." Indeed Sheridan would remain in the side for the next twenty-six League fixtures and was soon bossing games from midfield in a manner befitting a much more experienced player.

Although Leeds would lose both the League games that followed Sheridan's debut (against Barnsley and QPR), Leeds would lose only four of their remaining League fixtures that season. This only paints half a picture though – this sequence included only three home wins and also featured fourteen draws (including three sequences of four consecutive draws). In fact, over the course of the entire 1982-83 season Gray's men would actually draw twenty-one games and only Wolves (promoted as runners-up) lost fewer games. Yet again it was goal scoring that would prove to be Leeds' problem, a problem that was arguably never satisfactorily resolved throughout the entirety of Gray's reign.

With Leeds bereft of funds, and seemingly doomed to remain a Division Two side, a decent cup run was vital and although Leeds would not progress beyond the Fourth Round, their FA Cup adventure would nonetheless extend to four games.

First Preston North End were beaten 3-0 on 8th January in the Third Round at Elland Road (which was Leeds United's first home win since 30th October) a game in which Sheridan had opened the scoring after thirty-one minutes (with his second goal for the club), played impressively throughout and was given a standing ovation when he was replaced with seven minutes to go.

"Sheridan showed some of the pedigree of the old Leeds," Preston's boss Gordon Lee complimented after the game. "He used the ball sensibly and with a lot of thought which is nice to see in a young player."

Eddie Gray was equally enthused: "John is a smashing footballer," he said. "He shows so much composure that people forget that he is only eighteen. He has played a lot of games since he came into the side on 20th November. That's why we took him off when we were 3-0 up, to give him a break."

Leeds' reward for beating Preston was a high profile Fourth Round clash with the club's 1972 Cup Final opponents Arsenal at Highbury. Although a sustained run in the competition now seemed unlikely, it eventually took Arsenal three attempts to dispose of a spirited Leeds side and with the three ties watched by an aggregate of 85,000, the West Yorkshire club did procure some much needed revenue.

Despite the absence of the suspended Sheridan, Leeds managed to come away from Highbury with a 1-1 draw (Arsenal equalising within seconds of Leeds taking the lead). In the replay at Elland Road (again without the suspended Sheridan)

Leeds once again took the game to Arsenal and even thought they'd pinched it with an Aidan Butterworth strike deep into extra time, only for Graham Rix to break Elland Road hearts equalising with a skidding 30-yard free kick with virtually the last kick of the game. Worse was to follow for United when Arsenal won the toss to stage the second replay at Highbury.

It was a bitterly cold night at Highbury for the second replay and during a goalless first-half there was a snowstorm to add to the players' problems. Despite that, all contemporary match reports describe the returning Sheridan as playing a blinder – with his probing passing and his combination play with Eddie Gray particularly eye-catching – with Arsenal having their work cut out to keep him in check.

Although Tony Woodcock put the Gunners ahead after fifty-four minutes Leeds were in no mood to surrender lightly and began piling the pressure on the home side. Twice Sheridan went close to restoring parity, first curling a thirty-five yard free-kick was just wide and then, in the sixty-seventh minute, hitting a shot marginally wide as Arsenal's defence rocked back on their heels. The equaliser duly arrived in the seventieth minute when Arthur Graham floated a cross-cum-shot towards the Arsenal goal that Pat Jennings could only palm onto the crossbar and Terry Connor was on hand to slot home the loose ball.

Although both sides pushed hard for a winner it was to be Arsenal's night when, eight minutes from time Graham Rix struck the goal that finally ended Leeds' gallant resistance and put the Gunners through to face Middlesbrough in the Fifth Round.

Eddie Gray's men thus bowed out with their heads held high having more than held their own against their top flight opponents.

Sheridan in particular had acquitted himself superbly in his first game against top flight opposition, with Arsenal paying him the ultimate compliment of detailing former England international Brian Talbot to man mark him.

Out of the Cup, Leeds were now free to concentrate on their push for promotion but three consecutive draws following the second replay with Arsenal left them in ninth place and the Elland Road club were rocked further at the beginning of March when keeper John Lukic announced he wanted First Division football to further his international aspirations and put in a transfer request.

Lukic was promptly dropped (bringing to an end his record of 146 consecutive League games) and was replaced for the rest of the season by 35-year-old veteran David Harvey who Gray had latterly brought back to the club from Vancouver Whitecaps.

March saw Leeds hit something of a purple patch with four wins from five and after a hard-fought 2-1 win at Bolton on the first Saturday of April, Eddie Gray's side moved up to fifth place in the league with fifty-one points - seventeen fewer than leaders Queens Park Rangers, admittedly, but only a reachable eight points less than third placed Fulham.

Despite their win at Bolton, the performance illustrated not only what was good about Leeds but also what was so frustrating about their play during the 1982-83 season and ultimately why they were destined to remain a Second Division side.

"Leeds at Bolton were probably representative of their best and most irritatingly fallible," the Yorkshire Evening Post concluded. "They won the ball well then gave it away recklessly, often in the space of six strides. They defended splendidly and then left the sort of hair-raising gaps in defence which threatened to prise one [Nat] Lofthouse out of his seat and retirement, and they created chances in attack many times better than the ones which finally brought goals and a victory they deserved. When Leeds put it together, which may well be when fledglings like Martin Dickinson and John Sheridan mature, they could be a promotion side. And that had to be at least another full season away."

"John Sheridan was superb," another match report applauded. "Once he beat two men with a turn in midfield, left two more behind and then set Kevin Hird free with a magnificent pass. Once he took half a pace because there was no room for a full one and found Andy Ritchie [who had joined Leeds from Brighton in March for £150,000 in a deal that saw Terry Connor head the other way for £500,000] with a superlative pass over all of forty yards. Nobody else on the field aspired to that and John Sheridan was only eighteen!"

At this stage there was still nine games and twenty-seven points left to fight for, and although promotion remained, at best, only a faint mathematical possibility Gray refused to rule it out until the fat lady sang. "It's not a lost cause," Gray urged his team. "We have to hope that teams above us slip up, while we win all our matches from now on."

Perhaps inevitably it was not to be – although Leeds lost only two of their remaining nine games (at Queens Park Rangers and at home to Sheffield Wednesday), they won only once (at Burnley), drawing the other six games to finish in eighth place.

As far as club captain Kenny Burns was concerned Leeds' youngsters were then just a shade too young for promotion to have ever been a realistic goal that 1982-83 season. "I remember we had young players like Neil Aspin, John Sheridan and Dennis Irwin coming through," the former Scottish international later recalled. "Denis was not the quickest – clever, but not the quickest. John Sheridan had lots of ability, but I think he thought he was a better player than he was at the time. He was a young boy and thought he knew everything. But a very, very good passer of the ball. Scott Sellars had a nice left foot and went on to play in the Premiership. Neil was raw, but just gave you everything he had, a real honest player. Then, they were all a wee bit too young. If they were eighteen months to two years down the line, it would have been a great help."

With Leeds consigned to another season in the second tier it was perhaps inevitable that, arguably their remaining star players would be on their way: Arthur Graham hopped over the Pennines to join Manchester United for £50,000, Paul Hart joined Nottingham Forest for £40,000 and John Lukic headed to Arsenal, and great success (although international recognition would forever elude him) for a give-away £100,000.

Although the club undoubtedly needed the money, without such consistent performers it was always going to be increasingly difficult for Leeds to mount a concerted promotion challenge in 1983-84 and so it would prove.

Leeds started the season in dismal fashion, picking up a mere seven points from their first nine League games (a run which included six defeats, four of them consecutively) and also suffering the ignominy of being beaten 1-0 at Elland Road in the League Cup by Chester City who were then rock-bottom of the Fourth Division (in front of a paltry 8,106 crowd – although they did atone with a 4-1 win in the second leg). It was the club's worst run for twenty-six years, and without doubt the biggest crisis Eddie Gray had faced in his short managerial career to date.

"The worst period for me was unquestionably the early part of my second season," Gray recalled in his autobiography, "when we suffered four defeats on the trot in the League and were beaten by Chester in the League Cup. As we had been ahead in three of those games, the overall view seemed to be that we had a soft centre and that this was a refelction of my temperament and personality. The idea was that I was not ruthless enough to be a manager, which I am sure my players would have voted a myth, was summed up by a newspaper headline urging me to quit – "Call it a day, Eddie, the nice guys can never win.""

Fortunately for the Leeds players, who all liked and respected their manager, Gray was no quitter and Leeds stopped the rot by winning each of their next three games, beating Cambridge United (3-1), Barnsley (2-0) and Portsmouth (2-1).

Unfortunately it was in the game against Barnsley (a fiery local derby at Oakwell on 23rd October) that Sheridan's season was brought to a premature close when he sustained a broken leg after the Tykes' midfielder Stuart Gray caught him late on the shin midway through the first half.

Although Stuart Gray earned only a caution for his tackle on Sheridan he probably wished he'd been sent off a few moments later when a vengeful fifty-fifty challenge with Sheridan's midfield colleague Gwyn Thomas led to him being stretchered off with a suspected broken ankle. Ironically, Gray ended his evening in the next hospital bed along from the man whose leg he had broken!

Without Sheridan, Leeds plummeted down the table (winning only one of the nine League games that followed his injury) and went into their last game of the year, at home to Middlesbrough, fourth from bottom in the table. There was no doubt about it, Leeds were now involved in a fight against relegation. By the time Sheridan recovered there was a very real possibility that Leeds would be playing Third Division football.

Salvation, however, arrived in the familiar but unlikely form of Leeds legend Peter Lorimer, who returned to Elland Road in December on a free transfer from Vancouver Whitecaps where he had been, to all intents and purposes, winding down his playing career as player-coach.

Not only was Lorimer now thirty-seven years of age (and therefore a year older than his manager) but he had not played in either of the top two divisions for almost four years (having left Leeds in 1980 to join York City). In fact, when Leeds offered him the opportunity to return the veteran Scot seemed as surprised as anyone.

But after making telling substitute appearances in United's home game against Middlesboro on New Year's Eve (a 4-1 win) and in their 1-1 draw away at Manchester City two days later, it was impossible to ignore Lorimer's claims for a starting berth and the Scot would go on to start in each of Leeds' remaining twenty League fixtures.

"I suppose it could be taken as a sad reflection on the game to recall a player of my age," Lorimer remarked at the time, "but the most successful teams have one or two old pros and my role will be to help stop players running here there and everywhere and bring a sense of order and direction to our play."

Lorimer's impact was immediate, with the win against 'Boro marking the start of a seven game unbeaten streak and eventually a run of eight wins from eleven games that propelled Leeds away from the danger area. Age might have reduced Lorimer's mobility but his class remained undimmed, pulling the strings from midfield while youth team graduates like Irwin, Sellars and Wright (now all firmly established in the first team) did his running, and Leeds started to look like a decent team again.

In fact, United lost only four games in the second half of the season and steadily climbed the table to finish a fairly creditable tenth place with sixty points.

With Lorimer and Harvey proving so influential, the manager (who felt the dual role was beginning to catch up with him) decided that it was finally time for him to hang up his own boots, bidding farewell in the season's last game against Charlton Athletic. He had played over 550 times for Leeds, a figure which would undoubtedly have been more had severe injuries not cruelly sabotaged the middle of his career.

Ahead of the 1984-85 campaign, then, there was optimism around Elland Road that Eddie Gray's blend of youth and experience could lead finally lead Leeds back to the First Division.

Bolstered by the return of Sheridan (who automatically regained his place after recovering from his broken leg) and the addition of young centre-half Andy Linighan (a £25,000 steal from Hartlepool, Leeds' only acquisition of the summer, incidentally), Leeds hit the ground running at the start of the 1984-85 season, winning their first four matches against Notts County (2-1), Fulham (2-0), Wolverhampton Wanderers (3-2) and Grimsby Town (2-0) to storm to the top of the table.

But just when it looked like United were emerging as genuine promotion candidates, that maddening inconsistency that had characterised Eddie Gray's reign immediately resurfaced as they then lost their next three.

Gray's men responded to this run of defeats, however, in ruthless fashion, spanking Oldham Athletic 6-0 on 29th September at Elland Road (a game that marked the twenty-second anniversary of Peter Lorimer's Leeds debut as a fifteen-year old) with goals from Wright, Linighan, Sheridan and an Andy Ritchie hat-trick. It was the first time Leeds had hit six in a League game since a 6-1 victory over Arsenal in May 1973 (when Lorimer himself was the hat-trick hero).

There can be no doubt that Leeds were a very difficult side to beat around this time, indeed they lost only three matches between New Year's Day and the end of the season, but ultimately, Gray's men once again drew too many matches.

Nevertheless Leeds approached the business end of the season still in with an outside chance of promotion. They were rank outsiders, admittedly, but Eddie Gray was not about to let the season finish with a whimper. To add impetus and firepower to the push Gray brought in Ian Baird from Southampton and the striker duly opened his account with a goal in Leeds' 2-1 win over promotion chasing rivals Manchester City on 8th April.

With six games remaining United's manager once again tried to rally his troops, and called for his side to deliver a run of six straight victories, and the response of his players was immediate as Palace were routed 4-1 on 13th April – a game in which

Sheridan became increasingly influential as the match progressed, setting up Leeds's second goal with a wonderful bit of sorcery (collecting the ball by the corner flag before weaving his way past two opponents and curling a shot around the Palace keeper, his effort rebounding off the post for Scott Sellars to tap in) and scoring the final two – his second a marvellous 25-yard strike.

Strangely their emphatic win against Palace emphasised Leeds' failings rather than underlined their promotion credentials: "Leeds United's promotion flame continues to flicker," one match report opined, "but the manner of their victory emphasised why they are only outsiders. Before the inventive John Sheridan influenced matters, scoring twice in the last seven minutes, Leeds had struggled to make their extra class tell. Even with a First Division chance to rouse the passions, Eddie Gray's young side swapped the sublime for the indifferent at the swing of a boot."

Only Sheridan it seemed was spared criticism: "Rain quickened a greasy surface in the second half and John Sheridan became an inspiration. There seemed little threat as he took possession near the left corner flag, but he thought otherwise, spurting between Henry Hughton and Tony Finnigan and cleverly curling his side-foot shot around George Wood and against the far post. Scott Sellars, named Yorkshire's young player of the month, arrived on cue to provide the final touch. Two up after sixty-one minutes Leeds finally made things happen. Palace introduced the winger, Alan Irvine, and threw Tony Finnigan forward, but it was Leeds that continued to press, Sheridan putting Tommy Wright clear, only for the striker to drive directly at the goalkeeper. Wright did better seven minutes from time, keeping possession under severe pressure before manufacturing a left wing cross which John Sheridan slid in. Palace immediately pulled back to 3-1. Tony Finnigan tapping in after Mervyn Day had parried a Trevor Aylott header. Sheridan, though, had the final word. A tentative clearance left him thirty-five yards from goal and facing a penalty area packed with bodies. Sheridan relished the responsibility, evading a challenge, switching to his right foot and crashing the ball into Wood's top left hand corner of the net from twenty-five yards out. No wonder that Eddie Gray could confidently state, "We are better equipped than last year. The boys are a bit more experienced and can make things happen." They just need it to happen on a more regular basis, that's all."

Palace's manager Steve Coppell also put his finger on Leeds problems: "It is an unpredictable Second Division, and they are the most unpredictable side," he said. "They might destroy you but they always give you a chance."

Nevertheless the win against Palace had given Leeds the fighting chance of promotion that the manager had asked for. Could they pull off the challenge set by their manager by winning their last five?

It was not to be. A 1-1 draw at Brighton seven days later ensured the maximum haul of points demanded by Gray would not materialise and though they beat eventual champions Oxford 1-0 in their next match, Leeds would finish the season with a battling draw with Wimbledon, a win against Shrewsbury and a defeat at Birmingham to finish in seventh place on sixty-nine points – five points behind third placed Manchester City.

Leeds had undoubtedly finished the business end of the season strongly - losing only one of their last nine fixtures. Unfortunately three draws during this sequence would ultimately scupper their chances of promotion. If every one had been won then Leeds would have done it with a point to spare and it was a source of regret for Gray that he hadn't acted earlier to bring in Ian Baird who plundered six goals in six games at the tail end of the season.

Nevertheless Leeds finally had the look of a settled side, indeed nine outfield players would make more than thirty appearances that season (Denis Irwin, Gary Hamson, Neil Aspin, Tommy Wright, Peter Lorimer, Frank Gray, Scott Sellars and ever-presents Linighan and John Sheridan) and with Gray's fledglings maturing with every game, surely their time in the Second Division couldn't last indefinitely.

For Sheridan it had been another good season. He had bounced back strongly from his broken leg and had played in every one of Leeds' forty-six League and Cup fixtures (scoring six League goals) and his increasingly impressive displays had been rewarded with an Under-21 cap in March when he played in Ireland's 3-2 defeat against their English counterparts in a match played at Portsmouth's Fratton Park.

There is no doubt that progress was being made at Elland Road, albeit a tad too slowly for United's impatient board. A good start the following season was therefore essential if Eddie Gray wanted to keep his job.

The omens looked good. Gray had spent wisely in the summer, bringing in England Under-21 international midfielder Ian Snodin for £200,000 from Doncaster Rovers, which would prove to be a particularly astute piece of business (though Gray had to balance the books partially by allowing his brother Frank to join Sunderland for £100,000).

Despite starting the season with pretty much the same settled line-up that had come so close to promotion the previous season Leeds began the 1985-86 campaign in disastrous fashion.

An opening day loss at Fulham was followed by two disappointing home draws (against Wimbledon and Hull City) and a 6-2 hiding at Stoke. Another defeat at home to Charlton saw Leeds slip to 20th in the League and the writing appeared to be on the wall for Gray.

It was then however that Gray started to turn things around as his team embarked on a six match unbeaten run (winning three and drawing two in the League, and drawing 0-0 with Walsall in the first Leg of their Second Round League Cup tie), during which Gray gave another youth team product, full back Terry Phelan his debut.

Although Leeds were beaten at Huddersfield in the League (a game in which Sheridan was sent off by Macclesfield referee John Hough "for foul and abusive language"), Leeds then cruised to a comprehensive 3-0 win at Walsall in the League Cup on Tuesday 8th October.

One defeat in eight, however, was not enough for the Leeds board of directors, who almost indecently had come to the conclusion that Gray was no longer the man to take the club forward and three days after the win at Walsall the axe fell on the Scot, bringing to an end his three and a half year reign as manager and his twenty-two-year association with the club he had joined straight from school. The board voted 6-2 in favour of his dismissal because, club chairman Leslie Silver announced, fourteenth place in Division Two, "was not good enough for a club of United's stature."

Neither the fans nor the players were happy with the board's decision. Some of the younger players reportedly wept upon hearing the news and there was a near mutiny, of sorts. According to Lorimer the players refused point blank to work with the man the chairman had lined up as Gray's replacement, former Leeds Youth Team Coach Keith Mincher. On behalf of the team, skipper Lorimer even went so far as to hand a statement to the board in which he and the players asserted their view that Gray should be reinstated and condemned the timing and handling of the announcement. The statement did however contain a pledge that the players would continue to do their best for the club.

The fans meanwhile staged a massive protest in the Elland Road car park demanding Gray's reinstatement and Silver's resignation. They, like the players, believed that with the evergreen Lorimer alongside the willing young legs of Sheridan, Sellars and Snodin (who was already being tipped as a future England international), Gray's men had the makings of a side that were bound to out the club back on track in time, a view endorsed by the departing manager: "Bearing in mind that there were another thirty-one matches to go, and that the team had started to gain the physical strength we previously lacked, I was confident I was walking along the right lines."

Despite their rather cavalier attitude to keeping their players and supporters happy the board stood by their decision, although one of the original nay-sayers, director Brian Woodward did resign in disgust.

Coach Peter Gunby was put in temporary charge and Chairman Leslie Silver paid tribute to Gray's service: "Undoubtedly reaching this difficult judgement has placed the affairs of Leeds United at a crossroads. With the season less than a third complete there is still a great deal still to be accomplished during the coming months."

"I felt really sorry for Eddie," Sheridan later recounted. "He started off my career really and I, like many other players, have a lot to thank him for. I thought the world of him and the decision, I felt, was totally wrong. We were eight games unbeaten and we had just won away at Walsall the night before, so how could they sack him?"

The day after the deeply unpopular announcement, United beat Middlesbrough 1-0 at Elland Road thanks to a Lorimer penalty (which he later he admitted he had considered missing in protest) where fans again chanted for the reinstatement of Gray and the resignation of Silver.

The only way to appease the protesting fans, Silver decided, was to replace one Leeds legend with another and it was Billy Bremner, Don Revie's still-revered former captain, to whom the Leeds chairman now turned.

John just after his debut against Middlesborough FC in November 1982, received the man of the match award.

Chapter Two

The new man in the Leeds hot seat – the third Revie legend to be handed the reigns in succession - had entered management with Doncaster Rovers and had twice guided the South Yorkshire club to promotion from the Fourth Division (and one relegation from the Third).

Although Bremner could not have been more excited about accepting what was his dream job, according to his biographer the Scot was mindful that a) the task he would inherit was not an easy one and b) accepting it would smack of cashing in on Gray's bad luck, something Bremner was keen to refute: "Eddie and I were pals," he stated, "[and] I would have willingly stayed as manager of Doncaster Rovers if it had meant him keeping his job at Leeds. He had been battling against the odds for some time. The club were in a mess and trying to manage a club in those circumstances was like trying to sweep up dead leaves in a gale."

As Bremner recognised, the plain facts of the matter was that the club was still broke (so broke, in fact, that they were forced to sell Elland Road to Leeds City Council around this time, receiving £2.5 million in exchange for a one-hundred and twenty-five year lease). The promotion demanded and seemingly expected by the board would have to be achieved without any significant sums of money being spent on the team. Any strengthening would have to be done on a miniscule budget and counterbalanced by players leaving the club. Managing Leeds really did seem like an impossible job.

And so it proved. The first months in charge were, in all honesty, a disaster for Bremner. The new manager rang the changes, but victories were few.

Lorimer was put out to pasture after nearly 700 games and a club record haul of 265 goals (with Ian Snodin replacing him as captain), and players like Phelan, Irwin and Sellars soon found themselves increasingly overlooked for first team duty (although Bremner would hand debuts to Youth Team graduates John Stiles, Peter Swan and Bob Taylor).

In addition Bremner sold Andy Linighan to Oldham for a mere £55,000, while Martin Dickinson was offloaded to West Bromwich Albion for £40,000. They were replaced in the heart of Leeds' defence by Brendan Ormsby who came in from Aston Villa for £65,000 and David Rennie who was purchased from Leicester City for a further £50,000.

None of the changes did anything to improve Leeds' fortunes, as Bremner's men made quick exits from both the League Cup and the new Full-Members Cup while three straight defeats either side of the Christmas period (against Hull, Blackburn and Brighton) suggested that this would indeed be the season that Leeds finally escaped the Second Division, by being relegated to the Third.

Although a win against Oldham on New Year's Day brought respite, Leeds promptly lost five of their next six fixtures which included the ignominy of being dumped out of the FA Cup in the Third Round when they succumbed to a 1-0 defeat away to Fourth Division strugglers Peterborough United. This was the third year in a row that Leeds had exited the FA Cup at the first hurdle.

Although Huddersfield were beaten 2-0 at home at the start of March another winless streak of four games followed and Leeds worryingly found themselves in 18th position in the League with only weeks remaining of the season.

Fortunately, at the start of April, Leeds won three on the spin, which included consecutive away victories at Portsmouth and Bradford City and a home win against Millwall to inch themselves towards safety, and despite another three defeats in their last four games Leeds finished the season in fourteenth place – the exact same position they had been in when Eddie Gray departed and the club's lowest League finish since Don Revie's first full season in charge in 1961-62.

At the end of the 1985-86 campaign, Bremner came to the conclusion that swingeing changes would have to be made if he wanted to bring the glory days back to Elland Road. "Being manager of the club was totally different from before," Bremner ruminated. "Leeds was still a very big club with tremendous support, but there was a lot of work to be done. It was great to be back at Elland Road where everything was so familiar to me. At times I almost expected Don Revie to walk in and tell me to get out of his chair. Yet, somehow, the place seemed run down and I knew that the only way to build it up again was to get the right results on the park as quickly as possible. It was not enough to say we were safe from relegation. We had to be battling for promotion and I spent most of the summer working on the changes that would, hopefully, achieve that."

Indeed, it seemed like there was barely a day that went by during the close-season that someone wasn't either joining or leaving the club.

It had been clear from the previous season that Bremner had no intention of continuing Gray's policy of placing his faith in youth. Out, then, went most of the young players blooded and nurtured by Gray, all of them sold for a pittance. Denis Irwin moved to Oldham Athletic for £60,000, where he was soon joined by Tommy Wright for £80,000 while Scott Sellars moved to Blackburn Rovers for the ludicrously small sum of £20,000. Terry Phelan, meanwhile, was allowed to join Swansea City on a free!

That Irwin would go on to prove himself to be a player of the highest class, winning countless trophies with Manchester United and fifty-six Irish Caps during a long and distinguished career, that Phelan would also later command staggering transfer fees and also won forty-two international caps with the Republic of Ireland and that

Scott Sellars would be brought back to Leeds for £800,000 in 1992 is perhaps all that needs to be said about the wisdom of the decision to offload these players.

That said, Bremner was concerned only with the present not with potential. Bremner simply didn't have the time to build for the future. What Leeds needed, in Bremner's mind was some experienced, seasoned professionals and some honest to goodness battlers and of the promising youngsters who had burst onto the scene during Gray's reign only Sheridan and Aspin escaped his axe.

Also shown the door by Bremner was George McCluskey who moved to Hibernian, and Gary Hamson who left for Bristol City, both on frees, while £10,000 was received for David Harle who also joined Bristol City.

There were almost as many players coming in. Prolific scorer Keith Edwards was brought in from Sheffield United (for £125,000), defender Peter Haddock was recruited from Newcastle (for £40,000), experienced stopper Jack Ashurst was signed from Carlisle for £35,000 and Bremner returned to Doncaster Rovers to pick up winger John Buckley for £40,000. Bremner was also allowed to splash out £10,000 on keeper Ronnie Sinclair (from Nottingham Forest) and £15,000 on East-Stirlingshire right-winger Russell Doig.

At the start of the 1986-87 season it did not appear than any of Bremner's changes had made the slightest bit of difference as Leeds suffered two defeats in their opening three games. According to Bremner's biographer Bernard Bale it was at this point that the Leeds manager read his players the riot act, reminding them in the plainest of terms to pull their bloody fingers out. This rollicking seemed to do the trick too because Leeds would lose only one of their next ten League games to join the pack of clubs chasing promotion.

As far as Bremner was concerned the upturn in Leeds' fortunes was due primarily to the form of his midfield playmaker, who had also forced his way into Jack Charlton's full Republic of Ireland squad around this time following a string of brilliant performances. He even made the subs' bench for their game against Poland in November, although he would have to wait until the following year before winning his first full cap.

"There has never been any doubt about John's skill and it was only a matter of time before he developed into a quality player," Bremner praised. "I suppose his transformation this season is due to him adding consistency to his play. Perhaps it's due to the boy maturing. He's getting involved more. Whatever the reason I'm glad it's happened. I've been delighted with the way he's begun to fight for every ball, getting back to do his share of the defensive duties as well as being one of the most creative midfielders in the Second Division. He's certainly playing with a lot more authority these days and I'm glad my old pal and team mate has selected John for his national squad."

But just when it seemed that Bremner's men were mounting a serious assault on promotion their old inconsistency returned with three consecutive defeats in November against Millwall, Oldham and Birmingham.

Leeds bounced back to see off Derby County 2-0 at Elland Road on 29th November, a game notable for seeing the introduction of a party piece that Sheridan had been working on in training. Early in the game Leeds won a free-kick on the edge of the County box. Keith Edwards tapped it to Sheridan who coolly flicked it up with his right peg and, in the blink of an eye, volleyed it into the top corner. It was an outstanding piece of skill that would become something of a Sheridan trademark, a secret weapon to be pulled out of the hat as when the situation demanded it.

Leeds then lost 3-0 at West Brom the following Saturday, and although they responded positively by beating Brighton 3-1 seven days later (with Sheridan opening the scoring with a blistering twenty yard drive after beating two men), Bremner's men then made it five defeats in seven games when they visited Stoke City on 21st December.

The game against Stoke would be the nadir of Leeds' season and of Bremner's time in charge at the club. If Leeds were intent on avenging their 6-2 humiliation at the Victoria Ground the prevous season they utterly failed to show it. Leeds were 5-0 down by half time and although Baird and Sheridan scored second half consolation goals, Stoke eventually ran out 7-2 winners.

Although Leeds had been without Brendan Ormsby, Ian Snodin and John Stiles this did nothing to fully exculpate the defensive frailties that Stoke had exposed so ruthlessly and the performance was written off as "miserably inadequate, spineless and embarrassing" by the Yorkshire Evening Post, who also ventured, "Unless [Leeds] could produce a ring of steel to place round a suspect defence, promotion could be forgotten about for another year."

"It was one of those horror games," Bremner later lamented. "We were 5-0 down at half time. I couldn't believe what I was watching. Everything that we had instilled in the previous months seemed to have been forgotten, and Stoke had themselves an early Christmas party. At half time I had a few things to say and, as a result, the second half was not so bad. If you like we drew 2-2 in the second half. I prefer to think of that rather than remember it as a 7-2 beating. When you get into that goal difference at the end of the season, results like that can kill you off completely."

Bremner reacted swiftly in the New Year by selling the much sought-after Ian Snodin to Everton for £800,000 (a record fee received for the club) and spent some of the money on four new players: winger/full-back Mickey Adams (£110,000 from Coventry City), full-back Bobby McDonald (£25,000 from Oxford United),

Welsh international midfielder Mark Aizlewood (£200,000 from Charlton Athletic) and beanpole striker John Pearson (£72,000 from Charlton).

Fortunately Bremner's mid-season gamble paid off as the new men settled in quickly and Leeds suffered just four League defeats after Christmas and steadily climbed the table to rejoin the race for promotion or at least a place in the play-offs newly introduced by the Football League. More excitingly for the supporters however Leeds also made dramatic progress in the FA Cup.

The cup run had started on Sunday 11th January 1987 when Leeds had been were paired in the draw with GM Vauxhall Conference side Telford United, conquerors of Burnley in the Second Round.

Although Leeds had been drawn away, the Shropshire Police, fearing that they would be overstretched by Leeds' notorious hooligans at Telford's small Bucks Head stadium, advised the FA to switch the tie.

The FA agreed and, in a move that was widely condemned as a capitulation to the thugs, ordered that the tie be switched to West Brom's Hawthorns ground and, in a further bid to deter Leeds fans from travelling to the match, set the kick off time to Sunday lunchtime, while the Police set up road blocks to prevent ticket-less fans attending. In the event only 6,460 people turned up at the Hawthorns, chaperoned by three hundred police.

Due to icy, snowy conditions, the match almost certainly shouldn't have been played at all, but Solihull referee Vic Callow (presumably under pressure to get the match under way whatever the conditions) declared the playing surface fit for purpose following his eight a.m. pitch inspection. To be fair to Callow he was probably hoping that the cold weather might abate sufficiently to melt the frost but when the thaw failed to materialize it was clear that this would be no spectacle for the soccer purist; whilst Torvill and Dean might prosper on the surface, twenty-two professional footballers would not.

Although the conditions might have favoured the minnows, in actual fact both teams struggled on the frozen deck, particularly as the pitch, if anything, got worse as the game went on.

Although Leeds went ahead after eleven minutes thanks to an Ian Baird header, Telford refused to be overawed by either the occasion or their big name opponents and equalized in the fifty-third minute and might even have taken the lead on a couple of occasions as they pressed Bremner's side hard.

As the game approached its conclusion United appeared happy to settle for a draw, happy at the prospect of a replay at Elland Road and getting out of West Bromwich in one piece but then with only five minutes remaining Ian Baird scored his second of the game after being teed up by Sheridan to settle the tie. It was harsh on Telford who had more than made a game of it and indeed they would have snatched an equalizer had they not spurned a glorious chance at the death and the massive relief on the faces of the Leeds side, manager and supporters at the end of the game was visible for all to see.

The Fourth Round tie against Third Division Swindon Town on 3rd February was also a hard fought affair and Leeds came from behind to win 2-1 and were grateful that Mervyn Day had been in such inspired form on the day, pulling off as he did a string of marvellous saves.

United were put under tremendous early pressure by the home team and were a goal behind after only twelve minutes as Swindon threatened to over-run Bremner's side but Leeds were back in the game in the thirty-first minute when Jimmy Quinn headed past his own keeper from a Sheridan corner.

This seemed to knock a bit of the stuffing out of the Wiltshire side and after the break Sheridan (who was watched that night by Glasgow Rangers chief Graeme Souness, and Liverpool manager Kenny Dalglish) began to boss the midfield, no doubt impressing the watching Scots with the variety and accuracy of his passing.

Having gained the upper hand, Leeds then went ahead in the fifty-first minute when Ian Baird rose above the Swindon defence to score what would prove to be the winning goal.

Although Sheridan almost added a third with a moment of magic, beating a couple of defenders in a tight penalty area and firing in a goal bound shot that was deflected behind for a corner, the score line remained 2-1 at full-time earning Leeds a Fifth Round home draw with First Division Queen's Park Rangers on 21st February.

In front of a crowd of 31,324 – Leeds biggest crowd for five years – the atmosphere inside Elland Road was electric for that Fifth Round tie. "It is one of the biggest occasions we have had for sometime and there is a lot at stake," Billy Bremner said before the game, and his men were clearly fired up from the whistle, harrying and chasing every ball and showing the same hunger, desire and commitment that had made their manager such a formidable opponent in his time and much of the team spirit that had made Revie's side such redoubtable foes in the 1960s and the early 1970s.

Naturally United went into the tie as underdogs but it was they who took the lead on eighteen minutes through Ian Baird, who had bravely flung himself onto the end of John Pearson's flick-on to head home. Although Rangers equalised in the sixty-fourth minute thanks to a David Rennie own goal Bremner's men were not to be denied their due reward. Roared on by their vociferous supporters Leeds continued to attack and five minutes from time scored what turned out to be the winner when Sheridan's floated free-kick was flicked on by Pearson and skipper Brendan Ormsby timed his run to perfection to power a header past David Seaman.

"Leeds undoubtedly benefited by having an extra man in midfield," the Yorkshire Evening Post analysed, "as QPR adopted a 4-2-4 formation. Their young trio of John Stiles, David Rennie and particularly John Sheridan were always in command. Leeds won not by flowing football but by desire, less by skill than work rate and commitment... Leeds were decisive in defence and their passing, although only ambitious if John Sheridan was in possession, was reliable."

Leeds reward for reaching the last eight was a visit to Wigan Athletic on 15th March. For the second time during their 1987 cup run Leeds had to suffer the meddling hands of the FA, who were so anxious that Wigan's small Springfield Park stadium would be unable to cope with United's legion of travelling fans that they ordered the all-ticket game to be played on Sunday at noon.

Although the Third Division team started the stronger (with a strong, swirling wind behind them for the entirety of the first half) and fashioned some decent chances Leeds weathered the storm (thanks once again to a superb display by Mervyn Day, an FA Cup winner himself in 1975 with West Ham) and in the end ran out comfortable winners by two goals to nil courtesy of two long range second half strikes by John Stiles and Mickey Adams to seal Leeds' place in the last four for the first time in ten years.

Their Semi-Final opponents were First Division Coventry City and when the two teams met at Hillsborough on a baking hot Sunday on 12th April 1987, in front of a crowd in excess of 50,000 it would prove to be one of the most exciting Semis in living memory.

A clearly fired up Leeds side started strongly as they swept forward down both flanks and Steve Ogrizovic was quickly forced into action when he saved superbly from a header from John Pearson. But there was nothing the Coventry keeper could do in the fourteenth minute of the game when, following a Mickey Adams corner, David Rennie lost his marker and put his side ahead with a bullet header.

The Midlanders were rocked back on their heels and could barely get a kick for the next twenty minutes and only two more brilliant saves by Ogrizovic, acrobatically keeping out fierce goal-bound attempts from John Pearson and Brendan Ormsby, kept his side in the tie.

Coventry did eventually create chances of their own with Cyrille Regis squandering three gilt-edged opportunities from close-range while Keith Houchen saw a powerful drive fly over the Leeds bar from twelve yards.

Nevertheless the Leeds defence appeared to be coping fairly easily with the Coventry attack and there was little more than twenty minutes remaining on the clock when skipper Brendan Ormsby unfortunately made the error which was to turn the game on its head. Instead of hoofing the ball into the stands, as he would normally have done ninety-nine times out of a hundred, Ormsby instead attempted to shepherd it over the by-line. As a result Coventry's winger Dave Bennett was able to wrap a boot around Ormsby's legs and nick the ball before it went out of play and his cross was scuffed in by substitute Micky Gynn.

"It's nearly 20 years since the game and in all that time I've never tried to make an excuse for my mistake that brought Coventry their equaliser," Ormsby would later reminisce. "A long ball went over my head and I was trying to shield it over the line, Dave Bennett hooked his foot around my legs. It was virtually over the line but he kept it in by inches. My momentum took me running onto the track. Dave got up and crossed it across the face of the six yard box for substitute Micky Gynn to stick it in off his shin. I should have whacked the ball straight out of play, no doubt."

Having looked so solid prior to the Sky Blues' equaliser it then became Leeds' turn to come under sustained pressure as Coventry went all out for the winner. And it appeared to have come ten minutes later when Keith Houchen finished stylishly to leave United seemingly dead and buried. With one last roll of the dice Billy Bremner sent on substitutes Peter Haddock and Keith Edwards for John Stiles and John Pearson with just eight minutes remaining. Within moments his tactical switch paid off when Edwards, with virtually his first touch, headed in United's from Andy Ritchie's precise cross to send the game into extra-time.

Coventry emerged the stronger team in overtime and it was they who regained the lead midway through the first period when Dave Bennett scrambled the ball home from close range after Mervyn Day had stopped a Keith Houchen effort with his legs.

But United fought to the death, keeping up the pressure as Coventry tried to run down the clock and might have earned themselves a replay in the last minute when it needed yet another brilliant save from Ogrizovic to deny Keith Edwards a late leveller.

Instead Coventry held on to take the match 3-2 and make their first ever Wembley appearance which ended in an historic victory over Tottenham. Perhaps it was just one of those years when Coventry's name was on the cup.

Nevertheless Bremner's men had acquitted themselves superbly and probably more importantly there was no trouble from their much-maligned supporters.

Leeds United players traipsed off, some of them in tears, to a standing ovation from their own and Coventry's followers after an extra special Semi-Final which still rates as one of the among the most thrilling in the history of the tournament.

Even when speaking in 1992, by which time he'd played in and scored the winner in a Wembley Final. Sheridan still cited this 1987 Semi as the best match he had ever played in: "Regardless of the result, it was a very entertaining game," Sheridan recalled. "Either side could have won and we were unfortunate to lose. Leeds had enjoyed an easy run all the way and Coventry were the best team we'd met. But we were in control from the start and could have been three up by half-time. It was just a pity it stemmed from a mistake by us. But it was still a good game to play in. The atmosphere was unbelievable and I enjoyed that day very much."

"I could not be upset with my players, they were magnificent," a proud Bremner said after the game. "They ran their tails off, tackled like terriers and at the end they were totally exhausted. They had given all that they could give and nobody could ask for more than that. I was very proud of them and I was also proud of the supporters who had been tremendous from start to finish. Of course, I would have loved to have won the match, but I took a lot of encouragement from the way that the team had played. It told me that they were capable of even greater things."

A Cup Final might have slipped through their grasp but Leeds still had plenty to play for with eight games left of their League season.

Showing no hangover from their Hillsborough heartbreak United bounced back to win their next two fixtures against Shrewsbury and Ipswich (Sheridan scoring in both). Leeds then won three and drew one of their remaining six fixtures and on 4th May their place in the play-offs was all but mathematically confirmed with a 3-2 win at home to West Brom with goals from Pearson, Ormsby and a Sheridan spot kick (his fifteenth goal of the season, making him joint top League goal scorer with Ian Baird). It was Leeds' eighth successive home win.

It turned out to be an evening of memorable post match celebrations – Don Revie rang to congratulate his former captain, the fans wouldn't leave until Bremner and his players came back out after the match for a lap of honour (during which Sheridan was carried shoulder high around the pitch by a group of supporters keen to pay tribute to his massive contribution to the campaign), and Leslie Silver promised funds for the following season: "We'll break open the champagne bottles at the appropriate time," the Chairman pledged, "but whatever happens now it's been a marvellous season. We go into next season with confidence and there is money available to buy, too."

But Leeds knew they had to finish the job and they wrapped up their season the following Saturday with a 1-0 win over Brighton (with substitute Keith Edwards scoring the winner) to finish in fourth place on 68 points.

Joining them in the inaugural play-offs would be third placed Oldham Athletic, fifth placed Ipswich Town and nineteenth placed First Division club, Charlton Athletic.

Then, as now, the Play-Off Semi-Final would be a two legged affair. Leeds would play Oldham, while Charlton would take on Ipswich for a place in the Final. At the time the introduction of play-offs was not greeted with universal approval, with Oldham manager Joe Royle even describing the new-fangled format as grossly unfair, suggesting that the new system made for the longest cup competition ever. "You play forty-six games just to get to the Semi-Final," he seethed.

At the time there were many who felt he had a point. Oldham had looked like automatic promotion candidates throughout the campaign and indeed had never once strayed outside the top three. Not only were they a well-drilled outfit but their plastic pitch, though deeply unpopular with opposing teams, had made their Boundary Park home virtually impregnable.

They had also finished the season eight points in front of Bremner's men and had already beaten Leeds three times that season, twice in the League Cup and once at Elland Road in the League (Leeds had won the return fixture at Boundary Park). And with ex-Leeds players Andy Linighan, Denis Irwin and Tommy Wright, no doubt keen to prove a point or three, Royle's men were therefore hot favourites to progress.

Almost 30,000 crammed into Elland Road for the Semi-Final first leg and what they saw for much of the match was far from pretty. With so much at stake it was perhaps of little surprise that the opening exchanges were cagey, scrappy and littered with niggling fouls and off-the-ball incidents.

In one confrontation between John Sheridan and Mike Milligan both players received a stern lecture from Sunderland referee George Tyson after which the Oldham man was forced to the touchline to get a new shirt, as the one he'd taken to the field in had been ripped to shreds across his chest.

Indeed it was twenty-seven minutes before either side managed a telling shot on target when Andy Goram in the Oldham goal did well to repel John Sheridan's bending twenty-five yard free-kick.

As one contemporary match report succinctly put it, "the football was almost non-existent, with Leeds frustrated by Oldham's off-side trap and the fear of being caught on the break."

And it was via this tactic that Oldham almost went ahead in the sixty-fifth minute when Denis Irwin evaded three challenges inside the Leeds box but could only steer his twelve yard shot wide of the far post.

Leeds did manage to create a couple of chances in the second half - Ian Baird headed just wide for Leeds four minutes after Irwin's miss and an eighty-sixth minute volley from eighteen yards by Jack Ashurst was well saved by Andy Goram but those chances aside it looked as though Oldham's well organized defence, which had caught Leeds offside on fifteen occasions, would earn their side the goalless draw that would put them in pole position for the second leg.

But just when it seemed that Leeds would have it all to do on Oldham's plastic pitch the following Sunday lunchtime, Keith Edwards (who had come on as a seventy-second minute replacement for Andy Ritchie) surged in at the near post to glance a header past Goram from Sheridan's inch perfect free kick to seal a dramatic last gasp winner and hand Leeds a slender but important advantage. Elland Road exploded with relief.

The cynics didn't believe a 1-0 win would be enough, however, and Oldham remained firm favourites to progress. And Leeds travelling contingent of around 6,000 who had braved the cold and the rain must have feared the worst when, with the second leg only seventeen minutes old, Gary Williams headed home to level the aggregate score.

For long periods Oldham virtually set up camp in their opponent's half (Oldham corner advantage by the end of the match was eighteen-four), but Leeds hung on grimly until the eighty-ninth minute when Denis Irwin whipped over a cross from the right and Oldham substitute Mike Cecere put Oldham ahead.

With the aggregate score at 2-1 and with just seconds remaining the Latics were seemingly through and Leeds' promotion dream seemed over. Fortunately for Leeds the Oldham players let their concentration slip for one vital moment. With the Oldham fans and the Oldham players still celebrating what had seemed like the decisive goal, Leeds had just enough time left on the clock for one last punt.

With little time to think, Neil Aspin charged down the right straight from the restart and crossed for John Pearson to head down for Ian Baird whose blocked shot cannoned into the path of that man again, super-sub Keith Edwards who stroked the ball into the corner of the net to rescue his side and send the game into extra-time. It was the third time in successive matches that Edwards, a prolific marksman with his former club Sheffield United who had struggled to justify the money that had brought him to Elland Road, had come off the bench to score.

With the aggregate scores level, but with Leeds now sitting on a priceless away goal, all Bremner's men had to do was survive the additional thirty minutes and aside from Oldham's Kevin Moore hitting the crossbar with a header, the home side could not find a way past Mervyn Day and with Edwards' away goal counting double Leeds advanced to face Charlton Athletic (who had eliminated Ipswich) in the first ever Play-Off Final.

In those initial days of the play-offs, there was no Wembley showdown to thrill the fans. Instead the Final would again be a two-legged affair with the two teams playing each other home and away. The first leg would be played on a drizzly evening at Charlton's adopted Selhurst Park.

Bremner opted for containment in the first leg with former Charlton player Mark Aizlewood billeted at sweeper and lanky centre forward John Pearson using his height when defending set pieces. Defending in numbers, Leeds made few attacking forays, which was rather strange considering they had started with the latterly talismanic Keith Edwards. Although Charlton spent the majority of the game probing for openings, away from home they could muster little in the way of genuine penetration. It was not until the eighty-eighth minute that they were finally able to prise Leeds open when the stylish Colin Walsh, Charlton's most creative player, floated a left-wing free-kick (ironically conceded by Keith Edwards) into the six yard box. Journeyman striker Jim Melrose out-jumped the Leeds defence at the far post to head home.

Despite this setback, Bremner was happy with his team's first leg display and refused to criticise his players. "They were a bit down after the game but they soon seemed to get over it," Bremner stated. "If we had conceded a goal in the second minute of the game and then held Charlton to a 1-0 score-line it would have been hailed as a fine performance."

Indeed there was a feeling that Charlton, having shown nowhere near enough superiority in London, would find it very difficult to overcome a determined Leeds side in front of a packed and hostile Elland Road crowd and Bremner's side approached the return leg full of belief that they would be able to overhaul the first-leg deficit.

The second leg was another tense and fraught affair, though Charlton started brightly, silencing the home fans by creating a number of early chances that would have left Leeds with a mountain to climb had they been converted. But if Charlton had looked twice the side they'd been at Selhurst Park in the first half, Leeds slowly seized the upper hand and after fifty-four minutes, they finally went ahead on the night when twenty year-old striker Bob Taylor seized on to a loose ball in the Charlton penalty area. Although Charlton's captain Peter Shirtliff did his best to put the youngster off balance, Taylor got just enough of a nudge on the ball to send it trickling towards the line where Brendan Ormsby was on hand to prod the ball home.

The crowd of 31,395 (Leeds' highest of the season) turned up the volume as Leeds pressed for a second, though it was Charlton who arguably finished the game more strongly, collecting nine of their thirteen corner kicks in the last twenty minutes.

Leeds, though, stood the test well and, in fact, might even have nicked it at the death when Jack Ashurst punted the ball up-field for Keith Edwards whose acrobatic bicycle kick dipped, but not enough to creep into the net. The first ever Play-off Final thus ended honours even.

The two games against Charlton had been gladiatorial contests, with bookings and eye-watering challenges galore. "It's not football, it's a boxing match," Charlton's skipper Peter Shirtliff remarked. "There's no enjoyment whatsoever in these matches. People are just charging about crashing into each other because of what's at stake."

The draw left the FA with the sudden quandary of how to settle the tie. A short-notice replay was therefore hastily arranged at Birmingham's neutral St Andrews ground and it was there, on the Friday 29th May 1987, that the two teams would lock horns for the third time in less than a week.

In front of a crowd of 18,000 (with Leeds fans accounting for an estimated five-sixths) the pattern of the game was identical to the previous encounters with late tackles flying in from both sets of players.

Leeds suffered a major setback just before half-time, when skipper Brendan Ormsby was injured challenging for the ball with Charlton striker Garth Crooks and had to be carried off. Not only would Leeds miss his leadership and steadying influence at the back for the remainder of the game, but the injury turned out to be a serious one and he would play only one more match for the club.

Although Charlton had the edge in the second half it was Leeds who almost snatched it at the death when Keith Edwards almost scored another of his decisive late goals but Bob Bolder dived to make a fine save and take the game into extra-time.

"All we are saying is give us a goal," pleaded the Leeds fans and nine minutes into that first period their calls were answered when Leeds were awarded a free-kick twenty-five yards or so from the Charlton goal after Paul Miller had handled.

This was Sheridan territory and without any perceptible run up the Leeds play-maker precisely floated the ball over Charlton's five-man wall, beyond the reach of Bob Bolder and into the back of the net. With just twenty minutes remaining, Leeds had one foot in the First Division. The United fans again raised the decibel levels to roar their team home but just as victory and promotion was in sight it all went awry.

Leeds had retreated, getting every man behind the ball, hoping to cling onto their lead until the final whistle blew. For thirteen minutes United kept Charlton at bay and they were just seven minutes away from a return to the top flight when Charlton's skipper Peter Shirtliff, abandoning his defensive duties, popped up in the penalty area to thread a low shot from fourteen yards out through a crowded penalty area into the corner of the Leeds net for the equaliser.

From the restart Sheridan tried to chip Bob Bolder from the half-way line but his audacious effort sailed narrowly over.

Three minutes later, Sheridan conceded a free kick on the edge of the area after impeding Steve Gritt. It was taken short by Colin Walsh and curled in by Andy Peake and Shirtliff, in the middle of a crowd of players, forced in a brave diving header to put Charlton in front. The Charlton skipper's two extra-time goals were the first he had scored that season, and the first time he had ever scored two goals in a game and, ultimately, they would be enough to keep his side in the First Division.

For Leeds to have come so near and yet so far was a blow to the solar plexus after an exhausting fifty-five match season and it was clearly shared by the club's supporters who refused to leave St. Andrews until their heroes, who they knew had given everything, made a re-appearance. Some thirteen minutes after leaving the field, the team, led by Billy Bremner reappeared, heartbreak and despair written all over their faces, to acknowledge their supporters' desire to give them a final cheer. The defeated Leeds players were treated to a rousing reception and a spine-tingling chorus of "We'll support you ever more." In response the players threw their shirts into the crowd.

"I could not believe that we had lost out after all that," Bremner lamented. "I don't think that Charlton were in the game for most of the time. Their goals were well taken and the difference between the two sides was simply that they scored and we didn't, but it was cruel on my players and the Leeds fans who had travelled to Birmingham. Heads went down and there were tears, almost as if we had been relegated. I had to remind them all that, while we had not won promotion, we had turned a major corner in the fortunes of the club there were better days ahead. It took me back to the early days at Leeds when we were branded as the team who always went close but never actually won anything. We shut the critics up then and I knew we could do it again."

Having come, literally, within moments of both promotion and Wembley, it had been quite a remarkable season for Sheridan, his team-mates and the club's supporters. Finally, and gratifyingly it seemed that the sleeping giant had awoken from its hibernation and was ready to become a force again.

For taking Leeds to within a whisker of Wembley and promotion, Bremner's contract was extended before the start of the 1987-88 season and Sheridan (who had played in all but two of Leeds fixtures, had scored sixteen goals and was voted Leeds' Player of the Year) also decided to stay at Elland Road despite interest from both Arsenal and Spurs.

In a bid to take Leeds those vital steps closer to their goal Bremner again dipped into the transfer market in the close season, bringing in utility man Glynn Snodin (brother of former Leeds skipper Ian) from Sheffield Wednesday for £150,000, full-back Gary Williams from Aston Villa for £230,000, Jim Melrose from Charlton Athletic for £50,000 and Ken De Mange arrived from Liverpool's reserves for £65,000 (the latter two made little impact and were quickly sold on long before the end of the season).

After their impressive exploits of the previous season Leeds were red hot favourites to go up and Bremner's side started the season reasonably well with two wins and three draws from their opening five fixtures. However, they then went winless in four (losing to Ipswich and Hull, drawing with Huddersfield and losing to Middlesbrough) and it was soon abundantly clear that there was a serious scoring problem.

After nine League games, Leeds had scored only three goals (two of them by Sheridan both of which earned single goal victories, over Leicester City and West Bromwich Albion). How Bremner must have regretted his decision over the summer to allow his main strikers, Ian Baird and Andy Ritchie leave (Baird in a £285,000 move to Portsmouth, Ritchie in a £50,000 move to Oldham), but if he did it was strange that he should then compound his problems by allowing Keith Edwards to move to Aberdeen for a mere £60,000 after the 'Boro defeat.

Although Leeds beat Manchester City in their tenth match of the season and followed this up with draws with Stoke and Blackburn, consecutive defeats 3-1 at home to Villa and a 6-3 loss at Plymouth on 17th October saw Leeds slip ominously to sixteenth position in the table.

Although Sheridan missed the entire month of November due to injury, when he returned at the start of December Leeds embarked on a run of six consecutive victories that pushed them back into the top half of the table, with Sheridan contributing four goals.

Indeed with the fifth and sixth wins in that sequence (against Middlesbrough and Bradford) drawing crowds in excess of 34,000 to Elland Road there finally seemed a genuine optimism around the city that this could finally, finally be United's year.

Unfortunately following this run Leeds promptly lost their next three fixtures – at Hull City and at home to Barnsley in the League and against Aston Villa in the Third Round of the FA Cup.

On a brighter note it was during this period (in the 4-2 win over Swindon on 21st November) that a young, Leeds-born David Batty made his debut. Like Sheridan himself almost five years to the day previously Batty performed so well that he would remain in the side for the remainder of the campaign.

Sheridan's partnership with Batty would prove to be a highly effective one, reminiscent in many ways of the halcyon Bremner-Giles combination with Batty as the tenacious, combative ball winner and Sheridan as the ball-playing midfield schemer (who could also look after himself). It was a partnership built on mutual respect and one that Leeds could have shaped their entire future around.

"Sheridan was one of the few senior pros who was genuinely interested in us kids," Batty recalled in his autobiography. "I developed a real friendship with him, which we maintained through to our time together as first team midfield partners. Shez ... was a top man during my early days at the club. His status as a key player in the first team was endorsed by his sponsored XR3 car, a seriously trendy set of wheels. He also loved trendy clothes. But he wasn't big-headed; in fact, on more than one occasion he detailed one of us to drive his XR3 into town to pick up a new pair of trousers or a suit that had been altered. You felt you'd really arrived if you were the chosen one. I got so cocky that I would ask him if I could use his car when he was away overnight on first-team duty, and he used to let me. Such a thing would be unthinkable now. Looking back I like to think Shez appreciated what I went on to do for him when I broke into the team – namely, his running."

Despite Sheridan and Batty's burgeoning partnership the midfield men were powerless to prevent United's old inconsistency from reappearing and the team failed to keep up with their fellow promotion hopefuls throughout the rest of the season. Although Ian Baird returned from Portsmouth for a bargain £180,000 he could not repeat his scoring feats of the 1984-85 run in to haul Bremner's men back into the promotion race.

Although three wins and a draw in March put Leeds in the last of the play-off places, Bremner's men could only win two of their last six games and the season fizzled to an anti-climactic end with United seventh on sixty-nine points, one place short of the play-offs.

"We had a few injuries, but you cannot always blame every problem on injuries," Bremner excused. "We seemed to have lost confidence in front of goal. It wasn't that the team were playing particularly badly, but we just seemed to have a big problem with getting the ball into the net. That put extra pressure on our defence and we began to ship goals. In fairness, it was a rare thing to be able to select our strongest side. Mark Aizlewood had lengthy lay-off as did David Rennie, John Sheridan, John Pearson and Bob Taylor. It was not until they were all available together that we started getting some decent results again."

"We finished in a respectable position but on the whole the season had been disappointing," Bremner understated, "We had gone out of the FA Cup after one game and we had done little better in the League Cup. It was one of those seasons that was full of ifs and buts, and one which I was glad to forget."

Sheridan again topped Leeds goal scoring charts with fourteen goals from all competitions (twelve in the league, two in the Littlewoods Cup, seven from the spot) and his form had been good enough to earn him his first clutch of full caps for the Republic of Ireland – playing in the friendlies against Romania on the 23rd March (a 2-0 win, with his proud parents in attendance), Yugoslavia 27th of April (a 2-0 win), Poland on 22nd May (a 3-1 win – in which Sheridan scored his first international goal) and as a substitute in the goalless draw away at Norway on 1st June.

During the trip to Poland, however, Sheridan blotted his copy book with the Irish manager. Having gone to a night club in the team hotel for a social drink Jack Charlton had called time, reminding every one that they had an early flight the following day.

All the players obeyed Charlton's instructions and went to their rooms – everyone that is except Paul McGrath and John Sheridan.

"I hadn't noticed them leave," Charlton recalls in his autobiography, "so I went behind a pillar in the foyer of the hotel. And sure enough, the two of them eventually emerged, jumped into a taxi and headed into town. I chose to avoid a confrontation, for with a lot of drink inside them there could have been a nasty scene. Instead I went to see Mick Byrne and told him if the two players weren't up and ready to leave with us at eight o'clock the next morning, we would go without them. That of course was an empty threat for I knew that Mick would break the bloody door down if necessary to get them on the coach."

Charlton had been far from impressed with both players, but McGrath was far too indispensible to the Irish team for the manager to bear any meaningful grudge. Dropping McGrath would only be cutting his nose off to spite his face. Sheridan, on the other hand was far more expendable at this stage of his career and the manager marked his card.

While Sheridan performed well in this opening clutch of international games – indeed he found himself immediately being hailed as the natural successor to Leeds and Ireland's legendary playmaker Johnny Giles – in reality Ireland were blessed with a whole phalanx of superb midfield players such as Ronnie Whelan, Ray Houghton, Kevin Sheedy and, of course, McGrath. Even the legendary Liam Brady was still available for selection (although he was approaching the end of his playing career) and while Sheridan had done enough to earn himself a place in the Republic of Ireland twenty-man squad for the 1988 European Championships in Germany he would spend the entire tournament as a spectator.

At the tournament that summer the Irish were desperately unlucky not to qualify for the Semi-Final stage (the tournament was still then limited to eight participating nations). The Irish beat England (thanks to a Ray Houghton goal), drew with the Soviet Union (a game in which they had taken the lead through a sensational acrobatic scissor kick wonder goal from Ronnie Whelan and really ought to have gone on to win) and unluckily lost to eventual winners the Netherlands (thanks to a freakish late goal from Wim Kieft which ended Ireland's twelve game unbeaten run) and finished third in their group, albeit three points ahead of a pointless England.

Sheridan might not have secured a game at the Championships (though he did make the bench for the game with the USSR) but the thrill and experience, to say nothing of the honour of being involved in a major international tournament (and indeed the first one that the Irish had ever qualified for) would stand him in good stead for the future.

*****

Back at Elland Road, Billy Bremner was still in charge but there was a sense that Leeds would have to start the 1988-89 season with a bang if the manager wanted to keep his job.

Like so many during Sheridan's time with Leeds, the new season instead began dreadfully. If a 1-1 draw at home with Oxford United on the opening day of the season was disappointing that was nothing compared to the 4-0 spanking they received a week later at the hands of Portsmouth.

Sheridan (and the suspended Batty), though was spared blame as he had not played in either fixture because he was still recovering following an operation to remove a piece of cartilage in his right knee.

Despite being far from fit, Sheridan was rushed back into the team for the third match of the season against Manchester City on 10th September 1988. This was an important fixture not only because it was a Battle of the Roses clash between two of English football's biggest clubs (despite their second tier status) but also because Leeds had decided upon this game as the game where they would unveil their new Don Revie Stand in honour of their former manager who was invited to attend the match with former Manchester City coach and manager Malcolm Allison.

The two legends must have wished they hadn't bothered as the fare served up resembled a contest less between two sleeping giants as two bald men fighting over a comb.

It turned out to be a tedious foul-strewn match, referee Bob Nixon blowing his whistle for no less than fifty fouls, thirty-one of them against City, and seventeen more times for offside decisions and only twice for goals.

Behind to a Neil McNab penalty Leeds had to rely on a last-gasp face saver when Sheridan teed up Noel Blake in the eighty-eighth minute, the big defender notching

40

his first strike since joining United in the summer on a free-transfer from Portsmouth. "It was a great ball from John Sheridan," Blake complimented after the match. "I think Manchester City were playing for offside, but the ball landed at my feet and I just knocked it in."

Although Sheridan had looked rusty and far from fit he was virtually the only player capable of adding any sort of sparkle to what the Yorkshire Evening Post described as "a shambles of a game."

"John Sheridan's value to Leeds United," the Yorkshire Evening Post reported, "even when not fully fit, was underlined in a hard fought but far from attractive 'Roses' battle against Manchester City at Elland Road. The Republic of Ireland International was lacking in match practice and fitness after undergoing an operation for the removal of part of the cartilage in his right knee but he still managed to provide the occasional piece of much needed inventiveness. Regrettably for the League's fifth highest attendance of the day, 23,122, this ingredient was in short supply in a match that neither of these well supported sides dare lose. Stumbling starts to the season had left United and City without a victory to shout about and there was plenty of tension in the air, and on the pitch, as the two sides produced a foul-littered clash."

It left most spectators convinced that Bremner's side could forget any hopes of promotion unless he and the players could get their act together quickly.

The manager, however, claimed not to be too perturbed: "I was proud of the way the players kept going until the end," he would say after the City game. "At Portsmouth we just lay down in the second half, but we showed our spirit to get the equaliser against City. Even though we are not playing as well as we can I think that late equaliser will do us a lot of good. Because of the start we have made there was a lot of tension in the game. The players were up-tight and edgy, but I was delighted they stuck at it the way they did. Invariably the quality sides push their way into contention when it matters most and with that season even longer than before with forty-six matches, I don't think you can read too much into the form over the first couple of weeks. I expect ourselves and City to be there at the end of the season."

United followed this result with another draw at Bournemouth and then finally recorded their first win of the season against Barnsley in their next game. But United then lost 2-0 at home to Chelsea on 24th September which meant that after six games they were eighteenth in the League and though Bremner did guide Leeds to a 2-1 win in the first leg of their League Cup tie against Peterborough three days later it was not sufficient to save his job.

The following morning, almost three years to the day of Eddie Gray's sacking, Bremner was informed that his services would no longer be required and he was relieved of his duties.

Bremner had failed to deliver on the promise of the 1986-87 season it was true, but he had brought a degree of pride back to the club. In addition, like Gray before him, Bremner's time in charge had perhaps shown the board of directors that promotion could not be achieved on mere copper coins and petty cash. If the Leeds board really wanted to return to the top flight they would have to get their cheque books out.

After Bremner's departure Peter Gunby was again placed in temporary charge for three games, all of which were lost (against Brighton, Sunderland and Watford). As a result Leeds found themselves in a precarious twenty-first in a twenty-four team competition with just six points to show for their nine games played.

"The board felt it was time for a change" said chairman Leslie Silver who also paid tribute to the departing Scot: "I don't think there are many people with as much feeling for the club as Billy. Under Billy's guidance we came within a whisker of promotion two seasons ago and also reached the Semi-Final stage of the FA Cup and we all had hopes of building on those near misses. Unfortunately we again missed out and we must now find the right man to arouse the "sleeping giant" and take the club back to its rightful place among the game's elite."

That man proved to be Sheffield Wednesday's manager of six years Howard Wilkinson.

Chapter Three

Howard Wilkinson's arrival at Elland Road on 10th October was something of a surprise. Not only were Leeds in the relegation places in the Second Division but he was leaving a team that was comfortably ensconced in the top half of the First. To persuade a manager of Wilkinson's reputation to drop down a division and sign a four-year contract was therefore seen by many commentators as a major coup for Leeds United.

Major coup or not, according to David Batty many of the first team squad "shuddered" when they heard the news of Wilkinson's appointment and few if any of the players were genuinely excited at the prospect of working for him.

Wilkinson was known throughout the country as a thorough, organised coach and a hard, authoritarian taskmaster who believed that an emphasis on physical fitness on the training ground and a direct, long ball style of play were the best ways to win football matches, if not friends and neutral admirers. Even Wilkinson himself admitted that the foundation stone of Wednesday's success under his stewardship had been perspiration rather than inspiration.

Many players, it was even said, had been put off signing for him by the legends of his arduous training methods, the joyless style of football he espoused and his aloof, dour, schoolmasterly manner. Whichever way you slice it, Wilkinson did not sound like Sheridan's kind of boss at all.

But Wilkinson had not come to Leeds to make friends. Indeed he quickly offended many at the club when he controversially, some might even say sacrilegiously, ordered the removal of all the photographs of the Revie era that adorned the walls of the Elland Road foyer.

"Those pictorial memories of yesteryear appeared to me to be an emotional crutch," Wilkinson justified, "which too many people associated with the club had been prepared to rely on in times of adversity."

Wilkinson would also sever the last remaining link with the Revie era by dispensing with the coaching services of Norman Hunter, the last of the Don's good ole' boys still on the Elland Road payroll. Instead Wilko brought with him his own men, chief among them his long term sidekick and major-domo Mick Hennigan, the man who would orchestrate the commando style training ground routines he favoured.

"The basis of his philosophy at Hillsborough seemed to have been that as long as his players were fitter than any others," David Batty observed, "it would compensate them for not being as good, a sort of "we'll outrun, outfight and outlast them in the end" credo. It soon became clear that, at Leeds, we weren't matching up to Wilko's demands. So, under the watchful eye of Mick Hennigan, Wilko's 'Sergeant Major' we had to endure twelve minute runs flat out around the pitch – as warm-ups. With Wilkinson and Hennigan doggedly clocking every individual's performance, you had to complete a minimum eight, maybe nine laps of the pitch in those twelve minutes. In Bremner's days a twelve-minute run once or sometimes twice a week was the only running we would do in training. Now we were doing it as a warm-up every day. Hennigan, Howard's Mr Motivator, had previously worked as a pylon erector. There was many an occasion when I – and others – would have willingly pushed him off one if given the chance." Clearly Hennigan was not popular.

Wilkinson first took charge of Leeds on 12th October against Peterborough United in the second leg of their Second Round League Cup tie and duly got off to a winning start with a 3-1 victory. Leeds followed this up with three consecutive draws before chalking up their first League victory under the new manager when Hull City were beaten 2-1 at Elland Road (thanks to goals from Sheridan and Baird).

Although Leeds were then eliminated from the League Cup by Luton Town (losing 2-0 at Elland Road) and also made early exits from the Simod Cup and the FA Cup (losing 2-0 to Nottingham Forest in a game that Sheridan – making his 250th senior appearance - had performed superbly, no doubt impressing the opposition manager Brian Clough), it was League survival that was Wilkinson's priority.

When Wilkinson arrived, United were lying prostrated in twenty-first place in the League with just six points to show from their first nine games played. The new manager's methods might not have met with unanimous approval but there's no getting away from the fact that his appointment brought an immediate transformation in Leeds' League form.

In fact, not one of Wilkinson's first ten League games in charge was lost as his team put together a sequence of five wins and five draws to climb into the top half of the table (with Sheridan scoring three times during this period). Defeat to Shrewsbury on 10th December ended the streak but then Leeds embarked on another run during which they suffered only one defeat out of eleven to take them up to eighth in the table at the beginning of March.

With the threat of relegation long having been averted, Wilkinson was given the sort of money to spend that his two predecessors could only have dreamed about and he began his team-building programme before the season had even ended. His first major move in the transfer market was to bring in Scottish international Gordon Strachan from Manchester United for what would prove to be a bargain £300,000 (but still eclipsing any of Gray or Bremner's outlays). By his own admission Strachan had not been doing himself justice at Old Trafford and although the player was now thirty-two there was no doubt that he was still a class act and exactly the sort of experienced head in midfield the club had been lacking since Peter Lorimer. The purchase of Strachan would prove to be the making of Leeds under Wilkinson. A model professional who looked after himself, Strachan was also an inspirational leader and a supremely gifted midfielder.

Equally shrewd was Wilkinson's purchase of Tottenham's England Under-21 defender Chris Fairclough (for £500,000) and attacking midfielder Carl Shutt from Bristol City for £50,000 (with promising young forward Bob Taylor heading in the opposite direction for £200,000).

Both Strachan and Fairclough would play in every one of Leeds' final eleven fixtures that season and although injury would prevent Shutt from making more than three appearances that term he would quickly prove his value by scoring a hat-trick on his debut in the 3-0 win against Bournemouth (which briefly took Leeds into the play-off places) and scoring in the 2-1 defeat against Palace four days later.

There was one more new face on the scene as a young Gary Speed was handed his debut in the goalless draw with Oldham on the season's penultimate weekend.

With Strachan, Batty and Speed all now in situ, Wilko now had three quarters of the midfield who would win him the First Division title in 1992. The odd man out of the equation was John Sheridan.

Although Sheridan had played in all but four of the thirty-seven League games under Wilkinson that season, he would later admit that he had quickly became disillusioned with the new regime and the manager's unimaginative training routines, lengthy boring team talks, whiteboards, tactical gobbledegook and Revie-esque dossiers. In addition, it was also clear that Sheridan, who appreciated the passing game, was never going to become a convert of Wilko's more direct approach. For Wilkinson it was his way or the highway and Sheridan sooner or later was clearly going to be heading for the highway.

Having achieved a healthy tenth position on sixty-nine points, Wilkinson sat down with the Leeds board and argued his case for their financial backing (both in terms of a transfer budget and an increased wage bill), so that promotion could be achieved within two years (Wilkinson achieved it in half that time). Although the Leeds board had never extended the same courtesy to Gray and Bremner they agreed to back their manager.

With the purse-strings now loosened Wilkinson went shopping during the summer bringing in, among others, Mel Sterland, Chris Kamara and, in a move that raised more than a few eyebrows, Wimbledon hard-man midfielder Vinnie Jones, the latter signing clearly signalling that the manager wanted steel in his midfield, not silk.

The writing was on the wall for Sheridan and it was soon made plain that he and the other members of Leeds' old guard were not part of Wilkinson's future plans. These included Ian Baird, Bobby Davison, team captain Mark Aizlewood and Brendan Ormsby, who had finally returned to the side for the last game of the season for what would be both his comeback and his farewell.

According to Vinnie Jones' autobiography the atmosphere at Elland Road stank and cliques had formed with the old guard on one side and the new boys on the other (a view confirmed by Gordon Strachan). Matters reached a head when Jones, annoyed at the resentment festering within the old guard, confronted Davison and allegedly smacked him on the chops.

Summoned to the manager's office, expecting a rollicking or even his marching orders, Wilkinson told Jones: "You've disappointed me a bit, son. I've just been down to the players' lounge. Can't find one speck of blood in there."

If this was how Wilkinson really saw the old guard (though Davison would in fact remain at Leeds) then it was only going to be a matter of time before Sheridan was heading for new pastures.

According to Vinnie Jones the manager spelt it out to them in pre-season training when he announced his first team squad for the 1989-90 season. "He then told the others," Vinnie Jones recalled in his autobiography, "including Ormsby, Aizlewood and Sheridan: "You're over there. Do what you want. And you can get yourselves another club. You can go."

Sheridan had scored 52 goals in 264 games for Leeds in all competitions and this seemed a rather sad and peremptory way for his Elland Road career to end. Sheridan, however, was philosophical: "When Howard Wilkinson came in I didn't really fit into the way he wanted to play. He wanted us to battle our way out of the Second Division, which was fair enough."

"I never had a fall-out with Howard," Sheridan stated. "I didn't like some of the things he did and nor, I suppose, did he like some of my ways. I remember him taking David Batty and me to Roundhay Park to throw the ball up for us to head to each other. Just the two of us players. Why? But he had success and to achieve that he brought in different players to myself like Vinnie Jones and Chris Kamara. It was obvious I had to leave the club... I was unhappy. I didn't like the training methods and his style of football didn't suit me."

Since he was now free to leave, his destination was bound to be upwards. Sheridan's pin-point passing ability and his silky skills, quite simply, were made for the top flight where creative players get that little bit of extra time on the ball.

His progress had been monitored by several of the big clubs throughout his time at Leeds and now he was available for sale there was no shortage of suitors.

Initially Sheridan appeared to be on his way to Chelsea and he even attended and passed a medical to join the West Londoners. Although the deal that would have taken him to Stamford Bridge appeared wrapped up, Sheridan later admitted he didn't really want to play for Chelsea and was relieved when Nottingham Forest came in with an eleventh hour bid of £650,000.

Tempted by their on-the-deck passing game and the chance to work with their legendary but mercurial manager Brian Clough, Sheridan therefore turned down a move to London and signed for Forest.

With Forest having sold Neil Webb to Manchester United that summer the East Midlanders were in desperate need of a ball playing midfield schemer (although in this author's opinion Webb was never in Sheridan's class; not even close).

For Sheridan it seemed like a dream move. Well, it should have been a dream move, but for reasons that still remain vague and unclear Sheridan's time in the East Midlands turned into a nightmare.

Sheridan knew when he joined Forest that a first team place would not be his automatically. Despite the sale of Webb Clough still had plenty of midfield options and Sheridan would find himself vying with the likes of Garry Parker, Steve Hodge and Brian Rice for a place in the starting XI.

Nevertheless Sheridan went straight into the Forest first team, playing in all four games of Forest's pre-season tour of France – coming on as sub in the 4-3 win over Bordeaux Reserves on 31st July, and starting in the 3-1 win over US Villenave d'Ornon on 2nd August, the 1-1 draw with AS Angouleme on 5th August and the 2-2 draw with La Roche Sur Yon on 8th August.

Following their return from France Sheridan kept his place in the first team starting line-up (alongside Parker and Rice) in a 3-1 win against Notts County in the Nottinghamshire FA County Cup Semi-Final on 13th August and again in the 2-2 friendly draw against Leicester two days later.

But when the season proper started on 19th August, Sheridan was not even selected for the first team squad and instead found himself in the reserves. Forest's Central League season kicked off with a 4-2 win over Oldham on 24th August and it was Sheridan who set up goals one and four, and he then scored twice himself in an emphatic 9-1 win over Lincoln City in the Midland Senior League a few days later.

Although Sheridan continued to play well in Forest's reserves it was not until 20th September that he received another call up to the first team when he appeared in the Second Round first leg Littlewoods Cup tie against Huddersfield (even this must have been a late decision by Clough because the match programme does not include Sheridan in the team line-up). Sheridan played well and was even voted man of the match against the Terriers but despite this he still found himself back in the reserves for the remainder of his Forest career – aside from a friendly fixture at Kings Lynn when he scored in a 5-0 win.

To add to Sheridan's misery, since he was not getting first team football, he would also be overlooked by Jack Charlton for international duty during this time. With the World Cup less than a year away and having not played for the Irish since the qualifier against Spain in November 1988 (although he had won an under-23 cap in April 1989 against Northern Ireland, scoring a penalty in a 3-0 win), the chances of Sheridan being on the plane to Italy at this stage seemed less than remote.

Because there seemed to be no rhyme or reason behind Clough's decision to cold shoulder Sheridan there appears to be two different theories as to why this was so.

The first is that Clough simply didn't rate Sheridan, believing he had signed a complete no-hoper. "I played alongside him in the reserves at Coventry but I came off after an hour," Steve Hodge would elucidate in his autobiography, The Man with Maradonna's Shirt. "At Highfield Road there was a massive pillar in the dressing rooms and I'd had a shower and was getting changed when a livid Brian Clough came in with Ronnie Fenton. I don't know if he knew I was there but if he did he didn't care. I just kept quiet behind the pillar. He was talking about John Sheridan. "What have I signed him for!? He can't head! He can't tackle! He can't run! What the fuck have I signed him for?!"

The other and more plausible supposition is that Sheridan's face simply didn't fit. This was, to some degree, a pattern with Clough and certainly others had suffered at the hands of his caprices, such as Asa Hartford, Gary Megson and Danny Wilson all of whom had found themselves mysteriously ignored by the Forest manager soon after agreeing to join him.

Asa Hartford, for example, spent just sixty-three days at Forest and played only three games (all of which were won). Although Wilson did manage ten League games for Forest before he too was jettisoned, Megson wasn't so fortunate, spending five moths at The City Ground without making a single first team appearance, Clough having decided that the midfielder "couldn't trap a bag of cement."

Often with Clough, such incidents had less to do with a player's football ability and more to do with the Forest manager's whims as Patrick Murphy, author of His Way: The Brian Clough Story explains: "Clough was astonished to discover that Megson's pre-match nerves meant he was often sick in the dressing room and the process was repeated at half time. "He doesn't do that in my dressing room" was the sympathetic response and Megson was swiftly shipped out. The same with Sheridan. Clough did not appreciate Sheridan's downbeat attitude, his reluctance to smile, a body language that appeared sullen. When he failed to say a bright "good morning" to the manager and look as if he was enjoying life at Forest his time was up. It did not matter if you were the best player in your division – if you were not smiling and looking positive before a game, Clough would not keep faith in you."

Fortunately Sheridan was far too good a player to be languishing in Central League football, irrespective of Cloughie's opinion, and it was always only going to be a matter of time before someone came in for him. The man who came to his rescue was Sheffield Wednesday boss, Ron Atkinson.

There was only one small impediment. Sheffield Wednesday were at that point rooted to the foot of Division One with just six points from eleven games. "I was a bit hesitant," Sheridan admitted. "I didn't really want to come because the team was struggling at the time."

Initially Sheridan wanted to stay at the City Ground and fight for his place but when he was summoned to see the Forest manager, Brian Clough summarily told him Forest had accepted Wednesday's offer and that he did not consider him to be part of his first-team plans. His stay at Forest had lasted all of three months.

"Playing for Brian Clough was the strangest experience of my life," Sheridan later recounted. "I hardly ever saw him while I was a Forest player. He would turn up at the training ground now and again with his dog, but he never took any of the sessions. It was quite unbelievable, really."

"There were all sorts of rumours and stories flying around about why Clough sold me to Wednesday. But there had been no bust-ups between him and me. I hadn't been misbehaving or breaking any club rules. I think it was nothing more than that my face didn't fit. He did the same with Gary Megson and Asa Hartford. He had no sooner bought them than he sold them and that's what he did with me. But that's Brian Clough, isn't it? I'm disappointed it didn't work out, but I never got a chance. I couldn't show Brian Clough what I could do, playing in the Reserves and the third team all the time. It was made clear that I was not going to get in the side."

"I was playing really well in the reserves. Everyone else wanted me in the first team. Cloughie had it in his mind that he didn't want me in the team so that was that."

Clough did however have the good grace to give Sheridan a fond bon voyage: "I certainly don't regret signing John. We had a vacancy in our squad when Neil Webb left for Manchester United and we wanted to fill it. That said John knew he was coming here to compete with other quality players and he always knew the score about getting into the team. It took me all my time to find a place for Trevor Francis, and he cost us £1 million ten years ago. John goes from here with our best wishes and I sincerely hope he has a good future in the game."

A youthful John Sheridan on the cover of a Leeds United programme 1983

Chapter Four

After setting aside his initial misgivings about joining a team that were strong favourites for relegation, Sheridan was actually delighted to be joining Wednesday: "I joined Wednesday because they are a big club," he would say after putting pen to paper. "They are ambitious and want to win things, just as I do, and I want to be part of that. I'm grateful for Wednesday giving me a chance. I wasn't thinking of where they are in the League. They've got a lot of potential, a lot of good young players. A couple of wins can turn things around, and we can start to climb the table. The teams that Ron Atkinson has managed have all played football and that's another reason why I've signed. Ron told me that he just wants me to play my normal game. He has made me feel wanted – I haven't felt that for three months or so. I'll go out and do my best and try to help keep the club up."

This was not going to be easy. Wednesday had won only once and scored only twice in the League all season prior to Sheridan's arrival. And although they had beaten Aldershot 8-0 away in the League Cup (to atone for a dismal goalless home draw in the first leg) they had also been dumped out of that competition (which Nottingham Forest went on to win) in the Third Round by Derby County. Wednesday were goal shy and with club captain Nigel Pearson, usually a centre-half, deployed out of position in central midfield the Owls seemed utterly devoid of creativity.

As far as his new manager was concerned, Sheridan's arrival, therefore, could not have been timelier. "We've needed somebody in midfield who can pass and play a controlling role," Atkinson said. "We've been short of that basically since I've been at the club. The incentives are there for John – he was in Jack Charlton's World Cup squad, but he's been left behind a little after what's happened at Forest. Hopefully that experience will drive him on to achieve a position of respectability with us and get a place in the World Cup Finals."

In one of those delicious ironies that football so frequently throws up, Sheridan's debut for his new club would pit him against the team he had just left and in front of the very fans that had barely seen him play.

Sheridan knew he would be the centre of attention before the match but perhaps quite wisely refused to be drawn by the media on his thoughts about his controversial former boss. Sheridan instead insisted that he would prefer to do his talking on the pitch.

"At Forest there was a lot of pressure on me," Sheridan commented. "Every time I went out I felt I'd got to play really well to get into the side. I was probably trying too hard. It was getting harder and harder every week playing for the reserves. I shall just go out and play my normal game and do the best I can, though obviously it's going to be difficult going back after just signing for Wednesday. I still haven't played in the First Division yet. I'm just looking to starting to play again. There are no hard feelings. The only thing wrong at Forest was that I wasn't getting a game every Saturday. Everything else about the club was good. The things I was hoping to do at Forest, I'll now be doing for Wednesday. I'm still confident about my own ability. Ron Atkinson just wants me to play my own game. They play the passing game at Forest. I thought that was my game – but Cloughie didn't. I'm grateful to Sheffield Wednesday for being given a chance."

At the age of twenty-five Sheridan was finally going to make his First Division bow. With Sheridan lining up alongside fellow debutant full-back Phil King (bought from Swindon for £400,000), Atkinson made six changes to the team that had lost at home to Wimbledon the previous week, and immediately his side looked a much stronger outfit in all areas of the park.

It was inevitable that Sheridan would inspire his new team-mates to a sweet victory (would the footballing Gods have had it any other way?), although it was an own goal that provided Wednesday's winner when Terry Wilson put past his own keeper after Dalian Atkinson had shot against the post.

It was the Owls' first away win of the season and Sheridan's new boss couldn't have been more delighted with his two new signings: "Their debuts were as settled as any I've seen anywhere," Atkinson preened. "Sheridan is a quality player and he showed his quality. King looked as if he had played in the First Division all his career."

"We've now got a proper player in the team," Atkinson drooled when asked specifically about Sheridan. "Front players know there is someone who can slide balls through to them."

Incidentally, when one reporter asked Sheridan if Clough had spoken to him after the game, "No" came the brief reply.

In the following game against Charlton Athletic, Sheridan again caught the eye in a 2-0 win, providing the ammunition for David Hirst to finally open his account for the season with a brace. Even after just two games Hirst could tell he was going to benefit from playing with someone with Sheridan's passing ability. "We're playing to feet more," the striker remarked, "it's better service and a better system."

Although Wednesday suffered a reverse in Sheridan's third game for the club against Derby County, Sheridan's fourth game, a local derby against Sheffield United, was a game that few would ever forget.

Wednesday and United had long been kept apart in the fixture list, largely because they hadn't been in the same division since the 1979-80 season (when they were both in the Third) and they had not faced each other since a League Cup tie had paired them together in 1980. Now, having been drawn to face each other in the Zenith Data Systems Cup, the two rivals would finally get to face each other again in a competitive fixture.

Previously known as The Full Members' Cup and, later, the Simod Cup, the Zenith Data Systems Cup was a short-lived minor trophy introduced to provide extra fixtures for clubs in the top two divisions, or at least those who wanted them. Since entry was not compulsory the big guns like Liverpool, Manchester United, Arsenal and Spurs gave the tournament a wide berth but other teams were happy to take advantage of a possible route to Wembley as well as the opportunity it presented to increase their revenue. That at least was the theory. The competition, however, failed to capture the imagination of the public at large and struggled to draw significant crowds and it lasted only seven years before it was scrapped.

Not that any of that mattered on 21st November 1989. This was a Sheffield derby and one that both clubs desperately, desperately wanted, even had to win for their fans. With the Blades at that time cruising towards promotion in the Second Division and the Owls struggling in the First, pride, bragging rights and the unofficial title of Sheffield's number one club were all on the line. The status of the competition therefore was immaterial.

In front of 30,464, comfortably a competition record for a non-final, in an unsurprisingly fiercely contested and pulsating game Wednesday had twice taken the lead through Dalian Atkinson and Carlton Palmer only for The Blades to level on both occasions through Brian Deane and Bob Booker (the latter equalising Palmer's 86th minute strike with virtually the last kick of the game) to take the tie into extra time.

It was then that Sheridan would write his name into Wednesday folklore. Three minutes into overtime Sheridan gained possession of the ball in his own half then ran with it for sixty yards, burst into the United area, deftly cut inside two Blades defenders and finished with a curling shot into the top corner in front of a gobsmacked and delirious Kop.

It proved to be the match-winner and Wednesday for the time being had held on to their crown and Sheridan had become a Wednesday Hall of Famer after only three weeks at the club.

Sheridan, who later described the goal as the best of his career, stated: "For me that was an unbelievable goal because it's not like me to run from the halfway line. No one could catch me; I don't know who was chasing me. To say it was a Zenith Cup tie, it felt more like an FA Cup tie. There were over 30,000 people there and it was a great game".

Wednesday's next game was against Crystal Palace with Sheridan again in inspired form, capping another brilliant display by winning the penalty that salvaged a point. Better was to come the following Saturday against eventual champions Liverpool. With Sheridan utterly dominant in midfield Wednesday strolled to a 2-0 win to record their first home victory against the Reds for over a quarter of a century and move out of the bottom three. It was, as Sheridan later assessed, his best performance of that season.

Sheridan had settled in immediately at Hillsborough and had captured the fans' imagination and including his debut against Forest, Wednesday would win five and lose only three of the twelve League matches that followed his signing, as well as beating Wolves in the Third Round of the FA Cup.

In addition, since Sheridan's arrival, Atkinson's men had started to play some wonderfully attractive football, with Sheridan as the team's orchestrator. His vision and the precision of his passing was a joy to behold, setting up countless scoring opportunities for his grateful new team-mates, none of whom could believe Cloughie had let him go.

"A number of factors have contributed to our recent improvement," Ron Atkinson concluded, "but the biggest single factor has been John Sheridan's arrival. At last we've got a "proper player" in midfield, and John's got the respect of everybody in the team because they know he has the ability to make things happen, and it's good to see how well everybody is responding."

"I can't understand why Forest let him go because he's been inspirational for us," new team mate Alan Harper agreed. "He helps everyone by being so comfortable in possession. You're not frightened to give him the ball instead of wellying it up to the front players, which is what teams tend to do when they're struggling. If anyone was suffering from a lack of confidence it should have been John after what he went through at Forest. But he is responding to the challenge."

David Hirst also joined the fan club, placing his return to goal scoring form squarely down to Sheridan's signing: "John has given me more belief in myself. When players pass to your feet, as he does, it's a sign that they believe in you."

For his part, Sheridan was enjoying the responsibility of being the creative hub of the side, grateful to be allowed to play his natural game and thriving in the knowledge that he was rated and appreciated by his manager, probably for the first time since he'd worked under Billy Bremner.

"He has become the barometer of his team's performances," the Wednesday programme praised. "A set fair reading from Sheridan and the higher the pressure on the opposition. No wonder Atkinson wants his team to keep tapping the glass... The better he plays the better the others play and the more service he receives. That seems to be the pattern: a chain reaction with Sheridan and his fluent, quick witted style as the central cog." In other words, if Sheridan played well, Wednesday played well.

Wednesday had been bolstered further in November by the acquisition of Swedish international right back Roland Nilsson (a £375,000 purchase from Gothenburg). Not only had Nilsson earned himself instant cult status with Wednesdayites for choosing the Owls in preference to Manchester United but he was also, like Sheridan, what Atkinson would have described as "a proper player" – a world class right-back who would have been an automatic selection for virtually any side in Europe.

By the middle of January Wednesday had fought their way to fifth from bottom in the League, far from safety, admittedly, but making good progress, and with the squad strengthened again in January by the signing of former England striker Trevor Francis on a free transfer from QPR (where he had just lost his job as player-manager), all thoughts of relegation seemed to have evaporated.

As January turned into February, however, Wednesday suffered a dip in results, suffering consecutive defeats against Everton (the second in the Fourth Round of the FA Cup during which Sheridan was watched by Jack Charlton and his assistant Maurice Setters), drawing with Millwall and losing at Aston Villa to make it three defeats out of four.

What was so frustrating was that Wednesday were still playing the same attractive, open football that all Ron Atkinson teams were noted for. The problem was the Owls were not taking their chances, and were letting teams off the hook by conceding goals in games in which they'd dominated.

"We've certainly not been getting what we deserve," Atkinson complained in February. "Our performances are gaining us a lot of merit, but points matter more than plaudits – and we're not getting the points we so badly need. I wouldn't mind if we weren't playing well. But even our sternest critics are praising our style and skill. I wouldn't mind if we weren't dominating teams. But we are. Alas, too often when we're burying teams we're emerging with one point instead of three, notably in home games, while in away matches we're losing when our efforts have justified us coming back with something to show for them."

The Owls responded to this poor run of results with an unbeaten sequence of six games which saw a home win against Arsenal, a draw with Crystal Palace, a home win against Derby and a 4-1 thrashing of Coventry City, Sheridan scoring in the latter two fixtures. His goal against Derby was his first in the League for Wednesday and his first in the top flight and was particularly memorable - beating Peter Shilton with a long range screamer that the England keeper could do nothing about.

"It was a nice feeling to score, especially against Peter Shilton," Sheridan remarked after his goal against Derby. "I didn't think about a shot at first but when their defence backed off a bit, I thought I'd have a go."

Wednesday then completed their unbeaten run with an impressive home win against Manchester United and a draw at Wimbledon which moved them on to thirty-seven points, theoretically just one win away from the magic number of forty that usually guarantees First Division safety.

Since Sheridan had joined the club Wednesday had yet to lose at home in any of their eleven League games and with six matches remaining (and three at fortress Hillsborough), the Owls looked home and hosed.

Sheridan's form around this time was such that it was no longer possible for his Jack Charlton to ignore his claims for a recall to the national team, particularly since he had been assured that it was only his Forest nightmare, and thus the fact that he hadn't been playing first team football, that had caused him to be overlooked in the first place.

Sheridan finally received his overdue international recall for the Republic's game against Wales on 28th March 1990. As Sheridan was desperate not to miss out on a place in Jack Charlton's World Cup squad in Italy, he was naturally elated to still be in the manager's thoughts: "I'm very pleased to be picked again, with the World Cup coming up. I've been playing quite well; that's all I can do. I'm only in the squad. I don't know if I'll be playing yet. It's just nice to be back."

"I'd like to think I'll make the World Cup squad," he continued. "I wouldn't necessarily expect to play in the finals. Just going to Italy would be every player's dream. I've just got to keep playing well and I'm still getting used to the First Division. It is a different ball game. You get more time in possession but I'm happy about that. I'm pleased with the start I've made and I'm enjoying my football."

Nevertheless, it was clear that Sheridan had much to do to impress the Irish chief. Jack Charlton, it seemed, had yet to firmly make his mind up about the player and his thoughts seemed to echo the neutral's view that a flamboyant, extravagantly gifted ball player such as Sheridan was not exactly the sort of player who naturally suited Big Jack's style of play.

"Sheridan is a bit of an enigma," Charlton would write in his World Cup Diary. "When he does things well, he is in a class of his own – a magnificent striker of the ball who can lift a crowd with just one slide rule pass. Against that, however, he has some infuriating weaknesses which so far, have defied all advice. He hadn't played for us since that miserable night in Seville almost eighteen months ago when he suffered almost as much as I did in the 2-0 defeat by Spain. In fairness, we weren't the only ones who wished they were somewhere else that night. That, I felt, wasn't the true John Sheridan and he deserved the chance of proving what he could do before we set off for the finals."

However there was to be no fatted calf awaiting the prodigal midfielder. It seems that Sheridan had been away from the international scene for such a long time that he had forgotten some of Charlton's do's and don't do's.

"It had been a long time since he was with us," Charlton scribbled, "so long, in fact, that he appeared to have forgotten the squad rules. He turned up at our hotel ninety minutes after the appointed time and I saw red. It wasn't the reception I had planned to give him but rules are rules. If I let that incident go without question, the whole system might have disintegrated around me."

To the World Cup winner's credit this minor indiscretion did not prevent him from handing Sheridan a place in his starting line-up to face the Welsh and the Wednesday man not only played the full ninety minutes (to win his sixth cap) but acquitted himself well in a 1-0 win which stretched Ireland's unbeaten run in Dublin to eighteen games. It was like so many of Ireland's games under Charlton, however, a relentlessly dour evening, enlivened only by Sheridan's vision.

"It is fair to suggest that the number of good passes in the game could be counted on the fingers of one hand," Big Jack conceded, "and all of them came from John Sheridan."

Nevertheless it was clear that Charlton still regarded Sheridan as something of a luxury item. Whilst acknowledging that John had accounted for most of Ireland's best moves, Big Jack couldn't help but think there were areas where the ball player could improve.

"I've mentioned the fact that John Sheridan accounted for most of the telling passes that went in," Charlton elaborated. "John is good at that but on occasions such as this, I'm examining the negative as well as the positive and fuming over the things players are not doing. I want to see them put their foot in, track, defend and, when the opportunity presents itself, get forward and support. In short, I'm looking for the total player, not just one who catches the eye in flashes. It's amazing how often people go along to a game and see only the flashy bits. A player may sweat his guts out in a grafting role for 90 minutes but it's a pound to a penny the spectators will come away remembering the guy who does something spectacular every twenty minutes or so. And it's not only the fans who err on this point. All that is by way of saying that I'm not totally happy with Sheridan's display against Wales, despite the fact that many people seem to think he has had a good game."

Sheridan, then, still had much to prove if he wanted to be on the plane to Italy and the best way to do that was to continue performing to his very best for Sheffield Wednesday.

Sadly, back at Hillsborough just when any talk of relegation seemed preposterous, the wheels came off Wednesday's season in somewhat spectacular fashion with four consecutive defeats – against Tottenham (4-2), Southampton (1-0), Manchester City (2-1) and QPR (1-0).

Although a 2-1 win against fellow strugglers Charlton Athletic in their penultimate fixture took Wednesday to the "safety" of forty points, Luton Town, a place below them, had narrowed the gap to within three. All Wednesday therefore had to do was avoid defeat in their final game of the season at home to Nottingham Forest (winners of the League Cup the previous weekend when they beat Oldham Athletic), and even in defeat they would escape relegation if the Hatters failed to win at Derby County.

Even at this late stage of the season, relegation still seemed unthinkable. "At the time we went to Forest [in November] ... our situation looked pretty hopeless," Big Ron wrote in his programme notes ahead of the final showdown with Clough's men. "Those were the dark days and it seemed unlikely that we might have the chance to save ourselves in our final game. However since then we have achieved a great deal more than our current position might suggest. Our improvement raised our expectations and aspirations, and it is ironic that, just when I've never been more optimistic about our prospects for the future, we should be left with so much depending on what happens today."

In a turn of events that few would have predicted, the Owls crashed to a 3-0 defeat while Luton secured an unexpected 3-2 victory (thanks in no small part to a Peter Shilton clanger that gifted the Hatters their late winner). Having won their final three fixtures Luton (who had had three managers that season) survived and Wednesday went down with an inferior goal difference of just two.

It was the slenderest of margins and the cruellest of body blows (rendered more painful to Wednesday's fans by Sheffield United's promotion back to the top flight along with Leeds United) and a shock to almost everyone in the game. Over the course of forty-two games most relegated teams get what they deserve but it was almost uniquely different with Sheffield Wednesday that season. Indeed the whole country was surprised that such a talented team should go down. What had seemed inconceivable only weeks before was now a reality.

In the final analysis Atkinson put relegation down to Wednesday's poor, goal-shy start to the season: "It meant that despite the dramatic improvement we made from November onwards, we were left with little room to ride that unexpected run of defeats which began with the Tottenham game."

The most frustrating aspect of the relegation was the certain knowledge that Ron Atkinson's side were a good side, far too good for the second tier and one that would have been a decent outside bet to finish in the upper reaches of the First Division the following season had they stayed up.

******

The summer would give Sheridan the perfect opportunity to put the relegation to the back of his mind, namely securing a place in Jack Charlton's World Cup squad, which, as we have seen, was by no means nailed on. Fortunately, when Charlton handed Sheridan the chance to impress in a pre-tournament warm up match against Malta on 2nd June, the player stepped up to the plate and capped a fine performance by setting up Ireland's third goal for Frank Stapleton with a left-footed cross.

His manager was suitably impressed. "Sheridan stepped up considerably on recent displays," Jack Charlton wrote in his World Cup Diary. "He was tackling more effectively, tracking better and I liked the way he picked out Stapleton with the cross for that third goal."

Sheridan had thus done enough to secure his place in Charlton's World Cup squad, if not necessarily in his starting XI. "Compared to many of the other big names in Britain, Sheridan is still only an apprentice," Big Jack would aver. "And yet few players evoke the same sense of excitement on the terraces when he gets on to the ball in midfield. Sheridan can winkle out passes from five to fifty yards and the crowds love it. And yet he still has much to learn. For example, he still doesn't know how to shadow a player and avoid selling himself in the tackle. Those things irritate me but he now has a good tutor in the person of Ron Atkinson. In time, I think he will emerge as a great player for Ireland."

Therefore it was clear that Charlton still saw Sheridan as a squad player at this stage; and so it would prove at Italia '90 as Sheridan remained a spectator for all but the last few moments of Ireland's participation in the tournament.

Ireland had been drawn in the same group as England, the Netherlands and Egypt. Few gave Charlton's men a chance of progressing. They had beaten England in the European Championship Finals two years previously, it's true, but, and without wishing to take anything away from that splendid result, it seemed unlikely that England would be as poor, luckless and weakened by injuries again (or as pitiful defensively). The Netherlands were bickering as usual but still had a spine of world class performers such as Ruud Gullit, Marco Van Basten and Frank Rijkaard. Egypt meanwhile were a virtually unknown quantity, though they had served notice of their potential by beating Scotland 3-1 in a warm up game in Aberdeen and had played very well against England a couple of years previously in Cairo (despite suffering a 4-0 defeat).

In the group stages the Irish would draw all three of their games – 1-1 with England (Kevin Sheedy equalising Gary Lineker's early goal after a mistake by Steve McMahon had all but teed him up), 0-0 against a cagey Egyptian side and 1-1 with the Dutch (Niall Quinn equalising Ruud Gullit's classy opener after Dutch keeper Van Breukelen had spilled Van Aerle's back pass from Pat Bonner's route one punt).

This meant Charlton's side were through to the knock-out stages where they would meet Romania in the boiling heat of Genoa. Two hours of open play had failed to separate the teams (despite the dangerous presence of the often breathtaking Georghie Hagi in the Romanian side) and the match would be decided on penalties. After eight kicks the scores stood at four apiece, but then Pat Bonner saved the Romanian's fifth from Timofte and veteran Arsenal centre-half David O'Leary kept his cool to side-foot home the decisive penalty to send Ireland through to the Quarter-Finals of the World Cup. Their opponents would be Italy; the venue, Rome's Olympic Stadium.

This was without doubt the biggest game in the Republic of Ireland's footballing history and Jack Charlton's men (who were honoured by an invitation to meet the Pope three days prior to the match) were massive underdogs. The Italians possessed in Zenga, arguably the world's best keeper, in Maldini and Baresi two of the world's best defenders, in Donadoni one of the world's most stylish midfielders, in Toto Schillaci the tournament's eventual Golden Boot winner and in Roberto Baggio one of the world's most explosive and skilful players.

The Irish meanwhile, had yet to win a game in normal play and had scored only two goals in four games (both gifted to them by opposition blunders). Despite their evident need for a bit of flair, guile and creativity in the centre of the park (Charlton had been widely criticised for his pragmatism in this regard, particularly after the Egypt game which had seen a particularly poor performance from his side), Sheridan once again remained on the bench.

The Irish nevertheless started well and were matching the Italians in every department and even though they fell behind in the 38th minute when Toto Schillaci tapped in after Bonner had failed to hold a rasping drive by Donadoni, there was a sense that the Irish were far from out of it.

Unfortunately, the Irish could find no way past the Italian defence in the second half, although the Irish manager felt that his side's chances were repeatedly undermined by over-officious refereeing.

"We were winning the battle for midfield control," Charlton attested, "but every time it seemed that we competed for the ball in any kind of dangerous situation, the whistle for a foul against us... That kind of thing is soul destroying for any team. You think you have won the ball cleanly and fairly and the referee goes and takes it from you to give it back to the opposition. In these circumstances, it's very difficult for us to develop any real momentum. And that simply infuriated me. I genuinely believed that we had the players and the resources to win the game. I could still smell the final but suddenly we were beginning to run out of time."

With less that quarter of an hour remaining Jack Charlton finally gave John Sheridan his chance to see if he could prise open the Italian defence. Sadly it was not to be.

At full-time the score line remained 1-0 and it was the hosts who progressed to the last four where they lost on penalties to Argentina. For Ireland their amazing World Cup adventure was at an end.

Sheridan's tournament might have lasted only a few minutes but the player regarded it as a massive honour to have been involved at all: "I was only on for the last twenty minutes," Sheridan said, "but it was an unbelievable experience. It is every player's dream to play in the biggest competition of all and there I was in front of a huge crowd in Rome. It was brilliant, something I will always cherish."

By reaching the last eight Ireland had exceeded expectations and the morning after the Italy game Charlton and his squad flew home to Dublin where a ticker tape parade and an estimated quarter of a million people greeted the players as they made their way into the city centre on an open-top bus.

"It was quite extraordinary," Tony Cascarino would recall. "In the seven months since we'd qualified for the finals, the country had been ravaged by the most contagious fever since the foundation of the state. Football fever. Blotched in green, white and orange, we could not have been greeted more fervently if we'd won. And on that ht summer afternoon in June, there was no greater celebrity that to play for the team that Jack built. We were Masters of the Universe. Kings."

DELIGHT FOR JOHN SHERIDAN, AS HE OPENS THE SCORING WITH HIS 14th GOAL OF THE
SEASON.

ACTION REPLAY

*John after scoring, as stated above, his fourteenth goal of the
1986- 1987season against Birmingham City, a club he would later
play for. Taken from Leeds United programme.
The 1986-87 season was Sheridans most prolific for goals.
He finished with a total of 16 goals in all competitions.*

Chapter Five

Most managers get their P45 immediately upon relegation but Wednesday's newly appointed Chairman Dave Richards, declined Big Ron's offer to resign and made it his post-season priority to persuade Atkinson to accept an extension to his contract. With Wednesday's fans four-square behind him, Atkinson duly signed a two-year contract extension.

Keeping Atkinson at the club made it much easier to convince the players to do the same. Consequently there was only one major departure from the first team squad – that of Dalian Atkinson who moved to Real Sociedad for £1.7 million – a record fee received for the club. The rest decided, seemingly without hesitation, to stay and right the wrongs of the club's relegation. That Sheridan and Roland Nilsson both waived clauses in their contract that would allow them to leave upon such an eventuality says a great deal about them as men as well as professional footballers, and both enhanced their standing with Wednesday's fans by doing so.

As far as Sheridan was concerned, not only did he regard it as "the right thing to do" but he was also happy at Wednesday, felt loyalty towards the manager who had given him the chance to play first team football after his spell at Forest and also enjoyed the camaraderie he shared with his team-mates. "I was happy to stay," Sheridan affirmed, "and felt that was the right thing to do considering Ron had given me a chance at a time when my career had been at a low ebb."

But there was a collective sense of responsibility at Hillsborough. All the squad knew that this was no time to jump ship and the close season also saw popular long serving utility man Nigel Worthington agreeing upon a new contract while Hirst and goalkeeper Kevin Pressman both signed extension deals.

Atkinson spent some of the money brought in from the sale of his namesake to bring in former England Under-21 international striker Paul Williams for £600,000 from Charlton Athletic, spent £200,000 to bring in experienced Northern Ireland international midfielder Danny Wilson, who had been so instrumental in saving Luton from the drop the previous season and also brought in USA international midfielder John Harkes who had impressed whilst on trial with the club the previous season.

One incident, however, threatened to derail the manager's best laid pre-season plans and at the centre of it, regrettably, was John Sheridan. During the summer the Wednesday squad had travelled to Italy for a summer tour (where they would lose 3-0 to Genoa and 2-0 to Cremonese) during which Atkinson had permitted the players a night out, on the strict proviso that they stuck to an 11.30 curfew.

Two players, however, decided to defy the manager's instructions and when Ron checked the hotel bar as midnight approached, he was enraged to find John Sheridan and Carlton Palmer still in the bar supping. An altercation ensued and blows were traded between Sheridan and his manager. The following morning, Ron Atkinson assembled the squad, sans Sheridan, and told them that he was thinking of selling the player but he would let the players make the final decision. The players unanimously voted for Sheridan to stay.

Sheridan, naturally, apologised to his team-mates for letting himself and everyone else down and a line was drawn under the matter. The fracas could have created a rift within the squad but by choosing to stick together at this vital moment it made the team spirit even tighter.

With a strong team spirit and strength in depth in the squad, Atkinson's men were installed as bookies' favourites for promotion and there was a tangible mood of optimism around Hillsborough as Wednesday ahead of the new campaign, reflected in the fact that the sale of season ticket sales had topped £600,000 – a reported increase of twenty per cent!

Wednesday began the season with four successive wins – 2-0 against Ipswich, 5-1 against Hull City (with Hirst bagging four – the first time a Wednesday player had done this in the League since Derek Dooley in 1952, ironically also against Hull), 1-0 against Charlton (Sheridan scoring the winner with an outrageous long-range thirty-yard volley – his fiftieth League Goal) and 2-0 against Watford.

A draw with Newcastle followed and then another victory against Leicester City (4-2) made it five wins from their first six League games (three of these away from home).

Although Wednesday were then somehow held to a draw by West Ham (with their keeper Ludek Miklosko keeping the East Londoners in a game that Atkinson's side had totally dominated), the Owls returned to winning ways against Brighton (with Sheridan scoring Wednesday's second with a rare headed goal from a Trevor Francis cross) and Bristol Rovers (which saw Francis claim his first goal for the club).

After beating Plymouth in their tenth League game thanks in no small part to a Sheridan brace (the first a powerful shot, the second after cleverly eluding his marker and deftly sending the keeper the wrong way), Wednesday were sitting proudly at the top of the table.

The Owls eventually stretched their unbeaten start to the season to fourteen matches (during which they had also beaten Brentford home and away in the Rumbelows Cup – despite a skied penalty from Sheridan in the second leg) which had seen them tot up six successive away wins in the League and Cup (their impressive away form would be a feature throughout the season). Ron Atkinson's side had remained unchanged for their first seven League fixtures and they looked every inch a team that would reclaim their place in the First Division at the first time of asking, not always an easy feat as so many clubs have found.

It was not just the results but the manner with which they were achieved. Wednesday had stayed true to Ron's principles and were playing some really attractive, high tempo football. In a division where football playing teams don't always get their just desserts this was no small achievement and it was an approach that won them many neutral admirers. "People say that you can't play good football and win promotion at the same time," Atkinson attested, "but we aim to do just that. Our goals are at last coming from different parts of the field and that's a good thing."

At the heart of it all was John Sheridan whose form was devastating during the unbeaten start to the season, opening up defences at will and proving like so many of his colleagues that he was far too good for the second tier.

Since it was only a drop in division that Sheridan had suffered Jack Charlton continued to call him up for international duty. And Sheridan was able to add to his tally of caps when he appeared for Ireland in the friendly versus Morocco as a 65th minute substitute for Andy Townsend on 12th September and then started in the 5-0 European Championship qualifying win against Turkey the following month (Sheridan's only appearance throughout Ireland's unbeaten but ultimately doomed attempt to reach Euro '92).

The Owls finally lost their unbeaten start at Millwall losing 4-2 on 27th October (despite opening up a two-goal lead by half time) and this defeat was compounded by the loss of Roland Nilsson who suffered a serious knee ligament injury that would keep him out until the following April.

Wednesday, however, shrugged off the setback, drawing with Swindon in the first leg of their Third Round Rumbelows Cup tie (in which John Harkes came in for the injured Swede), salvaging a point in their next game at home to promotion rivals Oldham (thanks to two Sheridan penalties in the second half) and emerging 1-0 aggregate winners against Swindon to progress to the Fourth Round of the Rumbelows Cup thanks to Nigel Pearson who sealed the win with a header from an inch-perfect Sheridan cross.

Although the Owls were then beaten at Blackburn Rovers on 10th November, they won their next two League games against Swindon and West Brom.

Wednesday's League season then seemed to lose momentum as each of their next five League games were all drawn. In fact, seven of their next eight fixtures were drawn – five in the League, plus their Fourth Round League Cup tie with Derby

County and their Zenith Data Systems tie with Barnsley (from which Barnsley progressed on penalties, Sheridan and Steve McCall the penalty culprits for Wednesday). On a happier note the one game that was won during this period was the League Cup replay against Derby County in which the Owls put in an outstanding performance to advance to the Quarter-Finals.

Although Wednesday had become mid-season draw specialists they were not suffering defeats. In fact following the Blackburn reverse the Owls remained unbeaten in eighteen League and Cup matches.

Following the final draw of that sequence against Wolves on Boxing Day, Wednesday bounced back with four successive wins against Portsmouth, Middlesbrough (after which 'Boro boss Colin Todd described Wednesday as "the best side in the division"), Mansfield Town in the FA Cup and Hull City to reignite their promotion charge.

After the Hull game new signing Viv Anderson (who had just arrived on a free transfer from Manchester United and had taken the place of the suspended John Harkes) was clearly impressed: "It was nice to play in a team like that. All those players should be in the First Division."

The Owls followed this run with a goalless draw with Charlton to register their fourth consecutive clean sheet which was followed serenely by a fifth as Wednesday beat Coventry 1-0 in the Quarter-Final of the Rumbelows Cup with a late goal from Pearson (created by Hirst and Sheridan) to set up a Semi-Final date with Chelsea.

After five consecutive clean sheets the Owls defence blotted their copybook by conceding four in their next match against Millwall in the Fourth Round of the FA Cup. Fortunately Wednesday also scored four themselves (and had taken the lead three times) to take the London outfit back to Hillsborough four days later where the Owls won 2-0.

With one eye perhaps on their Semi-Final date with Chelsea in the Rumbelows Cup, the Owls then failed to win each of their next three games – away at Watford (2-2), away at Cambridge in the FA Cup (where Dion Dublin inspired his team-mates to a 4-0 giant-killing), and a defeat by Swindon at the County Ground.

This was hardly ideal preparation for the first leg of their Semi-Final with Chelsea at Stamford Bridge but underdogs Wednesday withstood an early barrage of pressure from the home side and with Chris Turner in inspired form between the sticks, the Owls defied the odds to take a 2-0 advantage back to Hillsborough thanks to second half goals from Shirtliff and Hirst.

Three days later came the return leg. Although 2-0 was a comfortable lead Wednesday could not afford to be complacent. Fortunately any lingering hopes of the pre-Abramovich under-achievers staging a revival were virtually banished in the thirty-fourth minute when skipper Pearson met Sheridan's pinpoint cross to powerfully head home.

With Cockney street chisellers already screen printing vast quantities of low quality Wednesday souvenirs Chelsea soon found themselves with a mountain to climb when Danny Wilson made it 4-0 on aggregate just before the interval.

Chelsea attempted to stage a recovery after half time and pulled a goal back through Graham Stuart, but without Abramovich's money to bale them out it proved to be a mere consolation and when Paul Williams made it 3-1 on the night (and an emphatic 5-1 on aggregate) with a cute dink over Dave Beasant in the Chelsea goal, Wednesday had cruised to their first major final for twenty-five years where they would meet Ron Atkinson's former club, Manchester United.

"The prospect of Wembley is terrific," Ron Atkinson stated. "The players will enjoy it, and so will I, but, essentially, it belongs to the fans. I'm delighted we've gone a long way towards repaying the debt we owe to those people who never deserted us after last season's disappointment."

If one result epitomised Wednesday's 1990-91 season, however, it was the game that followed, against rugged promotion rivals Notts County. Having set up their Wembley date with Manchester United they could and would have been forgiven for taking their eye off their League form. In fact, with their game against County following only three days after the Chelsea tie most sage football pundits would have chalked this up as a home banker for the Meadow Lane side. Instead Wednesday confounded the experts with a hard-fought 1-0 victory courtesy of an own goal from Danny Thomas who diverted a Sheridan free kick past his keeper.

After the game County boss Neil Warnock magnanimously echoed the thoughts of many when he said, "Wednesday are the best footballing side in the division," which, as a born and bred Sheffield United fan, could not have been easy to say.

The win against County was therefore the perfect psychological boost and the Owls followed this with a win against West Brom, sealed by a Sheridan spot kick on 9th March.

Despite having helped his side piece together another eight game unbeaten run (which included the Semi-Final wins), Sheridan would later concede that his form appeared to desert him around this time.

Sheridan was puzzled by his drop in standards: "My passing, which is my strongest point, has been letting me down a bit," he admitted. "Maybe it's because I've been trying for the miracle ball all the time. I was pleased with the way I began the season but after that I wasn't happy with my game at all, particularly in home matches – and I don't know why that should be."

If, as many thought, the natural rhythm of Sheridan's game had been disrupted by the close attentions of many a Second Division clogger and, as Wednesday's danger man, he did frequently find himself man-marked and therefore less able to find those split seconds to split defences as frequently around this time, then Sheridan, commendably, refused to use that as an excuse.

"I don't think man-marking is a factor," he said. "Teams generally are making it hard for us because our game is knocking the ball about."

He did however confess that having experienced life in the top flight he now found it more difficult to play in the Second Division, reiterating his belief that he and his team-mates were and always had been more suited to the pace and standards of the top flight. "It's difficult in the Second," he remarked. "I found last year that I had a lot more time on the ball. Hopefully we can go straight back because this team is more suited to the First Division."

As Sheridan was only too well aware the second tier of English football is a most unpredictable animal, then as now. The bottom clubs can beat the top clubs more often than they do at any other level, or at least it often seems that way, and so it proved when Wednesday succumbed to three defeats in seven days over the crucial Easter period to allow the chasing pack of Millwall, Middlesbrough and Brighton to make up ground. The Owls lost 3-2 against Wolves, 2-0 at home to Oxford (the first time they'd been beaten at home in the League, incidentally) and then 2-0 against Portsmouth. Perhaps more significantly in the latter game Carlton Palmer was sent off for arguing over the eighty-eighth minute penalty that resulted in Pompey's second goal. As a result, he would miss the Rumbelows Final through the automatic two game suspension he incurred. On the brighter side, the Owls could celebrate the reassuring sight of Roland Nilsson returning to the first team after his long injury lay-off.

For Sheridan, the Oxford game was the nadir of his season. Not only did he miss a penalty but it was his error that led to Oxford's second goal. Although skipper Nigel Pearson would say that "too many individuals had an off day at the same time," a small but vociferous section of Wednesday's supporters chose to single out Sheridan as their scapegoat and he was loudly booed. The fans patience with what they regarded as his seemingly lackadaisical attitude had reached its breaking point. Although Sheridan had acknowledged he was going through a period of poor form, this was no way to treat a player who was clearly one of their most talented and one who had contributed so much to get them to Wembley and nicely poised in the promotion chase.

Clearly Wednesday's fans had become so accustomed to his brilliance that they almost couldn't compute that Sheridan might have a bad game. Steady Eddie's are allowed to trot along but the flamboyant flair players are expected to do it week in week out which is not always easy when you're having lumps kicked out of you or, god forbid, having an off day. Either way it was not an enjoyable experience for the player.

"The fans were expecting us to win every game at home," Sheridan later recalled. "But in the Oxford game we were beaten 2-0 at home. We'd hit a little sticky patch. I missed a penalty early on and gave the ball away for their second goal and the crowd got a bit frustrated. They'd paid their money and a few of them gave me quite a bit of stick. I didn't expect it so I was quite surprised by it all."

Fortunately for Wednesday this unseemly episode did not harm Sheridan's confidence. The sacks of mail containing letters of support from Wednesday's true fans would see to that, as would the banner at Portsmouth that proclaimed: "There's only one Johnnie Sheridan." In addition, Sheridan would later admit that the barracking was the kick up the backside he needed.

"I'd got hundreds of letters the following week saying the fans had been out of order," Sheridan recalled some years later. "That was a big confidence boost. They had obviously been disappointed. It had been a crap game and I had a bad game. But then we played Portsmouth away and they were all shouting my name again."

After three defeats in seven days, though, Wednesday needed to turn things round quickly if they wanted to maintain their promotion push but at half-time in the game that followed against Blackburn – just four days after the Pompey defeat – their aspirations appeared to be in tatters as they went into the break a goal down. Lesser teams might have folded but Atkinson's men rolled their sleeves up and nine minutes into the half Anderson met a Phil King corner with a perfect header to level. Within sixty seconds, Sheridan received a precise pass from Hirst and lashed in a spectacular twenty-yard strike with the outside of his right boot that sailed past Bobby Mimms in the Blackburn goal.

The sheer relief etched in Sheridan's face as he celebrated spoke volumes, as did the reactions of his team-mates who had mobbed him en masse. Showing tremendous bottle, Sheridan would also step up to take a seventy-eighth minute penalty and retained his composure to wallop the spot kick into the top corner to further silence his critics.

"I had a good game against Blackburn," Sheridan later reflected. "When I scored the first goal, I was in two minds whether to do something to the crowd. But scoring was the best way to answer it, really, and then it was all forgotten. With the penalty I felt as though I was on form. Everything was going right for me, so I thought to myself: "Just whack it." It took a bit of bottle to take it after missing the one against Oxford. I thought: "Whatever you do, don't place it!" I was going to make sure I didn't miss it. So I whacked it!"

With form and confidence restored at precisely the right time Sheridan then helped Wednesday beat promotion rivals Middlesbrough 2-0 on 13th April (thanks to two late goals from Paul Williams) and his importance to the team was then reflected in Atkinson's decision to bench him for the following game against Newcastle four days later.

With Palmer already ruled out of the Rumbelows Final through suspension, Atkinson couldn't afford to lose his playmaker and the man who made the rest of the team tick.

It was, however, a decision that backfired somewhat as Wednesday went down 1-0. Without Sheridan the Owls' midfield found it difficult to create chances and it was only after the introduction of Sheridan and Francis late in the second half that Wednesday showed any sort of attacking threat. Atkinson would describe the match as Wednesday's "worst performance of the season" – hardly the best preparation for Wednesday's Wembley date four days later on 21st April 1991.

The League Cup was still taken seriously in those days by the so called big clubs and with the ban on English clubs in Europe having been lifted the previous season the UEFA Cup place it carried (though not to Wednesday as a Second Division club) was enough inducement for Alex Ferguson to field his strongest team. Manchester United had, in addition, never up until that point won the competition. This was not the era of fielding youngsters and fringe players and United were red-hot favourites.

But Atkinson's men were not going to Wembley simply to make up the numbers. Atkinson had drummed it into his players not to be overawed and to go out and enjoy the occasion and backed by 30,000 raucous supporters amongst the 77,612-strong crowd, there was a vague but tangible sense that Wednesday could upset the odds.

"I don't think we could have had a better manager to take us to Wembley than Ron," Sheridan opined later. "He'd been there a few times and he knew exactly how to do it. He managed the whole weekend. What I really remember was when we were on the coach... and we turned towards the stadium. Obviously, playing Manchester United you expect their fans to be everywhere. But all we could see was blue. It was unbelievable down Wembley Way. The support we had was frightening. The whole place was Sheffield."

When the game got under way Wednesday settled quickly. Far from being overawed by the big occasion, Wednesday looked comfortable in possession and organised in defence.

Although the football wasn't the free-flowing spectacle that many had predicted there was no denying that Wednesday looked a match for their illustrious opponents in every department.

"Some people suggested United might exploit the fact that Roland Nilsson had not been long back after an injury lay-off," Sheridan remembered, "but Lee Sharpe, who was one of the best young players in the game at the time, never gave Roland the anticipated run-around. I don't think I've played with a better full back that Roland. He was world class, and we never had any doubts about him coping that day. Anyway he had John Harkes backing him up as part of our game plan."

With both sides restricted to half chances, the game needed a goal to bring the contest to life and on thirty-seven minutes one duly arrived. When Lee Sharpe handballed on the edge of his own penalty area, the Owls won a free-kick in a dangerous position – and one from which Wednesday had actually practiced set-pieces in training.

The original plan was for Worthington to play it short down the touchline to Harkes, but when he spotted that the American was covered, the Northern Irishman opted to float one into the middle of the United box. When the ball came in Pallister headed it away from underneath Pearson's challenge and the ball fell on the edge of the area and into the path of the onrushing Sheridan who smashed a stinging, and ever so slightly out-swinging right footed half volley towards goal, and though Les Sealey, diving at full stretch, got enough on it to divert the ball onto the post, the sheer venom of the shot carried the ball into the net.

"Nigel Worthington took a deep free kick and he was trying to hit Nigel Pearson," Sheridan later recalled. "It was headed out by Gary Pallister and I just met it... I struck it well, but I thought their keeper had saved it. I couldn't really see it through all the bodies so I think the power must have been too much for him. It's just such an unbelievable feeling to score."

The blue and white half of Wembley went berserk and Sheridan wheeled away in delight and headed straight in the direction of Carlton Palmer.

"It was typical of the spirit in the Wednesday dressing room that we were all desperately disappointed when Carlton Palmer missed the 1991 League Cup final," Sheridan explained, "and, as Carlton was my particular pal, before the big game I promised to run straight to him if I scored that day. I suppose it was my way of saying he was part of the team even if he was suspended. That's why now, Carlton always comes into my thoughts whenever I recall the goal... I remember how Gary Pallister tried to head clear from Nigel Worthington's free kick and the ball dropped just nicely for me. My first time shot was one of those which can either go into the crowd or find the back of the net. But I knew I'd struck it well, and, though the goalkeeper got a touch, luckily the ball went in off the post. As I saw it reach the net,

I turned straight to the bench and started running towards Cartlon. I doubt if I've ever moved so fast in my life. Nobody could catch me, and Carlton was heading in my direction just as fast – it was a marvellous moment I'll never forget."

After the break United tried to find a way back into the game but Wednesday were in no mood to surrender their advantage. United did manage to get the ball in the net when Hughes blatantly pushed into Chris Turner as he met a cross from Mike Phelan, barging both the Wednesday keeper and the ball over the line. Wednesday's fans hearts were in their mouths when the referee initially appeared to signal a goal and you could almost hear 30,000 Wednesday fans breath a sigh of relief when they realised he had correctly blown for an infringement.

Aside from that it's a measure of Wednesday's performance that afternoon that United were only able to carve out one other significant chance in the entire game and it came eight minutes from the end when Denis Irwin cross eluded Hughes but not his strike partner Brian McClair who connected with a bullet header from ten yards out that Chris Turner did well to touch over the bar at full stretch.

In fact, Wednesday might have settled matters when substitute and long-standing club servant Lawrie Madden was set free on the right by Sheridan and Hirst but the chance went astray.

Minutes later the referee blew for full time and Wednesday had won their first major honour for fifty-six years. While the Old Trafford men might have played below their best, everyone agreed that Wednesday had fully deserved their victory. It remains, to this day, the last time a club from outside the top division has won one of England's two major domestic cups. To put Wednesday's achievement into an even more impressive context, just a few weeks later Manchester United would beat Barcelona with the same team that had finished the match against the Owls to lift the European Cup Winners' Cup.

"We looked a good side – very professional," Atkinson said after the match. "I knew that if we played well we would be a match for anyone and we played well today....we haven't looked out of our depth today. We said we would pass the ball around and we tried to do that... we played with control and kept the ball moving. We had to play a different type of game in midfield, which we did very well. We had to keep behind the all, keep the ball and pass it. Chris made a magnificent save but prior to that we had three or four situations where we might have extended our lead. It was a super goal that decided it."

"Manchester United were the firm favourites," the match-winner beamed, "but they knew they hade a game on their hands that afternoon, and nobody could deny we were worthy winners. We'd gone into the match full of confidence and really believed we could do it. What a thrill it was for a Stretford lad like me to have helped beat United at Wembley!"

"A lot of my mates were behind that goal. One or two of them jumped up because it was me who had scored. It was good for me to score the winner – especially against Manchester United with me being a Stretford lad. My Dad had a bet on me scoring. I got a bit of stick afterwards from all my mates, but I think they were happy for me. If anyone was going to score they were happy for it to be me. I still get stick from them, especially after they've had a few bevvies."

Nigel Pearson (who was named man of the match) led his team up the thirty-nine steps to collect the trophy (handed over by Tracy Bateman winner of the coveted Rumbelows Employee of the Year award) and then the players did a lap of honour – pausing at the Wednesday-filled end of the stadium to share the moment with their ecstatic fans.

Atkinson's men celebrated long into the night at their London hotel that evening, but the boss refused to let his players take their eyes off the main goal: promotion and consequently postponed the heroes' welcome planned for the following day in Sheffield. "We'll accept the plaudits when we've completed the job that really mattes," he party-pooped, "getting back to the First Division."

Happily, Atkinson's players were of the same mind. "We were deadly serious about getting promotion," Sheridan confirms. "The Cup was a wonderful bonus, but bouncing back to the Old first division at the first attempt was the priority, and we all felt we simply had to achieve that to compensate for the terrible disappointment of being relegated the previous season."

Seventeen days later that promotion target had been achieved as well. After drawing with Leicester, Wednesday then beat Barnsley and Millwall, and after drawing with Port Vale, the Owls went into their last two games needing just one point to secure a return to the top flight at the first time of asking and promotion was duly sealed with a 3-1 defeat of Bristol City on 8th May.

Three days later Wednesday brought their season to a close at Oldham where the Lancashire side came from 2-0 down to seal an injury time win with a penalty to earn them the Second Division Championship ahead of runners-up West Ham and third placed Wednesday.

For Sheridan, third place was something of a travesty: "Although we finished third in the table in 1990-91, we were the best team in the Second Division by far. Of course, believing ourselves to be a First Division side didn't automatically mean we'd get promotion, because many good clubs had gone down and struggled for a few years before achieving that goal."

"[But] we started well and were in the top three nearly the whole season. We knew we were too good for that division and we did well to get out at the first attempt. But we had too many good players to stay in that division."

To add further gloss to such a memorable season Wednesday's reserves won the Pontins (Central) League title for the first time in thirty years and their Juniors reached the FA Youth Cup final for the first time. In addition four of Wednesday's players were selected in the PFA's Second Division Team of the Year: Pearson, Hirst (who scored thirty-two goals that season to bring him to the attention of the national selectors), Palmer and Sheridan.

For Sheridan it had been a season to remember. Aside from a brief dip in form during the Spring he had performed marvellously, a fact reflected by the fact that his place in the Irish squad had not been jeopardised by a drop in division and what's more he had featured in all forty-six of Wednesday's League games (forty-five starts and one appearance from the bench), the only ever present that campaign. In fact Sheridan only missed the Second Round first leg Rumbelows Cup tie against Brentford throughout the entire season.

Sheridan's midfield partner, Carlton Palmer was also virtually ever present – missing only one League game and the Cup Final. Sheridan and Palmer made a formidable and highly complimentary partnership with the latter's tackling and tireless running providing the perfect platform for the former to make the plays.

Sheridan might have been the eye-catching schemer, but he was not big-headed and he knew all too well that it takes eleven good players to make a successful side.

"We were all good footballers," Sheridan asserted. "We had people who were good at different things. I was playing with Carlton. He was the runner of the team and I was the passer so we suited each other. Roland was a brilliant player. I'd say he and Denis Irwin are the best full backs I've played with. Roland came to Wed at the same time as me and Phil King, and the three of us felt we helped the team. He was a brilliant player, a fitness fanatic. I just used to click with him. He knew where I wanted the ball and I knew where he was. He was a clever player who made things look easy. Ron loved him. Then there was Barney [Nigel Worthington]. He and Roland were both fit lads. Nigel had played under Wilko and played a different way to Ron. But he and Kingy played nearly every game that season and the balance that those two had was unbelievable. Like I say, we were playing with great confidence. Those two had a great understanding. Then there was Roland and Danny [Wilson] on the other side. And Nigel Pearson, he was brilliant. As our captain that season he got all the lads going in the dressing room. Always messing about and pestering us. A good captain and a great player as well: solid as a rock. Hirsty was on fire as well. He was as good as [Alan] Shearer at the time."

And the rapport wasn't just limited to the playing pitch, the camaraderie was just as strong off it and Sheridan retains only the fondest of memories about his team-mates to this very day: "We had some good players in the changing room – they were always taking the piss out of each other. If we were going out for a drink there would be between ten and fifteen of us going out. We all stuck together."

Having postponed their Town Hall love-in after their return from Wembley everyone was looking forward to their rescheduled civic reception on 31st May to honour what was now a tremendous double achievement. The celebrations however would be crimped more than somewhat by the shock news that Atkinson would be leaving Hillsborough to take over at Aston Villa (who had fired their coach Josef Venglos earlier that month).

When he was offered the job, Atkinson initially prevaricated and it seemed at first that that the efforts of chairman Dave Richards and director Cliff Goodwin, who counselled him against leaving a good job half finished, and the efforts of the fans who pleaded with him not to go had been successful in persuading him to stay at Hillsborough. Big Ron even went so far as to inform the media that he had decided to stay, stating: "I'd have to be barmy to think of leaving this club."

But Atkinson would confess later that inside he was being torn apart and in the end just could not turn down what he described as his ultimate 'I wish job.'

"To be truthful, I doubt that I have ever dealt with a greater, or more demanding, dilemma in all my years in the game," Atkinson would explain in his autobiography. "Just weeks earlier, I had celebrated the most successful season in Sheffield Wednesday's modern history: promotion back to the First Division combined with winning the League Cup. Maybe as manager I could be accused of a shade of bias, but I genuinely felt we had the foundations to build one of the country's best teams. And that, pure and simple, was my big dilemma. Because, amid all the euphoria at Hillsborough, I had suddenly received a phone call that was to alter the whole focus of my career once more. It came, via an intermediary, from the chairman of Aston Villa, the aptly named "Deadly" Doug Ellis... offering me what I had always wanted: Villa, you see, were my club; I had followed them since boyhood. Now, on my seven o'clock drive to Sheffield every day, I suffered the agony of zooming past their training ground. That, I accept was my fault. I could have solved it with a move to Yorkshire, but it still amounted to my daily dig in the ribs, the reminder of what I had privately considered Villa to be my ultimate destiny as a manager. So when the bait was dangled I was hooked.... It was a case of my heart ruling head in many ways. Personal desire, rather than professional considerations, pushed me remorselessly in one direction."

It was therefore perhaps inevitable that one week later Atkinson handed in his written resignation and the next day he was unveiled as Villa's new manager.

"I have to admit," he said, "that it really was a big wrench leaving because I had been as happy in Sheffield as anywhere in my career; but it was a decision I had to take, and my consolation is that I feel I have done a good job at Hillsborough and leave the club in better shape than I found it. I hope that in years to come the supports will look back and say I set Wednesday on course for better things."

Instead, there were many at the time that regarded Atkinson's actions as treacherous, and certainly the timing of departure was atrocious but when the dust had settled most supporters did indeed acknowledge that he had been a force for good at the club, not simply in terms of winning that elusive major trophy and promotion but he had also bought in several players who would serve the club regally for several years to come (many of them having been lured to Hillsborough in the first place by the chance to play for him). Indeed he had also virtually singlehandedly introduced a sense of purpose and ambition to the club, to say nothing of his philosophies of attractive football, the sort not seen at Hillsborough for many years. Added to which no-one could doubt that he had also brought a touch of glamour and colour to the club, raising Wednesday's profile and expectations considerably, and most importantly he left behind a team that was full of ability, quality and potential that they would almost, almost fulfil. And if all that wasn't enough it was also Big Ron who suggested his replacement: Trevor Francis.

"At that time he had been with the club for two years," Atkinson recommended, "knew all the first team players, appreciated that the playing staff was sound and was familiar with the whole workings of the place. He understood, like me, that teams only needed tickling along to be a success."

Sheridan was sad to see Atkinson go and admitted he had been surprised that the Wednesday board had appointed Francis as his replacement. Later he would regard Atkinson as the best manager he ever played under. Sheridan had also been upset that since he was away on international duty (appearing as a sub in Ireland's 1-1 friendly draw with USA in Boston on 1st June) he never got the chance to say goodbye before Big Ron cleared out his desk: "I was away with the Ireland team at the time so I didn't really know what was going on. The first I knew about it was when I read it in the papers. It was a shock to the system, I couldn't believe it really. We were doing so well, looking forward to playing in the First Division. We had a great bunch of lads. We had great support. We'd been getting crowds of 30,000 every week and everyone was just disappointed at the way he did it. I was really disappointed because I thought he was a great manager. I got on really well with him and all the lads got on well with him."

"He knew how to treat players, that was his strength. Training was enjoyable all week. Even if you were playing five-a-side it had to be played the right way. And he'd let you have a pint when you wanted a pint if it was done the right way."

"In my view, if Ron had stayed at Wednesday another three or four years, we would definitely have won more major honours. There was no messing about with Ron, he knew how to treat players and get the best out of them. We did well under Trevor in the next two seasons, but Ron had that extra something which I'm sure would have taken us that little bit further."

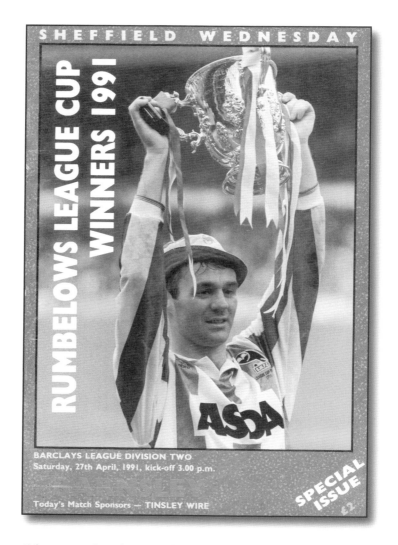

John, pictured on the cover of a Sheffield Wednesday programme special issue, holding the Rumbelows (League) Cup aloft.

Chapter Six

Wednesday might have returned to the top flight with a new manager at the helm, but aside from that little would change. Trevor Francis knew he had inherited a good squad and spent his first summer in charge sensibly adding depth to the squad, rather than making wholesale changes in personnel.

Having lost highly promising reserve team central defenders Jon Newsome and David Wetherall to Leeds in a bargain basement combined £275,000 deal (a decision which proved particularly galling when Wednesday had to pay Norwich £1.6 million to bring the former back to Hillsborough in 1996), and Lawrie Madden and Peter Shirtliff to injury, it was clear that the area Francis most needed to strengthen was his back line. Oldham's England Under-21 defender Paul Warhurst was therefore brought in for £750,000, equalling the club's record purchase which was then surpassed with the £1.2 million capture of England International goalkeeper Chris Woods from Glasgow Rangers. Before the summer was out Francis had also brought in striker Nigel Jemson from Nottingham Forest (for £800,000), seventeen-year-old midfield prospect Chris Bart Williams from Leyton Orient (for £350,000) and Julian Watts from Rotherham (for £80,000). Meanwhile Nigel Pearson, Carlton Palmer and Viv Anderson were all persuaded to accept new contracts.

No-one would have been surprised to discover, when the fixtures for the season were announced for the 1991-92 season, that Wednesday had been drawn to play Ron Atkinson's Aston Villa at home on the opening day. With feelings of bitterness still rife in certain sections of the Hillsborough crowd, Wednesday were desperate to put one over on their former boss and get the new era off to a winning start but although they led 2-0 at half time with goals from Hirst and Wilson, it was another Hillsborough old boy – Dalian Atkinson – who emerged the hero, scoring the equaliser (after Cyrille Regis had reduced the arrears) and setting up Villa's late winner for Steve Staunton.

This setback aside Wednesday started the season respectably, winning four of their opening seven fixtures, which included a 4-1 thumping of QPR (in which Sheridan opened his account for the season with a thunderous volley and in which the usually goal shy Carlton Palmer netted an unlikely hat-trick!) and an away point against eventual champions Leeds United.

With the new manager keen to maintain his predecessor's philosophy of playing open, attractive football the omens for the season ahead looked good for Wednesday. For Sheridan however, Francis's first season in charge would be a difficult and frustrating one.

After just six games of the season, Sheridan, who had been struggling with knee problems, joined up with the Republic of Ireland squad to take on Hungary on 11th September (a game which the Irish won 2-1) during which he suffered an unrelated injury which required a cartilage operation on his return to Sheffield. The initial estimate was that he would be out for a month but as it turned out Sheridan's injured knee would continue to limit his first team appearances for virtually an entire year.

Initially his injury did only keep him out of action for eight games – during which Wednesday did well, winning four and drawing two. Nevertheless, Sheridan went straight back into the side for the visit to Luton Town on 19th October. It would be a Roy of the Rovers style return. Luton were leading 2-1 with only a minute remaining when Sheridan dusted off his trademark free-kick routine. Receiving a tapped free kick some twenty-five yards from the Luton goal, Sheridan flicked the ball up and unleashed a dipping volley high into the net. It was an outstanding piece of skill that would later win him the Chairman of the Supporters' Club Goal of the Season award.

"It got us out of jail today," Sheridan's grateful gaffer applauded after the game, "it was a bit of a special way to end the game. John practices that in training – he's very confident of scoring from it."

"It was my first game back after injury," Sheridan later recalled. "I'd done my knee playing for Ireland. I wasn't fully fit and I shouldn't have played really. But the opportunity was there. The kick was in the right spot. I'd done it in the reserves a few times so I just thought I'd give it a go."

Although Sheridan played in thirteen of Wednesday's next sixteen games, the reality was that his knee was still not right. In fact Sheridan played throughout this period despite being barely seventy-five per cent fit according to his manager and between games was training only once a week and spending the rest of the time on the treatment table.

It says much, then, for his ability and character that during this period Sheridan was able to help guide Wednesday to impressive League wins over Manchester United, West Ham, Chelsea, Wimbledon and Everton. Indeed in spite of being only three quarters fit it's worth mentioning that against Chelsea he had completely overshadowed their captain Andy Townsend (one of his chief rivals for a place in the Irish side) and against Wimbledon Sheridan had scored both goals in a 2-0 win (one a penalty).

Although Sheridan played and scored in the 2-0 victory against Preston in the Third Round of the FA Cup on 4th January and also scored the consolation goal in the 6-1 thumping by Leeds eight days later, he was then left out of the Owls side that beat Villa by a single goal.

Although Trevor Francis's programme notes the following week asserted: "I made changes at Villa. We needed a bit more aggression in certain areas of the field, but my team choice was also dictated by the Villa Park pitch, which made it necessary to look for a different type of game, so explaining why I left out Chris Bart-Williams and John Sheridan," there was a more pressing need to leave Sheridan on the sidelines, namely a second operation on his troublesome knee.

 "No one could have complained had John said he wasn't fit to play," Francis commended, "but he would have kept going until the end of the season before going back to the specialist. However, I felt it unfair to him to delay things any longer, and, the operation having removed the troublesome piece of cartilage; hopefully he will be back to full fitness in a few weeks and contributing his specialist skills to the final months of our programme."

The surgery would keep Sheridan out for twelve matches and without him there is no doubt that the Owls struggled – bowing out of the FA Cup at home to Middlesbrough on 4th February, being spanked 7-1 by Arsenal at Highbury (despite the fact the score had been deadlocked at 1-1 after seventy minutes!), losing 3-0 to Oldham Athletic and going down 3-1 in the Sheffield derby at Hillsborough on 11th March.

Despite these setbacks Wednesday were still handily placed in the League to mount a charge on a UEFA Cup place at the very least, and if the teams above them faltered there was still even an outside chance of winning the League title. The Owls therefore needed Sheridan to return as quickly as possible and after a twenty-minute cameo for the reserves against Bradford City on 24th March (carving Bradford open with his first touch of the ball, incidentally) and an hour long minute run out against Liverpool reserves a week later (in which he scored from the spot), he was finally able to return to first team duty at Nottingham Forest on 4th April where he helped Wednesday to a 2-0 win.

Including the win against Forest, with Sheridan restored to the side (though not yet to full fitness) Wednesday would remain unbeaten for the remaining seven games of the season. After the win at the City Ground, a draw at Coventry was followed by successive wins against Manchester City, Southampton and Norwich (in which Sheridan scored from a narrow angle to take his tally from his injury-ravaged season to seven, six of them coming in the League). This put the Owls on seventy-three points with two games remaining, only two behind second placed Manchester United (on seventy-five) and three behind Leeds (on seventy-six).

It must have been ironic for Sheridan to watch his former club Leeds spending their way to glory, having spent most of his time at Elland Road in a team that had been assembled by little more than shrapnel, but creditably Sheridan bore no hard feelings or jealousy towards his old club.

"I was very disappointed when I left Leeds," Sheridan commented as the season went down to the wire, "but things have now worked out well for both of us. My partnership with Bats [David Batty] could have been a good one and we're still great mates. But Howard Wilkinson had his own ideas and he's spent the money well. Good luck to Leeds if we don't win the title I hope they do. Most of all, I'd be happy to see them take the championship for the fans. I saw how loyal they are because I was at Leeds in hard times. Even then we could still get crowds of over 30,000. The support was unbelievable. The fans waited a long time for money to be spent on the team. I was there for seven or eight seasons and my only disappointment looking back is that what is being done now could have happened five years earlier."

It must have been ironic for Francis, too, to watch Eric Cantona proving so influential in Leeds' title charge. The controversial Frenchman had been given a trial by Francis in January but made only one appearance for Wednesday in an indoor six-a-side competition. When Francis dared to suggest to Cantona that he would like to extend the trial so he could see him play on grass (video players apparently having not yet been invented), the insulted Frenchman headed for the exit and drove up the M1 to Elland Road where he was snapped up by Howard Wilkinson without a second's hesitation.

To be fair to Francis, he did already have a playmaker around whom he could reliably shape his team (fitness permitting) and would shortly buy another one, and there was enough goals in an injury-free David Hirst to make the signing of Cantona appear if not unnecessary, then hardly vital. Cantona, too, was an individual, a peacock, and his signing might have upset the balance of Hillsborough's time-honed camaraderie. All of which is just a theory and a case of what might have been for others to contemplate. Certainly Francis would claim to have no regrets.

Wednesday's penultimate fixture of the season was an agonising 1-1 draw with Crystal Palace (who salvaged a point thanks to a late, late Mark Bright goal) and although Manchester United's defeat to Liverpool and Arsenal's draw at Chelsea over the same weekend did guarantee the Owls European football and at least third place, any lingering hopes of the title were banished when Leeds beat Sheffield United at Bramall Lane the following day to become champions for the first time in eighteen years. On the final weekend of the season Manchester United beat Tottenham to secure the runners-up spot while Wednesday could only draw 0-0 with Liverpool and had to settle for third place.

Still, third place was a very creditable finish indeed, indeed it was Wednesday's highest League finish for thirty years and it also brought European football back to Hillsborough for the first time since the 1963-64 season when they'd appeared by invitation (rather than qualification) in the Fairs Cup.

While it may be fair to say that Wednesday's third place finish had far outstripped expectations, by finishing only seven points behind Leeds it is nonetheless tempting to fantasise about what might have been had Sheridan been available for more than twenty-three of Wednesday's League fixtures. After all Wednesday had accrued forty-four points with Sheridan in the side and only thirty-one without him. It is not too fanciful, then, to predict that had Sheridan been available more his creativity might have been able to turn draws into enough victories and narrow defeats into enough draws to secure the extra eight points needed to have brought the title to Hillsborough.

Sheridan himself was, modestly, not so sure. "It was a great achievement for Trevor to finish third in his first season and get into Europe. We had a great season but we had a few hammerings....Maybe with Ron [Atkinson] having more experience we could have won one or two games by doing different things. But, to be fair, I don't think we could have done much better."

That said, even for a newly promoted team Wednesday hadn't over-achieved – third place was no fluke. Wednesday had a good side full of ability, hunger and goals, and one in which virtually every member of the team had reaffirmed their right to compete at the top level.

These were exciting times at Sheffield Wednesday and it was a measure of the club's ambition and cachet at that time that in the summer of 1992 they were able to attract a player of Chris Waddle's calibre to the club. "I wanted to sign for Wednesday" Waddle announced after his £1million move from Marseille where he had spent the past three seasons. "I like the way they play football. I have a lot of respect for the manager and the club."

For Sheridan the chance of linking up with one of the most naturally gifted footballers of his generation was a mouth-watering prospect and he couldn't wait to play alongside the England winger. First, though, he would have to get himself fully fit.

Although Sheridan signed a one-year contract extension during the summer he spent the close season recovering from yet another knee operation. As a result the improved contract contained a clause stipulating that he had to prove his fitness over twenty games.

As he was still recovering from his surgery Sheridan would miss the start of the 1992-93 campaign and he would not appear in a Wednesday shirt until 13th October when he had a forty-five minute run out for the reserves against Notts County.

In Sheridan's absence, Wednesday suffered a poor start to the inaugural Premier League season – winning only four of their first thirteen League games. Francis, though, refused to panic, insisting that results did not reflect his team's performances. Having lost Hirst, King, Pearson, Waddle and Sheridan to injury throughout this period he knew that it was just a matter of getting everyone fit before his team showed their true colours. Still, when four wins out of thirteen became four out of nineteen there were many tipping the Owls for another relegation.

It was not until 27th October that Waddle, Sheridan and Hirst were all finally available to make their first appearance together, and when they did Wednesday fans were soon drooling as their attacking thrust helped rout Leicester City 7-1 in the Third Round of the Coca Cola Cup.

Despite the score line and manner of the victory it was the return of Sheridan that most delighted the Wednesday manager: "Frankly, the most important things that came out of the game included getting John Sheridan back," Francis stated. "It was good for us, but especially for John himself to get the psychological boost of a return after six months of worry and doubt. Some people anticipating he would be on the bench after so little match practice in the reserves, were surprised that he started the game, but there are times when I feel it is better for a player to be on from the beginning and John proved it. He gave everyone a lift and did very well before we brought him off after nearly seventy minutes."

Sheridan also returned just in time to take part in the Owls' first European campaign for decades. Having disposed of Spora Luxembourg 10-2 on aggregate Wednesday had been paired with Kaiserslautern in the Second Round in October. As an unused substitute Sheridan had watched his team-mates lose 3-1 in the first leg in Germany. Hirst had given the Owls an early lead but then the game was turned on its head by two controversial refereeing decisions – first the Germans equalised courtesy of a highly dubious penalty (following a Viv Anderson tackle which appeared to be out of the box) and then three minutes before half time David Hirst was undeservedly sent off courtesy of some textbook German cheating by Marco Haber who writhed, pole axed, on the ground after the most innocuous challenge imaginable.

Nevertheless, thanks to the away goal they were still in the tie when the Germans visited Hillsborough for the second leg.

Without the suspended Hirst and the ineligible Mark Bright (recently signed from Crystal Palace in a deal which saw Paul Williams head the other way) Francis pressed Paul Warhurst into service as an emergency striker and Wednesday twice led through Danny Wilson and Sheridan (who curled in a sensational twenty-five yard free kick) only for the Germans to equalise on both occasions and seal a Third Round tie with Ajax. Unfortunately for the Owls this would be their last appearance in a major European Competition to date, so they were unable to learn the cute tricks that the Germans were so adept at – getting men sent off, time wasting, diving in the box etc. To be fair Kaiserslautern were also probably a better side.

"At 1-0 I thought we had a very good chance," Francis sighed after the match. "When you score a goal away and two at home, you feel you should have done a bit better. The tie was lost in Germany when David Hirst was sent off."

Fortunately Wednesday were quickly able to put their European disappointment behind them, and including the win against Leicester, embarked on a run during which only two League and Cup games were lost out of twenty-five. During this period (with Waddle and Sheridan ever-present), Wednesday's form was simply irresistible, and between mid-December 1992 and April 1993 they were far and away the best side in the country, and easily the most entertaining. "We were playing with confidence," Sheridan recalled proudly. "We were going out and expecting not to get beaten no matter whether we were playing Manchester United or whoever."

Much of the credit for this must go down to the combination play between Sheridan and Waddle. Their fleet-footed craft, intelligence and artistry created countless chances and dozens of goals.

During this run Wednesday made excellent progress in both domestic cup competitions, disposing of QPR in the Fourth Round of the Coca-Cola Cup, and making short work of Cambridge and Sunderland in the FA Cup and having languished in the bottom six in the League prior to Sheridan's return an away win at Chelsea on 30th January propelled Wednesday up to ninth in the League.

Four days later when Wednesday had disposed of Ipswich 1-0 in the Coca Cola Cup Fifth Round Replay to advance to the last four of the competition, Trevor Francis decided he had seen enough of his playmaker's form and fitness and decided to activate Sheridan's contract extension one game earlier than planned.

Sheridan, however, had not entirely shaken off the injury and was frequently playing through the pain barrier: "The truth is I rushed back too quickly," he would later reveal. "We had signed Chris Waddle that year, and I think I hurried my return because I wanted to play with him. I was okay in the matches themselves, but the reaction afterwards was not what it should have been. The trouble of course, is when the team's winning, you want to be part of it, and you tend to try to make light of the aches and pains."

One game Sheridan certainly did not want to miss was the first leg of the Semi-Final of the Coca-Cola Cup against Kenny Dalglish's expensively assembled Blackburn Rovers side which might well be recalled by those who saw it as one of Wednesday's best ever performances. Although Blackburn had gone ahead early in the game, Wednesday responded with a spell of devastating, one-touch attacking play and deadly finishing. In sixteen first half minutes the Owls scored four times - Harkes headed the equaliser, a Sheridan flick gave the Owls the lead and then Warhurst struck twice in four minutes. In fact Wednesday looked like scoring every time they went forward.

Although Carlton Palmer scored an own goal shortly before half-time, 4-2 was an undeniably healthy lead to take into the second leg. The gloss on a memorable evening was however taken off in the second half when Nigel Pearson broke his leg, an injury that ended his season. Indeed Pearson would only play five more games for Wednesday (the following season), the last of which saw him break his leg again, effectively ending his Hillsborough career.

The Owls were without doubt the form team in the country around this time. Following their defeat to Leeds on 12th December, Wednesday went unbeaten in sixteen games (spread across all competitions), a run which included an astonishing thirteen victories, eight of these consecutively.

Towards the end of February the Owls were sitting fourth in the League (with games in hand on the teams above them (Aston Villa, Manchester United and Norwich), seemingly had one foot in the League Cup Final and were through to the Sixth Round of the FA Cup (having seen off Southend in the Fifth Round three days after their 4-2 win at Blackburn).

What was all the more remarkable about these statistics was that they were achieved without the regular services of their first choice strikers, Hirst and Bright, for much of this period. In their stead Chris Bart-Williams and Paul Warhurst had deputised and it was the form of the latter that been one of the keys to Wednesday's remarkable run of form, particularly in the cup competitions. Warhurst had had a short spell up front earlier in the season and had thought that Francis had been joking when the idea of converting had been put to him in training and only agreed to make the switch with reluctance. Strange, then, that he should take to the role as if to the manor born. Blessed with pace, strength and bravery that made him a real handful for defenders and an instinctive finishing ability, Warhurst was a revelation, finishing the season with eighteen goals from all competitions. It was the tactical masterstroke of the season, although it was not to be without repercussions for the manager.

Although Wednesday's unbeaten streak finally came to an end on 3rd March with a 1-0 defeat away at Coventry, the Owls quickly bounced back to earn a hard-fought 3-3 draw with Derby County in the Sixth Round of the FA Cup and a 1-0 win at Ipswich. Particularly pleasing about the latter result was that it was earned in the absence of many of Francis's senior players (including Sheridan), rested ahead of their Semi-Final second leg with Blackburn Rovers.

When Blackburn arrived at Hillsborough four days after the Ipswich game it momentarily seemed like Wednesday's progress to a second League Cup final in three years was not the foregone conclusion it had seemed, when Blackburn reduced the aggregate arrears with a goal after thirty-four minutes. Fortunately second half substitute David Hirst restored Wednesday's two-goal advantage with twenty-two minutes left to play and then Bright added a second on seventy-three minutes to put the Owls through to their second League Cup Final in three years, where they would meet George Graham's Arsenal.

The Lancastrians' Sheffield misery was then compounded when they were dumped out of the FA Cup at the Quarter-Final stage on penalties by Sheffield United at Bramall Lane two days later. As a result, with the draw having already been made, the Owls knew that if they could see off Derby County in their Sixth Round replay they would meet their fiercest rivals from across the city in the Semi-Finals of the competition for the first time in history.

The city of Sheffield was therefore relying on Wednesday to make this dream tie a reality and the Owls didn't disappoint, with Paul Warhurst volleying home a sublime pass from Sheridan in the 23rd minute to score the only goal of the game. Wednesdayites now had two Wembley dates to look forward to... at least.

First up was their Semi-Final appointment with Sheffield United. Staging the Semi-Finals at Wembley had only been introduced in 1991 when Arsenal and Tottenham were paired together in the last four. Now that they had drawn each other again in 1993, Wembley was again chosen as the venue for their match while Elland Road would play host to the Sheffield derby.

This decision caused uproar in Sheffield – this was the biggest Sheffield derby in history, Sheffield's very own Cup Final – and it was view shared by many (though not by this author) that the national stadium was the only fitting place for such an historic (and, to date, unique) occasion, and the FA were besieged with telephone calls, faxes and letters from the Steel City demanding the tie be switched to Wembley. Both the Sheffield clubs also desperately wanted to be afforded the same courtesy as their North London counterparts and with the backing of their local politicians successfully lobbied the FA to get the venue changed.

Sheffield United's desire to switch the tie seemed baffling, both then and with the benefit of hindsight. The comparatively tighter confines of Elland Road would surely have offered a more traditional derby atmosphere and "ordinary" match feel in which the Blades were much more likely to prosper. Wednesday's team was packed with players who had experience of Wembley (and winning experience, to boot) whereas United's side had only three (Alan Cork, Franz Carr and John

Pemberton) who had played on the hallowed turf. Their desire to switch the tie seemed to hand the Owls a potentially crucial advantage, as United manager Dave Bassett would later acknowledge in his autobiography.

Sheridan and his team-mates couldn't believe their luck when they found out that the Blades actually shared their wish to get the tie switched: "We couldn't believe they wanted to play at Wembley," Sheridan said, "Elland Road would have been a right battle because we were a footballing side and they were hardworking. But they wanted to play it at Wembley which suited us down to the ground, and on the day we proved that."

Sheffield supporters, though, made the city proud and proved what it had meant to them to get the game moved south, creating an electrifying (and trouble-free) atmosphere that was enough to make some of the players hair stand on end as they came out of the tunnel.

"Coming out of the tunnel the noise was frightening," Sheridan recalled. "It was louder than against Manchester United for the Rumbelows. There were balloons everywhere. The atmosphere was probably one of the best I've ever played in."

Wednesday got off to the perfect start within sixty-two seconds of the kick-off when they were awarded a free kick after Pemberton had fouled his former Crystal Palace team mate, Mark Bright. Even though the free-kick was some thirty yards out, Chris Waddle audaciously decided to go for goal, and duly curled the ball into the net much to the surprise of everyone in the ground, the players included. Standing over the ball alongside Waddle was John Sheridan who, naturally, remembers the moment well: "Chris just said he was going to hit it. I thought it was a bit too far out, actually. But he got so much power and bend on it. I think with it being so early in the game it took everyone by surprise. It flew in and was a great start for us."

The early breakthrough gave Wednesday confidence, and they started to play the Blades off the park, creating numerous chances to kill the game off, with Warhurst twice hitting the woodwork. Despite Wednesday's demonstrable superiority, at 1-0 down the Blades were still in the game, and a minute before half-time they grabbed a scarcely deserved equaliser when Alan Cork latched on to a long ball from Franz Carr and beat Chris Woods with a shot that just about trickled over the line and into the net.

In the second half Wednesday continued to dominate and also continued to miss chances, with Bright and substitute Hirst being particularly culpable in this regard. As United rocked under the pressure, seemingly inhibited by the venue of legends, how they must have wished they were at Elland Road as the wide open spaces suited Sheridan and Waddle down to the ground. Fortunately with Alan Kelly in seemingly invincible form, denying Hirst, Sheridan and Bright with a sequence of marvellous saves, the game was still there for the Blades to nick it against the run of play.

The game went into extra time and two minutes into the second period Wednesday won their umpteenth corner and it was from this that they finally found their way past the resolute Kelly. Sheridan had up until that point taken every corner but on this occasion a combination of frustration and fatigue got the better of him and he gestured for John Harkes to try his luck instead. The American delivered his kick to the near post and Mark Bright – who had missed so many chances throughout the match – headed the ball down, past Kelly and into the net.

"I can remember having a real go at Brighty," Sheridan recalled of the events leading up to the match-winning moment. "He'd just missed a couple of chances. It was out of frustration, really. Anyway, the next corner came along. I was supposed to take all the corners but I was on the other side of the field and I couldn't be bothered to run over. So I sent Harkesy over to take it, and luckily enough it landed on Brighty's head and he'd got the winner."

There was no way back for the Blades after that and it was the Owls who would head back to Wembley on 15th May for a showdown with Arsenal (who had beaten Spurs in the other Semi – ensuring both of England's domestic cups would be contested by the same two sides for the first time). Sheridan had laid the ghost of 1987 and his team had been worthy winners. "I know it was only 2-1 on the day" Sheridan believed, "but it could have been six or seven. Alan Kelly had one of those days, he was world class."

A fortnight after their Semi-Final triumph the Owls returned to Wembley on 18th April for their Coca-Coca Cup Final date with Arsenal.

Wednesday started the brighter and almost went in front after only four minutes when Paul Warhurst smacked a shot against the post. Five minutes later the Owls did go ahead. Having been awarded a free kick on the edge of the Arsenal penalty area, Sheridan fed King whose low centre was only half cleared and Harkes pounced to score. Unfortunately Wednesday could only hold on to the lead for nine minutes before Paul Merson lashed in a curling twenty-five yard equaliser.

Both teams continued to create chances throughout the first half but the score at the break remained 1-1. The second half was a much more subdued affair and chances were noticeably fewer and further between, the closest Wednesday came being a Sheridan free-kick that was well saved by David Seaman.

A tight and rather turgid contest was then settled in the sixty-eighth minute when a low cross from Merson was diverted by Carlton Palmer into the path of Steve

Morrow, who despite never having scored for Arsenal prior to the game, kept his nerve to knock home the loose ball from eight yards.

It was somehow typical of their tame second half performance that Wednesday could find no response in the remaining twenty or so minutes other than a couple of half chances and it would be Tony Adams and not acting Owls skipper Viv Anderson (whose head was swathed in a blood soaked bandage after injuring himself in a collision with Ian Wright) who would lift the Coca-Cola Cup.

Wednesday had not done themselves justice in the game, a fact that the manager was all too quick to acknowledge: "We didn't deserve to win," Trevor Francis admitted bluntly. "We didn't pass the ball well. Arsenal did not play well either. They did not take us apart and the winning goal, unfortunately, was a mistake from Carlton Palmer."

"The League Cup wasn't a good game," a disappointed Sheridan would regret. "It was a scrappy game. I think, to be fair, there wasn't much in any of the games, but we didn't play the way we knew we could play."

Having been distracted by the cups it was perhaps inevitable that Wednesday's League form would suffer and it did. In fact, Wednesday would register only two wins (against Southampton and Arsenal) from their concluding eleven League fixtures to finish in seventh place.

This did not meet with Wednesday's expectations, admittedly, but, in further mitigation, the build up of fixtures caused by their cup successes meant that at the start of May, for example, Wednesday had been forced to play five games in eleven days – concluding their League campaign with a 3-1 defeat away at Queen's Park Rangers.

Five games in eleven days was hardly the most ideal preparation for an FA Cup Final appearance and neither was the fact that only one of these games was won (ironically against Arsenal).

Nevertheless the FA Cup Final promised to be a nicely poised affair between two evenly matched teams. Arsenal had won the Coca Cola Cup Final, but the Owls had triumphed in the most recent League game between the two sides. Arsenal had plenty of big game players such as Ian Wright, Paul Merson, David Seaman and inspirational skipper Tony Adams, but Wednesday had plenty of potential match-winners, too. Arsenal were a strong defensive side, but Wednesday had proved time and again that season that they had the craft and creativity to carve open even the very best defences on their day.

Francis had only one major selection headache. Having lost Peter Shirtliff to injury, Francis had asked Warhurst to revert to defence. For reasons that seem too obscure to fathom, Warhurst decided to take this innocent request very badly indeed; childishly throwing his crayons out of his pram and later revealing to a tabloid newspaper that he had considered walking out on the team on the eve of the Final! It is every boy's dream to play in the FA Cup Final, indeed it's every professional footballer's dream and most would have given their high teeth to play whatever the position. Evidently Warhurst didn't share this sense of honour and given the arc of the player's subsequent career, his reaction now seems like the actions of a deluded prima donna. Certainly Warhurst's own view that he "was being treated like a piece of shit" rings hollow to this very day. Either way the situation was hardly helpful to Wednesday's Cup Final preparations and indeed had Warhurst gone through with his self-centred and asinine plan to walk out it could have totally derailed them.

According to Ian Wright's autobiography the Gunners preparations, meanwhile, went swimmingly and the striker would also reveal that his team-mates had been fired up for the game by some loose words from the Wednesday manager: "Wednesday did a brilliant job of shooting themselves in the foot in the preparation for the second final," Wrighty bristled. "Trevor Francis came out with the theory that we'd only won because we'd stopped their flair players in the first match. Now pardon me because I may have been missing a few things over the years, but isn't that the whole point? Should we have just sat back and let Chris Waddle and John Sheridan make forty yard passes all day, or let Brighty have all the chances that his heart desired? Rubbish! We had a game plan and we stuck to it brilliantly, and George wasn't going to change a thing second time round."

In other words the FA Cup showdown on 15th May was to prove another dour encounter.

As they had in the Coca-Cola Final, Wednesday started well but this time it was Arsenal who took the early lead courtesy of a set-piece, when Wright got in front of his marker to nod in Andy Linighan's flick on from Paul Davis's chipped free-kick.

Arsenal, who had made 1-0 wins such a speciality, predictably attempted to shut up shop but the Owls slowly regained the initiative after the break and their persistence against Arsenal's stifling tactics was rewarded after sixty-two minutes when Hirst equalised following a move started by Sheridan. With the scores level at the end of ninety minutes the game went into extra time and but this too proved insufficient to separate the teams. Wednesday had probably shaded the encounter and had certainly played most of the attacking football (reflected in a corner count of twenty-seven) but it had been a poor game to watch.

In those days the traditions of the FA Cup Final were still sacrosanct and so the two sides headed to a replay the following Thursday. Had the game been staged nowadays the first game would have been settled on penalties which if nothing else would have at least spared Wednesday fans the torture of having to watch Arsenal for the fifth time that season.

As with the first game Arsenal again took the lead through Ian Wright (who latched on to a long ball and sprinted between Wednesday's makeshift central defence of Palmer and Warhurst to clip the ball over Woods and into the net) but again the Owls equalised when Harkes found Waddle and the winger's goal-bound shot was deflected by Lee Dixon past David Seaman on sixty-nine minutes.

Wednesday pushed on in search of the winner and Bright hit a post and could, and almost certainly should have won it for Wednesday at the death but side-footed wide when it seemed easier to score.

Instead the game again went into extra time and just when it looked like matters would have to be settled by a penalty shoot out Arsenal nicked it with mere seconds remaining, when a Paul Merson left wing corner was met by Andy Linighan who directed his header towards goal. Woods did get his hands to the ball but was somehow unable to prevent it from crossing the line. It was an agonising and cruel conclusion to 240 minutes of action, that on the balance of the actual football played, the victors had scarcely deserved.

How had Wednesday come so close to end up with nothing? "Arsenal at the time were all about stopping teams from playing and they were very good at it," Sheridan believed. "If there was one team we didn't want to play, it was Arsenal. If we could have played anyone but Arsenal then we'd have won both cups. They knew they had to stop Chris Waddle. I think we should have won the FA Cup replay. We were absolutely gutted to lose both cup finals. It showed on our faces at the end of the replay. It wouldn't have been so bad if we'd managed to win one of them. I was ready for penalties in the replay. What a time for them to score."

"My memory of the FA Cup Final replay," Sheridan later recalled, "is that we should have won it because we had the chances; and it was very disappointing when Arsenal snatched the winner in the last seconds of extra time. There was nothing between the teams, really. At the time the goal went in, I was turning my thoughts to the penalty shoot-out, because I had been designated to take our first spot kick, I would rather have seen us lose on penalties than to be defeated in the way we were. It was very cruel."

If there's any consolation, the George Graham Arsenal side would now probably remembered at best by a shrug of the shoulders (as the chant of "Boring, Boring, Arsenal" and Tony Adams raising his arm aloft for some illusory off-side washes over one's senses) while the Wednesday of Waddle and Sheridan et al are probably remembered even by neutrals as an exciting footballing side that was often a treat to watch.

Added to which Wednesday could take more positives than negatives out of what fans to this day must surely look back on as a vintage season, debatably Wednesday's best ever. Jubilation had ultimately mixed in unequal measure with disappointment but there had been no shortage of drama.

One might argue (without strong conviction) that Wednesday's seventh place finish in the League was disappointing after the promise of their mid-season form (and the third place finish of the previous year) but I doubt there were many Wednesday fans who resented their concentration on the cups. In fact seventh was highly respectable given their disastrous start to the season and the absence of so many key players throughout the entire marathon 63 match campaign in which the Owls had lost only sixteen times and had scored a whopping one-hundred and six goals.

The signing of Chris Waddle had proved a massive hit, capturing the imagination not only with Wednesday fans, drooling neutrals and envious rivals but also with the nation's football writers who voted him their 1993 Player of the Year. In fact the only person in the country he was unable to seduce with his brilliance was the England manager, Graham Taylor, who stubbornly and foolishly preferred to pick virtually anyone else, including, to this author's eternal dismay and incredulity, future Wednesday player, Andy Sinton.

His partnership with John Sheridan, in particular, had been a spectacular success and with those two in tandem (and, if only, a fit David Hirst), Francis could at least boast a side that other teams genuinely feared.

While Sheridan was rightly quick to acknowledge that the Owls were far from being a two man team, he, too, was also quick to acknowledge Waddle's massive influence. "We still had a great balance in the team. There was myself and Chris as ball players and Carlton and Harkesy got through all the leg work. You've got to have different types of players and it just seemed to work. But Chris [was] a world-class player. [You] only [had] to give him the ball and let him get on with it. The opposition would put so many players on him it was amazing."

It was a season that had ultimately represented tangible and continuing progress and having come so close to those two major honours it genuinely seemed that Wednesday were on the cusp of really big things.

"Keep giving us your support," Trevor Francis asked the fans that had gathered beneath the balcony of Sheffield's Town Hall where his team had been given a civic reception to commemorate their achievements, "because I forecast good times for Sheffield Wednesday in the next few years. We have proved to ourselves that we are now one of the top sides in the country and we are here to stay. We won't be satisfied until we bring the championship to Sheffield."

At the time this did not feel like empty rhetoric, but with expectations now sky high, Francis would have his work cut out to honour his promises.

Chapter Seven

Following Wednesday's defeat in two Cup Finals, Trevor Francis convinced himself that big changes needed to be made at Hillsborough. Out went Viv Anderson and Danny Wilson to join Barnsley as player-manager and player-coach respectively and they were soon followed out the door by Peter Shirtliff (who joined Wolves for £250,000) and John Harkes who had fallen out with the manager and joined Derby County (for £800,000).

To replace them Francis spent big, bringing in a new defensive pairing: Andy Pearce came in from Coventry for £500,000 and, as a further confirmation of Wednesday's ambitions, England international Des Walker was lured to Hillsborough from Sampdoria for a club record outlay of £2.7 million, which Francis then matched to bring in left-winger Andy Sinton from QPR. To balance the books somewhat Paul Warhurst, still sulking after the FA Cup Final snafu (despite being restored to his evidently preferred attacking role at the start of the new season), was sold to Blackburn for £2.75 million when the campaign was just four games old.

Despite the changes Wednesday again made a poor start to the season losing 2-0 away at Liverpool on the opening day (with Carlton Palmer getting sent off after only 12 minutes) and then drawing 0-0 with Villa (with Sheridan operating on the right hand side of a three man midfield). In fact after defeats to Arsenal and West Ham (the latter without Sheridan) and a 1-1 draw with Chelsea, Wednesday found themselves second from bottom in the League with only two points (and one goal) from five games.

Wednesday did rediscover their scoring boots in a 3-3 draw with Norwich (a game in which the Owls had led three-nil) and a 4-2 reverse at Newcastle but it was not until the eighth game of the season that they could finally celebrate a League win when they beat Southampton 2-0 with goals from Sheridan (a penalty) and Hirst.

In the space of a few weeks the Owls were then rocked by injuries to three key players. First Pearson broke his leg again in the game against Southampton and would never play for the Owls again, while Hirst, who had not been training, saw a specialist who recommended surgery on his Achilles. This latest setback would keep him out of action until late January and even then only for five games before he needed another operation that would rule him for the rest of the season.

Although Sheridan would take part in Wednesday's draw with Blackburn Rovers, the defeat against Manchester United and both legs of their Coca-Cola Cup Second Round tie with Bolton Wanderers (from which Wednesday would emerge with a narrow 2-1 aggregate win), he too would join the long-term injured after joining up with the Republic of Ireland squad for their vital World Cup Qualifier against Spain on 13th October.

Although Jack Charlton's side were at that time sitting top of their group with seventeen points, they also knew that if Denmark won, as they were expected to do at home to Northern Ireland, defeat in Spain would leave qualification resting on Spain's ability to beat Denmark in their final fixture, with the Irish themselves needing to take something out of a tricky tie against Northern Ireland at Windsor Park – where few neighbourly favours would be expected and no quarter given. On the flip side if the Irish beat Spain they would qualify for the 1994 World Cup.

What, then, could have been a night of celebrations, instead turned out to be a miserable night for the Irish and a night of mixed fortunes for Sheridan. With Sheridan starting on the bench, Charlton's men found themselves two goals down after sixteen minutes and matters quickly became worse when Kevin Moran hobbled off with a groin injury.

The Irish then found themselves three down in the twenty sixth minute and cruelly the goal came from an error of judgement by Sheridan (who had replaced the stricken Moran).

When the Spaniards broke quickly down the right, Sheridan tracked back to intercept the cross and kick it to safety. Unfortunately he failed to spot Denis Irwin covering behind him and he miscued the ball into the path of Julio Salinas, the only Spaniard in the vicinity of the Irish penalty area. Salinas duly accepted the gift, rounding Bonner to finish in style. With not even a third of the game gone, the Irish found themselves 3-0 down and staring down the barrel of a spanking that would seriously threaten their goal difference, and consequently their chances of World Cup qualification.

Fortunately the Irish steadied their ship with Sheridan in particular putting his earlier error behind him with a highly impressive all round display. This was not enough to prevent many Irish fans from leaving early and plenty had already left the ground when Sheridan's performance was rewarded with a consolation goal on seventy-two minutes, latching on to Ray Houghton's cute lay off and side footing home from six yards.

Sheridan had played well, impressed his national manager and scored the goal that would prove so crucial in the final qualification reckoning. Unfortunately it was during this game that he picked up the thigh injury that would keep him out for several months. In fact aside from a seven minute cameo for Wednesday in the 3-3 draw with Leeds on 30th October Sheridan would take no further part in the season until 20th March.

Whereas Wednesday had struggled in the past without Hirst and Sheridan this time they embarked on an impressive run of form. In fact between the Coca-Cola Cup Second Round second leg victory against Bolton on 6th October and their win at

Tottenham on 5th February the Owls lost only two games out of twenty six (and one of those their obligatory defeat Arsenal), a sequence which saw them register fifteen wins, climb to sixth in the League and progress once again to the Semi-Final of the Coca-Cola Cup.

What was even more remarkable about this sequence of results was that Francis's side was often even further decimated by injuries. When they played Coventry on 20th November, for example, they were forced to do so with Carlton Palmer playing as a makeshift striker and 39-year-old Trevor Francis making an appearance (his last for the Owls) from the bench. Indeed when they played QPR in the Fourth Round of the Coca Cola Cup they did so with only fourteen fit players!

It was not until 1st February that Sheridan was deemed fit enough to return to action, lining up for the reserves alongside Hirst in a 2-2 draw against Derby County. However it was not until 20th March that he was ready to return to the first team.

Although Wednesday had been doing well in Sheridan's absence after the win at Tottenham on 5th February, the Owls went seven games without a victory, a run which had seen them slide down the League table and lose both legs of their League Cup Semi-Final against Manchester United (bowing out 5-1 on aggregate).

Seven winless games became eight when Sheridan finally made his first team reappearance against Blackburn. Nevertheless, despite the 2-1 reverse Sheridan made an impressive return, matching his tenacious former team-mate David Batty tackle for tackle and helping his side keep the eventual League runners-up under wraps for long periods, until, perhaps inevitably, he ran out of puff and was replaced by Phil King on seventy-six minutes. The score line was then 1-1 but a late winner from Newell sealed the points for Kenny Dalglish's title contenders.

For Sheridan it was just a relief to be back on a football pitch: "I thought I wouldn't play again this season" he admitted, and added that he feared he might miss out on a place in the Republic of Ireland squad for the World Cup (the Irish having qualified for the world cup in Sheridan's absence on goal difference by drawing 1-1 with Northern Ireland at Windsor Park in November). "It's been a relief. Every time I started training again, I found it just too painful to strike the ball. I was all right running, but as soon as I began kicking, the problem would return. When I was injured I thought it was just a strain to start with. But it turned out to be a rupture... Hopefully the problem has now gone for good, although I've yet to feel one-hundred per cent in my general fitness."

Fortunately, despite not being fully fit, Sheridan was still very much in Jack Charlton's plans, the Irish boss naming him in his Irish squad for the friendly match against Russia just three days after his Wednesday comeback against Blackburn.

Sheridan, however, had to pull out and instead continued his road back to full fitness with a friendly game for the Owls against Real Madrid in Cordoba. Even though the Owls went down 3-1, Sheridan did score a sensational free kick reminiscent of his effort against Kaiserslautern the previous season.

Following the Blackburn defeat, Sheridan's return seemed to inspire a dramatic upturn in Wednesday's fortunes as Wednesday won each of their next four games against Chelsea, Everton, Swindon and QPR with Sheridan scoring against the two West London sides.

In fact from that point on Wednesday (without the injured Sinton and Waddle) remained unbeaten until the end of the season, winning five and drawing four of their last nine games to finish in seventh place.

Once again seventh place (and reaching the Semi-Final of the League Cup), was highly commendable given their persistent misfortunes with injuries and their extremely poor start to the season. The team had also scored a staggering ninety goals (seventy-six of them in the League – Wednesday's highest tally for thirty years!), which is rather extraordinary when you consider Francis's side had again been without Hirst, Sheridan and Waddle for extended chunks of the season and it must have been particularly gratifying for the manager to see squad men like Gordon Watson, Chris Bart-Williams, Ryan Jones and Graham Hyde come into the side and make their mark.

Although Sheridan had struggled to regain full fitness and had been replaced in several of the games that followed his comeback he had done enough to be given the opportunity to stake his claim to a place in Jack Charlton's World Cup squad when he was selected to start against the Netherlands in a warm-up match in Tilborg.

With central midfield men like Andy Townsend, Ronnie Whelan and Roy Keane seemingly above him in the pecking order, and having contributed so little to the qualifying campaign (appearing only twice – as a substitute in the away win against Latvia and the home defeat to Spain), it was essential Sheridan made this appearance count, and he did, playing superbly well throughout, teeing up Tommy Coyne to score the winner in a famous 1-0 win and earning high praise from his manager.

"In midfield there was the spectacle of John Sheridan in full spate," Jack Charlton would write in his World Cup Diary. "There were a lot of good players on the park at Tilburg, and it says much for Sheridan that he looked in a different class to any of them. Whether he was finding that extra yard of space for himself, changing the direction of the play with just one flick of the ball or sorting out the final pass through the middle, he was brilliant, and from a relatively early stage I'm sure that

Dick Advocaat, the Dutch manager, had identified him as one they had to stop... Try as they would, however, they couldn't put him out of the game and, fittingly, it was Sheridan who found the little touch of magic to provide the cross for the goal which won it for us early in the second half."

A few weeks later, on 24th May, Sheridan was given another opportunity to shine against Bolivia at Lansdowne Road. With so many central midfielders at his disposal Jack Charlton had jettisoned his favoured 4-4-2 formation and had devised an experimental 4-5-1 system to accommodate at least three of them (with one deep lying in front of the back four). With skipper Townsend and young tyro Keane undroppable in the manager's eyes it therefore seemed to be a straight fight between Liverpool's Ronnie Whelan and Sheridan for the spare berth.

Against the Dutch Charlton had handed the deep lying play-maker's role to Whelan (behind Townsend and Sheridan) and the Liverpool man had done the job excellently. Now Charlton passed the baton to Sheridan.

Not only did Sheridan perform with authority in this unfamiliar role against the South Americans, he also struck the winner in the closing minutes. Tony Cascarino knocked the ball down for Terry Phelan and when his shot struck a defender the rebound ran into Sheridan's path and he lashed it in from twenty-five yards out.

"When John catches the ball properly, he can be deadly from that kind of range," his delighted manager applauded. "Right from the moment the ball left his foot, he knew he was on a winner and the Bolivian goalkeeper never moved a muscle until the ball had hit the net. It was a goal to win any game, and with so little time left there was simply no way back for the Bolivians."

Skipper Andy Townsend was also impressed with the way the new-look midfield was shaping up. "'We have got a good balance," Townsend stated after the Bolivia game. "John likes to knock the ball around while Roy and I have the job of getting up and supporting the lone striker. It means being more patient but we are not the sort of team that likes to sit back. Jack always wants us to do the driving and pressing."

Five days later Sheridan kept his place for Ireland's warm-up match with Germany in Hanover and caught they eye again as Ireland upset their hosts to win 2-0 with goals from Tony Cascarino and Gary Kelly. Sheridan had more than done enough not only to secure his place in Charlton's twenty-two-man squad but in the starting line-up, too. His performances had simply made it impossible for Big Jack to leave him out.

"John Sheridan may occasionally have felt that he was never going to establish himself in the team but all that changed on the day we beat Holland in Tilburg and I realised there was no way that he could continue to be kept out," Charlton affirmed after he had named his squad, "even if it meant going in with an extra midfielder. As a distributor of the ball, he's always been in a class of his own, but back in the early days he wasn't too keen on tracking opponents. He is now prepared to do this and is a much better player for it."

Before the Irish flew to America there was one more warm-up game to squeeze in against the Czech Republic and Sheridan again started the match (this time alongside Andy Townsend in a 4-4-2 formation with Roy Keane rested). The 3-1 defeat the Irish suffered confirmed to Jack Charlton that he simply had to continue his 4-5-1 experiment at the World Cup. With both Sheridan and Townsend instructed to push on, the Irish missed someone to anchor the midfield and diminutive inside-forward Martin Frydek, operating behind two front men, wreaked havoc.

It was a disappointing way to wave goodbye to their home fans, though Jack Charlton did feel that it did serve to take some of the pressure off his players and the following day, on 6th June, the Irish squad flew to Orlando, Florida to acclimatise to the heat and humidity before the action proper began on 18th June.

Ahead of the tournament Sheridan was convinced that Ireland could make a big impact for the second tournament running: "We caused a surprise by getting to the quarter finals last time. But people are now taking a lot more notice of us. It'll be harder this time because other teams will be wary. But I'm still confident we can get through to the later stages."

Republic of Ireland had been drawn alongside Italy, Mexico and Norway in Group E which was immediately dubbed the group of death due to the parity of the sides. Norway were a strong, well organised side with plenty of English-based players (not unlike the Irish), and Mexico were an enormously skilful side with bags of pace (and some wondrously talented individuals), and while Arrigo Sacchi's Italy were strongly tipped not only to win the group but also the competition, the Irish would have one crucial advantage: the crowd.

With so many locals of Irish and particularly Italian descent both sides were made to feel welcome by the 72,000 crowd inside New Jersey's New Meadowlands Stadium, but there can be no doubt that the Irish fans were in the vast, vast majority, with Irish tricolours draped virtually from every pillar to every post. Four years previously the two nations had met in Rome but now it was almost as if the Irish were the home team.

For all that, the Italians contained in their team some veritable footballing Gods such as central defenders Franco Baresi and Alessandro Costacurta, left full-back Paolo Maldini, midfielder Roberto Donadoni, Giuseppe Signori (a prolific striker for his club Lazio) and, of course, European Player of the Year, the Divine Ponytail, Roberto Baggio. In fact the Italians had such a strong side that the brilliant Sardinian Gianfranco Zola could not force his way into the starting XI.

The Irish would be fortunate on two more counts ahead of the Italian game. Firstly under their coach Arrigo Sacchi, an obsessive tinkerer, these footballing deities frequently found themselves fielded out of position or hamstrung by rigid tactical systems and, secondly, the Irish had some quality players themselves, and were arguably stronger than they had been four years previously. Indeed the likes of Paul McGrath, Roy Keane, Denis Irwin, Ray Houghton and, of course, Sheridan would not have looked out of place lining up for rather than against the Azzuri.

Ireland took to the field for the game against the Italians with their robust 4-5-1 formation: Bonner in goal, full backs Denis Irwin and Terry Phelan, centre-halves Phil Babb and Paul McGrath, Steve Staunton and Ray Houghton on the flanks, Sheridan, Townsend and Keane in central midfield (with Sheridan and Townsend pushing on and Keane in front of the defence) and Tommy Coyne operating as the lone striker.

The game was only eleven minutes old when first Costacurta and then Baresi failed to clear a raking long pass from Sheridan and the ball fell to Ray Houghton who chested it down, swivelled and swung his weaker left boot to lift it quite majestically over the head of Gianluca Pagliuca who was yards off his line, under the bar and into the net to put the Irish ahead.

Although the manager feared that his side had scored too early, the Italian fight back never really materialised. Italy's midfield was sluggish, predictable and unadventurous throughout the first half, and their defence fragile, while their opponents were determined, organised and resilient, particularly in defence. Phil Babb would never again play as well, alongside the cool, vigilant head of Paul McGrath, while full backs Irwin and Phelan looked assured and totally unruffled. But it wasn't just the back four; Ireland defended as a team with Charlton's five man midfield content to conserve their energy by venturing forward in rationed bursts. Tommy Coyne meanwhile had the game of his life – holding the ball up when required and running himself into the ground, so much so that he would collapse on the team bus after the match.

Sheridan, too, was playing a blinder, dropping deep to deny space for and limit the effectiveness of the vaunted Baggio, whom he also clattered with a couple of crunching tackles. In truth, it was all rather thrilling.

In the second half, the Italian boss brought on Massaro to partner Baggio, and switched Signori to the left. For a while this seemed to inspire the Azzuri as they upped their tempo, and looked a little more penetrative but still could find no way past Ireland's immovable defence. In fact far from wilting under the pressure and the heat, Charlton's men began to counter-attack and could and perhaps should have doubled their advantage. First Houghton forced Pagliuca into making a sharp save and then, when Keane got to the bye line and pulled the ball back for the unmarked Sheridan in the 72nd minute the Wednesday man seemed certain to score.

Alas, Sheridan leaned back a shade too much and his close range shot cannoned off the bar and rebounded to safety.

Fortunately the Irish were not left to rue Sheridan's miss, and the final twenty minutes or so were remarkably stress free. By the latter stage Italy had simply run out of steam and ideas as the Irish recorded a famous victory, their first ever over Italy and, bizarrely, despite reaching the Quarter-Finals of the 1990 tournament, their first ever at the World Cup. It was sweet revenge for their defeat in Rome four years previously.

"For a country the size of Ireland to beat Italy," Jack Charlton said after the game, "well it doesn't happen very often, does it? It was very special and probably surpasses all my playing achievements in terms of emotion."

The Irish then flew to Florida for their meeting with the Mexicans. Although they had now beaten Holland, Germany and Italy away from home in recent weeks, beating the Central Americans was always going to be a tough ask. With the game played in the searing and oppressive heat of Orlando's Citrus Bowl Stadium, the Mexicans would be used to it, the Irish, especially being far from the youngest team at the tournament, would not.

Despite that the unchanged Irish side played quite well for the first thirty-five to forty minutes, closing down the Mexicans in midfield and occasionally putting some good moves together themselves. With a little bit more luck the Irish might even have gone ahead after ten minutes when Terry Phelan and Roy Keane combined down the left but Tommy Coyne could not get on the end of the latter's inviting cross.

Throughout the tournament getting water to the players was a persistent problem. It was easier to throw water bags to the wide players but getting them to the central players was much harder, particularly since sundry FIFA jobsworths obstinately refused to allow Charlton's assistants to throw bags on to the pitch.

"We had a letter from the FIFA people, the medical side," Big Jack recounted, "and it said that in those temperatures, unless the players received water every fifteen minutes they were liable to go into a coma from which they're not likely to recover. Well, I took that seriously, but nobody else did."

In light of these factors it was inevitable that the heat would get to the Irish as the game went on and three minutes before the break Luis Garcia put his side ahead with a neat twenty-yard finish.

The Irish recovered their composure in the second half and Sheridan might have equalised. With Mexican's flamboyant keeper Campos yards off his line, Sheridan attempted a chip but having been forced to take his shot early he couldn't quite get the accuracy required and the chance went begging.

Shortly afterwards Mexico went two-nil up when a rare defensive lapse by Denis Irwin led to Luis Garcia doubling his side's advantage, squeezing the ball past Bonner off the foot of the post.

With goal difference looking likely to be vital in Group E, Charlton brought on McAteer and Aldridge in attempt to salvage something from the game. Amid televised scenes that were far more memorable than the match itself the inept FIFA factotums momentarily refused to allow Aldridge onto the pitch which led to some foul-mouthed ranting from the striker and some ill-tempered exchanges between Charlton and the feckless officials (which led to fines for both Aldridge and Charlton and a suspension from the dugout for the manager for the following game).

"We had a problem against Mexico when I wanted to bring John Aldridge on," Charlton elucidated. "We tried to give a note to the fourth official so we could make the substitution but it was taken by a guy in a blue jacket and yellow hat, who suddenly appeared and said: "I'm the FIFA man." The delay was because he was Egyptian and couldn't pronounce "Aldridge." I was stuck in my technical area. I couldn't cross the yellow line, but he came to me. He was shouting at me. He actually pushed me, and I got fined for that, which was a nonsense. FIFA just make up the rules as they go along - that was the real problem."

Fortunately for Ireland, Aldridge managed to put the row with the jobsworths behind him when he was eventually allowed to enter the field of play and with seven minutes remaining it was his fine header from a cross by Jason McAteer (who had been intelligently released by Sheridan) that reduced the arrears. The Irish then finished the match strongly and might even have stolen an equaliser through Townsend but Campos, the flamboyant Mexican keeper, was able to deny the Irish skipper's blistering drive with a flying save.

The Irish returned to New Meadowlands stadium for the Norway game. With both full backs suspended Charlton had to shuffle his pack – bringing in Leeds' Gary Kelly at right-back and McAteer at right midfield and switching Staunton to left-back and Houghton to left midfield. Up front Aldridge would come in for Coyne and, as a reward for running his socks off in the first two games in a more advanced role, Sheridan would play in front of the back four with Keane pushing forward.

With so many Premier League players involved (Norway included ten English-based players in their squad, seven of whom would play some part in this game) a very British style match had been predicted by the pundits, and with both sides struggling for goals and operating similar playing styles (getting men behind the ball in numbers, for example) it was inevitable that they would cancel each other out and so it proved. I remember the game – which unsurprisingly ended goalless - as an almost excruciatingly dismal game. Since England had abjectly failed to qualify I was, like so many other people, rooting for the Irish, although university exams prevented me from watching as many games as I would have liked. The game versus Norway then was meant to be my treat for revising admittedly not very hard (as my second year exam results would bear testament to). The only chance of note fell to Sheridan but his cute little twenty-yard chip just went over. That said, since it was virtually the only moment in the entire match that could be remotely described as "a talking point" it was repeated over and over again on the television.

With the Italians and the Mexicans drawing 1-1 in the other game, it meant that all four teams in Group E finished with four points and an equal goal differential of zero, the only time that has ever happened in World Cup history. Having scored one less goal than the other three teams, it was Norway who headed home, while Ireland, Mexico and Italy all progressed to the Second Round, and in the Italians' case all the way to the final where they lost on penalties to Brazil.

The Second Round pitched the Irish against the Netherlands. The Irish had proved only a few short weeks before that the Dutch were beatable, but then even at their very best the Dutch are fundamentally always beatable, due, as a general rule, to the internecine squabbling that has effectively wrecked their chances of success at virtually every major tournament they've qualified for in living memory. In addition the Irish had also shown that they were a good side, and while they might not have been favourites against the Dutch there was genuine hope that they could progress to the Quarter-Finals, where a mouthwatering clash with Brazil awaited the winners.

The game would be played on Independence Day and Orlando's Citrus Bowl was the venue and once again Charlton made changes – bringing back Coyne and Phelan in place of Aldridge and McAteer.

Unfortunately it was a day when defensive errors would cost the Irish dear. First Phelan undercooked a header back to Pat Bonner which Marc Overmars capitalised upon to set up Dennis Bergkamp to open the scoring on eleven minutes and then on forty-one minutes future Sheffield Wednesday man Wim Jonk waltzed through the middle of the park, dropping his shoulders and gliding past Sheridan as he went, and aimed a hopeful 35-yard shot straight at Bonner which the Irish keeper inexplicably contrived to spill into his own net.

The Irish did their best to force their way back into the match in the second half but squandered their half-chances and though they thought they had pulled one back with roughly ten minutes to go through McGrath, the referee disallowed it because the defender, in his opinion, had raised his foot too high. At the final whistle the score line remained 2-0 to the Dutch.

Jack Charlton's side had performed well for the second World Cup in succession and with a bit more luck might have at least equalled their Quarter-Final achievement of 1990. As in 1990, pundits everywhere would talk about Charlton having performed miracles to take his team as far as he had but this seemed to be based on the fact that the Republic is a small country and basically overlooked the fact that he had some bloody good players at his disposal.

Jack Charlton believed that the weather and one simple rule change prevented his side from progressing further in the competition (as they might well have done so had the competition been staged on a different line of latitude): "On the eve of the World Cup FIFA changed the rules so that the goalkeeper could no longer pick up the ball, and that knackered us up completely. Our game was all about playing the ball behind our opponents' defence and putting them under pressure, but we wanted their keeper to pick the ball up if our attacks broke down because while the ball was in his hands you had a few seconds to readjust your players and get back into position. If we pushed up and the goalkeeper kicked the ball straight away, he could knock it behind us - and our centre-backs weren't the quickest. That rule, that simple little rule, totally knackered everything. Our last game was against Holland, who played a possession game. They didn't give the ball away. We weren't like that, but you can't have people running all over the place chasing the ball in the temperatures we were playing in."

Ireland's exit from the competition ultimately marked the end of an era. The ageing members of the side, Sheridan included, would, one by one, drift away from the international scene over the next few months and years and having been unable to replace the vast majority of them with like-for-like replacements, in 1995, Charlton too would step down. In fact the Republic has only qualified for one major tournament since Charlton's time in charge - the 2002 World Cup under Mick McCarthy. The Charlton era, to which Sheridan had made a significant contribution, then, is rightly remembered as the "Golden Era" of Irish football.

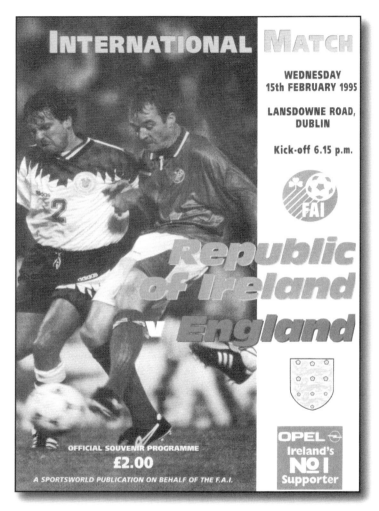

John appearing on the cover of the Republic of Irelend versus England programme.
Sadly, this game was abandoned due to crowd trouble.

Chapter Eight

It was a new look Wednesday that returned to Premier League action at the start of the 1994-95 season. Out, allowed to leave, went Nigel Pearson (who joined Middlesbrough for £500,000), Roland Nilsson (who returned to Helsingborg because of domestic reasons) and Phil King who rejoined Ron Atkinson at Aston Villa. Wednesday's longest-serving player Nigel Worthington and Carlton Palmer would also join the exodus, switching to Howard Wilkinson's Leeds United for £325,000 and £2.7million respectively. This was not just half a side; it was also the heart of the side.

In their stead came Ian Nolan (from Tranmere for £1.5 million), Peter Atherton (from Coventry for £800,000), and Romanian international Dan Petrescu (from Genoa for £1.3million) to form an almost entirely new back four, while Ian Taylor and Swedish international Klas Ingesson arrived from Port Vale and Bari respectively, to, well, at least theoretically, put pressure for places on Wednesday's midfield.

Unlike the previous seasons when the likes of Woods, Waddle and Walker had been brought in, none of the new men were the sort of signings to set the pulses racing and with Waddle also out injured with Achilles trouble (he would not reappear for the Owls until December) there was a pessimism abound that Wednesday no longer had a squad capable of challenging for trophies.

As far as the fans and some of the senior players were concerned, quality was not being adequately replaced. "Before they were buying proven players," Chris Waddle later commented. "All of a sudden we were bringing in unproven, potential players and that was the difference. It was a tricky time because we were an oldish experienced side but we still had a couple of years left in us and I would have liked to have seen us bring in one or two not five or six."

Sheridan agreed: "I think we got rid of too many players too soon. Several lads went who shouldn't have gone. The addition of one or two players to supplement those we had would have enabled us to profit from a blend of new blood and experience, but some experienced men were allowed to leave when, really, I doubt if any of the really wanted to go."

Wednesday made their usual poor start to the season losing 4-3 at home to Spurs on the opening day, and succumbing to a 3-2 defeat at QPR four days later (despite Sheridan scoring with a rare header). Although the Owls then opened their account by winning 1-0 away at Wimbledon it would be their only victory in their first eight League games.

Although Wednesday won their ninth and tenth League games of the season against Manchester United (1-0) and Ipswich Town (2-1), Wednesday won only one of their following six League games. During this time they would again lose Hirst to an injury that would keep him out of the side until early April.

Despite their faltering League form, Wednesday had made tentative progress in the Coca-Cola Cup, disposing of Bradford in the Second Round and Southampton in the Third. But when they drew Arsenal in the Fourth the writing was on the wall as far as their aspirations for that trophy and they duly succumbed to a 2-0 defeat.

Oddly enough the game against Arsenal on 30th November had been one of their better performances around this time, a game in which Sheridan's vision and passing was much to the fore but no-one could finish off his moves: "We lost the game ourselves, missing three great chances," summarised Sheridan (who had been appointed captain for the game and the two that followed in the absence of Des Walker). "We're giving one hundred per cent but it's just not going for us... we can't give any more."

With Hirst still absent Francis's side were simply not scoring. In previous seasons goals had come in abundance and from all areas of the park but by the end of Coca-Cola Cup defeat to Arsenal no Wednesday player had more than three goals to his name in all competitions.

Francis responded to this alarming statistic by buying Guy Whittingham from Aston Villa in a part/exchange deal that saw Ian Taylor head the other way, and half-decent player though Whittingham was, his signing seemed to underline the lack of ambition that was now spreading its tendrils throughout the club. Although Whittingham bagged two in each of his first two games for Wednesday he would not score in any of his subsequent twelve.

The return of Waddle for the match against Crystal Palace on 3rd December did provide a lift and, with Sheridan and Waddle reunited, Wednesday enjoyed a spurt of good form. They won all three matches over the Christmas period: beating Everton 4-1, Coventry 5-1 and Leicester City 1-0 to move them up to ninth in the table.

The game against Everton actually marked the start of a ten game unbeaten run in the League and Cup during which Wednesday briefly moved up to seventh in the League, exacting a measure of revenge against Arsenal at the very end of this sequence at last with a 3-1 win on 4th February.

The Arsenal win, however, turned out to be the high point of Wednesday's season. From then on in the only way was down.

If the course of a season can be said to change by one match, then for Wednesday in 1994-95 it was undoubtedly their FA Cup Fourth Round replay with Graham Taylor's Wolves at Molineux.

Although the first match between the sides at Hillsborough had ended in a goalless stalemate, the Owls had had enough chances to win (including an eighty-eighth minute Chris Bart-Williams penalty that was well saved by Jones, the Wolves keeper), so Wednesday ventured to Molineux with some confidence that 1995 could yet be their year in the oldest knockout competition of them all.

That dream however was then shattered in quite remarkable circumstances. The game (which Sheridan started on the bench, just as he had in the win against Arsenal four days earlier) had ended 1-1 after extra-time and had headed to the lottery of penalties.

With Bright, Whittingham and Pressman all converting their kicks (the latter two in particularly emphatic fashion) and with Wolves missing their first two, Wednesday appeared to be coasting. 3-0 up seemed an unassailable lead, but Andy Pearce then hit the crossbar, Bart-Williams' kick was saved, and Wolves held their nerve to level matters and take the drama into sudden death. The man who volunteered for Wednesday's sixth was Chris Waddle, the man who had skied *that* penalty for England in the Semi-Final of the 1990 World Cup against the West Germans.

Although Waddle had volunteered willingly to take one of the penalties, as he walked from the centre-circle he looked far from confident and later admitted that the traumatic memory of his miss in Turin was weighing heavily on his mind. "I decided that whatever I did I had to hit the target," Waddle later elucidated, "so I tried to place it by making the keeper go the wrong way. As it was, he guessed correctly and saved it. Everybody said I shouldn't have been involved, but if that was the case, then I had no right to be on the pitch. If the same thing happened again I still wouldn't bottle out."

When Don Goodman stepped up and put away his penalty Wolves had emerged 4-3 winners and Wednesday were out of the FA Cup. The players trudged off the field disconsolately, visibly shaken by what had just happened – nobody more so than Chris Waddle.

"The disappointment of losing when you've had chances to win and led 3-0 in the shoot-out, is an emotionally shattering experience," Trevor Francis lamented, "which ranks with how we felt after Arsenal's last minute goal in extra time at Wembley two years ago."

Nevertheless, at that stage Wednesday still had much to play for. Francis's side were still eighth in the League, and although it had become a straight shoot out between Blackburn and Manchester United for the title, there was a not insurmountable amount of daylight between the Owls and the teams immediately above them. After all, there was still fifteen games and forty-five points left to fight for. A UEFA Cup place was still within their grasp if they could put together a decent run. Something from the season, therefore, could yet be salvaged.

Instead, with confidence in tatters after their Cup exit, Wednesday lost seven of the nine games that followed it and nothing either the manager or the players could do could halt the slide. Lady luck was blowing on some other guy's dice.

After defeats against Blackburn (in which goalkeeper Kevin Pressman was sent off for the second time in five weeks), Villa and Liverpool (the latter with Sheridan again on the bench), Francis decided to change his tactics, opting for three centre halves, two wing-backs and a three-man midfield. In the manager's wisdom this left Sheridan as the odd man out and he sat out the next two games and incredibly found himself demoted to the reserves!

Sheridan, however, took being made the scapegoat by the manager in his stride: "[Trevor] was trying to change the team around; the players who'd been there a while were sometimes being dropped or left out. He was having arguments with one or two players when he was leaving them out but players are always moaning when they're being left out. But I didn't fall out with him, we got on all right."

At first Francis's changes appeared to have stopped the rot as Leeds were beaten 1-0 at Elland Road on 4th March and Norwich were held to a goalless draw at Carrow Road four days later.

Four points and two clean sheets were something on which to build but Wednesday's revival proved to be brief as they lost their next two fixtures: at home to Wimbledon (1-0) away to Palace (2-1).

Francis then brought Sheridan back into the side but even that didn't make any difference as Wednesday extended their losing streak to four with defeats at Manchester City (3-2) and then an embarrassing 7-1 hammering by Nottingham Forest at home.

Wednesday's season was unravelling at breakneck speed and the manager's future was now hanging by a thread. Indeed with the fans loudly chanting "We Want Francis Out" on the terraces, and with the tabloids filling their pages with rumours about Francis losing the dressing room, player unrest and open revolt, his departure seemed a matter of when and not if.

Stung by the humiliation by Forest, the Owls did then bounce back to beat Leicester 1-0 but then picked up only two points from their next four matches. They failed to score a solitary goal in the process (losing 2-0 to Coventry away, drawing 0-0 with Everton and Southampton, and losing 1-0 at Manchester United).

To make matters worse, as they approached their final game of the season, Wednesday were still mathematically involved in the battle to beat the drop. In the event a 4-1 win against Ipswich Town (and other results on the same day meant they would not have been relegated even if they'd lost) saw them finish thirteenth.

It had been a desultory, shambolic end to the season. For Wednesday fans finishing thirteenth and scrapping against relegation until the last game of the season was no longer acceptable after having their expectations raised in recent seasons. It was also clear that most of the manager's new signings had failed to live up to the standards set by the players they'd replaced. With Francis seemingly starting to lose unconditional faith in his creative players towards the end of the season, Wednesday no longer really had a side capable of playing the fluent attacking football which their supporters had become accustomed to.

As far as the fans were concerned the manager had to go, and six days following the end of the season, on the morning of the Cup Final, Dave Richards (a chairman who prided himself on listening to the voice of the fans) duly handed Tricky Trev his marching orders.

It could be argued that Francis had been unlucky, certainly with injuries to key players, pretty much throughout his time in charge at Hillsborough. David Hirst, for example, started only seventy-four of Francis's one-hundred and sixty-eight League games in charge, while Sheridan likewise missed huge chunks of the manager's four-season reign, ditto Nigel Pearson and Chris Waddle.

One thing Francis could not blame on the slings and arrows of outrageous fortune, however, was his unpopular decision to a) dismantle too hastily the squad he had inherited from Ron Atkinson and b) replace these stalwarts with players who were, quite blatantly, nowhere near as good.

Nevertheless, in the final analysis, I'm sure Wednesday fans would swap being rooted in the third tier of the English football with being fifteenth in the Premiership (and challenging for trophies). Certainly Wednesday fans and several of their senior players might now look back on Francis's dismissal as being a case of better the devil you know.

The man chosen as Francis's replacement was Luton Town manager David Pleat. Although Sheridan didn't know it at the time, Pleat's arrival would spell not only the end of his tenure at Hillsborough but, in the fullness of time, the end of Sheffield Wednesday as a top flight side.

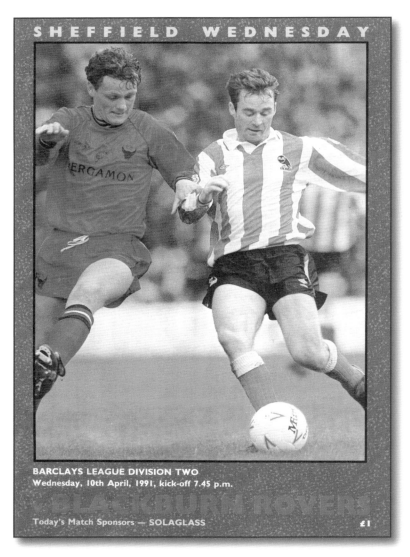

*John, appearing on the front cover of a 1991 Wednesday programme.
The player he is vying with was to become a Wednesday player a few
years later, Jim Magilton.*

Chapter Nine

From the moment David Pleat was appointed, it was clear that he intended to run things his way. His blueprint for success, however, was labyrinthine and recondite. Of course, no one can ever be really sure what his master plan entailed but it seemed, at least to the untrained eye, to involve the systematic freezing out of his experienced and established star players before replacing them one by one with sundry yes-men and mediocre overpriced, over-waged foreign imports.

Within two years Mark Bright, Chris Waddle, David Hirst, Chris Woods and John Sheridan had all left the club and in their place came the likes of Mark Degryse, Darko Kovacevic, Dejan Stefanovic, Reggie Blinker, Steve Nicol, Benito Carbone and Mark Pembridge.

Perhaps there was method to Pleat's apparent madness. He was the boss and if the older players thought he was a joke figure (and certainly none of them seem to have anything good to say about him, in fact quite the contrary), like virtually everyone else on the nation's footballing terraces, then stamping his authority on the club was going to be a very difficult task indeed. Ridding the dressing room of those he perceived to be malcontents would therefore have to be Pleat's priority. "That's what Pleaty wanted," Sheridan later sneered, "players who wouldn't answer back"

At the end of the day every new manager wants to bring in his own men – the fact that Pleat brought in new faces wasn't really the issue; it was the ones he brought in that was the problem.

Nevertheless Sheridan (who had added two more international caps to his collection over the summer, appearing in the goalless draw against Liechtenstein and the 3-1 defeat against Austria) actually featured in all of Pleat's first six League games in charge. He played in front of the defence as a deep lying playmaker as he had previously done for Ireland, a role which the player relished. Ominously, however, he was substituted in two of these games, and was relegated to the bench for the three that followed – a goalless draw with Manchester United and defeats to Leeds and Middlesbrough (Sheridan would only leave the dug-out in the latter two).

Pleat quickly got it into his head that he could start with Waddle or he could start with Sheridan but he could not start with both and the second game of the season against Blackburn would be the last time the two fans' favourites would start a game together for Wednesday. Instead Pleat looked to his new signings Mark Degryse and the combative but lightweight Welsh international midfielder Mark Pembridge to provide the craft and ammunition!

From this point it was clear that Sheridan did not feature in Pleat's long-term plans. There was some talk of a new contract but it was a derisory offer. The manager seemed to want to have his cake and eat it, he didn't want to pick Sheridan but selling him might make him look bad – not only would the fans get on his back (which the thin-skinned Pleat clearly wanted to avoid at all costs) but there was also the very real possibility the player might come back to haunt him if he sold him to a rival club. Pleat's diabolical solution was to slap a prohibitive price tag on Sheridan.

If Pleat's zany plans had brought success on the pitch, the fans might have shown more faith in him but the plain facts of the matter are that the only things Wednesday were serving up were mediocre results and abysmal football. For a manager who had tasted little if any tangible success in a long and perversely enduring career it is odd that he stuck to his guns and continued to ignore the one central midfielder player capable of turning around his team's fortunes. Indeed, aside from one brief substitute appearance in the 2-2 draw with Manchester United on 9th December, Sheridan languished in the reserves.

He might not have figured in Pleat's plans but he was still considered good enough to play for the Irish national side. He duly took his place in their starting line up against old foes the Netherlands in their European Championship Play-Off game on 13th December at neutral Anfield.

Following the World Cup, Sheridan had been a virtual ever-present throughout Ireland's attempts to qualify for Euro '96, starting in eight of their ten fixtures: the 3-0 win away against Latvia, the 4-0 home win against Liechenstein, the 4-0 away win against Northern Ireland (in which Sheridan scored a fine individual goal – his last for his country) and the disappointing home draw against the same opponents, the impressive 1-0 home win against eventual Group winners Portugal, the inept away draw with Liechenstein and both of the home and away games against Austria that each ended in 3-1 defeats. The home defeat against Austria, incidentally, represented the first time Ireland had been beaten at home in a qualifying game for either the World Cup or the Euros for seven years!

Although Sheridan would miss the 2-1 home win against Latvia and the 3-0 defeat away at Portugal, Ireland would finish second in their qualifying group on seventeen points (their goal difference was superior to that of Northern Ireland in third place by one solitary goal) and thus Ireland had qualified for the winner-take-all play-off with Holland.

In what was effectively a last throw of the dice, Charlton decided to start with virtually the same team that had lost to the Dutch in the World Cup in Orlando. Sadly there would be no last hurrah for the men who had served their manager so well over the years and the Dutch would again emerge 2-0 winners and as a result it would be they and not the Irish who would progress to compete in Euro '96.

Charlton pondered his future for eight days before deciding to step down as Ireland's manager on 21st December.

The popular manager had taken Ireland to the finals of three major tournaments, as well as, at one point, sixth place in the FIFA rankings. He had been manager of Ireland for ninety-four games during which he had won forty-seven, drawn thirty and lost only seventeen times.

Sheridan would also call time on his international career after the game with the Netherlands. He had played thirty-four times for the Republic of Ireland (a haul which would surely have been more but for injuries and the fact that Roy Keane and Andy Townsend had so often stood in his way), scored five times and had played in two World Cups, and in truth the Irish have missed someone of his guile and creativity ever since.

Sheridan has forever retained nothing but fondness for his time with the Republic, as well as the tremendous sense of honour that came with representing his country. "I have loads of memories," he would say in 2005. "I went to a lot of countries and saw how other people live. I wasn't sad when it was all over, just proud that I had been part of a magical time, playing against great teams and great players. It doesn't get any better than playing for your country and I will always see it as a terrific achievement."

*****

Sheridan returned from international duty and went straight back into the Wednesday reserve team and was in fact playing so well that one can only shake one's head in disbelief that the foolhardy Pleat showed no interest in restoring him to the first team. Although Sheridan admitted that he never once knocked on the manager's door demanding to know why he was not in the team and quietly got on with his business inside he was seething, miserable and desperate to get away.

"It was the things that Pleat used to say to me when I was playing in the reserves that pissed me off," Sheridan later explained. ""I love the way you get the young lads playing," he'd say and then every Saturday he'd leave me out. He was telling me in the office that I was a better player than some of the others, but that he had to play them because he was looking to the future. I was getting on for thirty-one or thirty-two but I knew I was better than the players he had in that team and I think the fans knew that as well. I just didn't get on with him at all. I never argued with him. I just didn't get on with him."

Having been starved of first team football for so long, when the opportunity arose to join Barry Fry's Birmingham City on a month's loan in February 1996, Sheridan jumped at it.

Birmingham had been vying for promotion from Division One earlier in the season but by the time Sheridan arrived at St. Andrews they appeared to have settled for mid-table obscurity (they finished the season in fifteenth place). Nevertheless they had reached the Semi-Finals of the League Cup and since Sheridan hadn't been selected by Pleat to participate in any of Wednesday's short journey to the Fourth Round, he was free to make his Birmingham debut in the Semi-Final first leg at St Andrews on Sunday 11th February. Standing in the way of Birmingham's passage to Wembley was Leeds United.

Leeds had achieved a great deal since Sheridan's departure in 1989 (notably winning the old First Division in 1992), but 1996 was really the fag end of Wilkinson's time in charge at Elland Road and his team were no longer the force they had been earlier in the decade. Nevertheless a few familiar faces were still on board including John Lukic, Gary Speed and the man who had ultimately replaced Sheridan as Leeds' schemer, Gary McAllister. Also in the Leeds line-up was Sheridan's former midfield partner Carlton Palmer. Leeds would start as overwhelming favourites to reach the Final.

If beating his former team was incentive enough for Sheridan, there was an extra motivating factor for Birmingham City, too. The draw had kept them apart from their fierce local rivals, Aston Villa, who been paired with Arsenal in the other Semi. It seemed a good omen for Fry's men as the only major trophy the Blues had ever won up until that point had come way back in 1963 when they had beaten Villa in the League Cup final.

At first everything appeared to be going Birmingham's way. The Blues refused to let their Premier League opponents settle and went in at the break a goal up thanks to a 25-yard screamer from Kevin Francis. Leeds however clawed their way back into the match and the equaliser duly arrived when Tony Yeboah finished stylishly after latching onto a long punt up field from the Leeds goalkeeper. Leeds were then gifted the lead when another former Leeds man Chris Whyte headed into his own net. Leeds ended the night 2-1 up but Barry Fry's side were still in the tie. Even Tony Yeboah admitted that the Blues had "frightened the life out of us".

After a 1-0 defeat to Stoke (in which Sheridan started) and a goalless draw with Barnsley (in which Sheridan was used as a sub) in the League, Birmingham travelled to Elland Road for the second leg on 25th February.

Backed by 4,500 travelling fans, Birmingham took the game to Leeds, looking for the opening that would square the tie. Six minutes after the break, with the game still goalless, they thought they'd found it when Ian Richardson found himself just ten yards out with only the keeper to beat. Unfortunately for the Blues Lukic blocked both the shot and with it, effectively, went Birmingham's chances of reaching the Final. Within a few minutes Leeds had scored twice through Phil Masinga (following an error by Michael Johnson) and a Tony Yeboah scissor kick to make it 4-1 on aggregate, leaving the Blues needing a miracle.

Creditably Birmingham refused to capitulate and were offered a glimmer of hope when, with more than half an hour left, Sheridan was tripped in the Leeds box by Gary Kelly. Birmingham, though, had had a dismal recent record of converting penalties and sure enough Steve Claridge, still dazed after a collision with the referee minutes earlier, could only send his spot kick against the foot of a post. Brian Deane's late header made it 3-0 on the night and Birmingham's Wembley dream was well and truly over and their wait for that second major trophy would have to wait fifteen more years. Arguably more painful than Claridge's missed penalty, Richardson's sitter, Whyte's own goal and Johnson's defensive blunder that had all contributed so much to their defeat was the fact that Villa had seen off Arsenal in the other Semi (Villa would win an embarrassingly one-sided Final 3-0).

Despite the fact that Birmingham had not managed to win any of the four games in which Sheridan had played, the player himself had impressed and when he returned to Sheffield he surprisingly found himself instantly recalled to first team duty.

Wednesday had at that point just lost six out of their previous seven games and had seemed so utterly bereft of creative inspiration that Pleat obviously decided he could no longer keep slicing away at his nose to spite his face.

Having spent so long on the sidelines, Sheridan entered the match determined to prove to every last one of the 22,964 spectators in attendance that Pleat had been wrong to freeze him out. In the event, Sheridan played a blinder and was at the heart of everything good about Wednesday's play as the home side ran out 2-0 winners thanks to goals from Whittingham and Hirst.

"I had a brilliant game," Sheridan recalled with satisfaction. "The fans were getting on his back for leaving me out of the team. I'll never forget how he came into the changing room after the game and said: "Boy, you made that look easy." He'd left me out for five months. I think he'd really wanted me to have a shit game."

After his display against Villa, it was now impossible for the manager to consign him back to the reserves and Sheridan duly kept his place for the visit to Southampton which Wednesday won 1-0 to record successive wins for the first time that season.

That, unfortunately, was as good as it got. Although Sheridan would play in every one of Wednesday's remaining seven fixtures except for the last game of the season, the Owls would register just one more win that season (at home to Arsenal) and Pleat's first season in charge limped to its moribund conclusion.

On 27th April, against Everton, Sheridan started a Wednesday match for the last time. It was not a fitting swansong – the Toffeemen won the game 5-2 and Sheridan was substituted.

Incredulously, Wednesday even went into their final game of the season away at West Ham as one of the four teams facing relegation. Fortunately in Pleat Wednesday had a manager who knew all about last day Houdini routines and a 1-1 draw was enough to see his team crawl to safety. Wednesday thus finished the season in fifteenth place – two places lower than the position which had gotten Trevor Francis the sack the previous season. Inevitably there were calls for Pleat's head. This time however the Wednesday chairman eschewed listening to the fans and decided to stick by his manager.

With the Owls far from convincing during the pre-season the calls for Pleat's head only got louder and a rumour went around that if Wednesday lost their first four games of the season Pleat would be sacked with Chris Waddle installed as the bookies' and fans' favourite to succeed him. The fixture list suggested that a large majority of Wednesdayites would get their wish. In their first four games Wednesday were due to play Villa at home, Leeds and Newcastle away and then Leicester at home.

Instead Wednesday and Pleat confounded the pundits and, indeed, all logic, by winning all four to sit proudly atop the League and Pleat had, if only temporarily, been vindicated.

Sheridan had been an unused sub against Villa and Leeds, was absent from the squad that faced Newcastle, came on as sixty-sixth minute sub against Leicester and in the following game – a 2-0 defeat to Chelsea – Sheridan came on as sixty-second minute replacement for Ritchie Humphries. It was to be Sheridan's last appearance in a Sheffield Wednesday shirt. After that it was back to the reserves.

If Sheridan had not been in Pleat's long term plans, why had he not been allowed to leave on a free transfer in the pre-season when he stood a better chance of sorting out a decent deal elsewhere? Several weeks into the season, managers at other clubs had spent their summer transfer budgets, as Pleat would have known all too well, and Sheridan was thus placed in a needlessly difficult position.

Fortunately, salvation arrived when the opportunity arose to join Bolton Wanderers on loan (for a "hire" fee of £20,000). In truth Sheridan couldn't wait to get away. Not only was he tired of playing reserve team football but Bolton were top of the League in Division One. In addition the move also offered him the chance to play alongside his old friend and former Leeds team-mate Scott Sellars.

It was nevertheless still a massive wrench for the player to be leaving Hillsborough:

"When my time came to go," Sheridan later admitted, "I left with a certain reluctance. Of course, I was disappointed about not being in the side, and, in truth, the promise of first-team football elsewhere was the crucial issue, but I knew I was leaving a place where I had had some wonderful times and a club which meant a lot to me. What did hurt was the way it all happened. When I moved to Bolton ..., I just walked out the door as if I was going home like on any other day in the previous seven years. But I knew I wasn't coming back tomorrow, and somehow it was as if it didn't seem to matter to anybody. Nobody said thank you, and, well, I just felt so disappointed."

Sheridan had played 232 times in all competitions for Wednesday (plus 11 as sub) and he had scored 33 goals. Sheridan would always look back at his time with Wednesday as the most successful of his career, the club where he had played his best football. And Wednesdayites agreed. When they were asked to vote for their player of the 1990s in 2002 Sheridan came out on top of the poll and he would always be given an ovation whenever he returned to Hillsborough either as a player or opposing team's manager.

While Sheridan could now look forward to getting his career back on track at Burnden Park, it was however made plain to the player that the loan move was a one-month agreement only. Wanderers' boss Colin Todd was not, at that stage, interested in making the deal a permanent one.

The sticking point appeared to be the amount of money David Pleat was demanding - £200,000 plus £100,000 if Bolton were promoted, which was seen by Colin Todd as a bit steep for a thirty-two year-old midfielder with a history of knee problems. In addition, Todd had a number of central midfield players already at his club and oddly appeared keen to avoid selectorial headaches.

Nevertheless Todd knew he was getting a player of proven and undimmed quality who would only enhance his side's promotion push and saw the move as a chance for Sheridan to advertise his wares, if not for Bolton, then elsewhere: "John has the know-how and the experience," Todd attested. "He is an excellent passer and moves the ball well, which is the way we play. I know he can play; now he's got the opportunity to convince other people he can still do it."

"It's a chance for a few people to have a look at me," Sheridan agreed. "Hopefully I can help Bolton carry on what they have done already this season. I'll play a few games and take it from there."

Sheridan would make his Bolton debut against Birmingham City, who having parted company with Barry Fry were now managed by former Wednesday boss, Trevor Francis. Although Sheridan scored a debut beauty, the Wanderers lost 3-1 to register only their second defeat of the campaign.

Sheridan also scored in his second game for the Trotters, netting from a deflected corner after eleven minutes in a 2-2 draw with Crystal Palace (which had seen the Londoners score twice in as many minutes to recover from a 2-0 deficit).

Oddly for a side that had been threatening to run away with the First Division Sheridan would not enjoy a win in any of his first five League games for Bolton, as his new team followed the Palace result with three more draws (against Oxford, Sheffield United and Barnsley).

Nevertheless the consensus of opinion was that Sheridan had performed superbly well and immediately hit if off with the Bolton fans and his new team mates, forming a promising central midfield alliance with Alan Thompson.

"I have not enjoyed my football this much for two years." Sheridan asserted. "Bolton is a great club with some terrific players and the football they play suits me perfectly."

Sheridan might not have been able to inspire a League win during his short loan spell but on 27th November he would be in the thick of the action in an unforgettable night when Bolton took on Tottenham Hostspur for a place in the last eight of the Coca-Cola Cup.

In front of a packed and passionate Burnden Park crowd Bolton lived up to their giant-killing reputation by thrashing the Premier League big boys 6-1.

With the score at 2-1 at the break, Bolton showed their Premiership opponents no mercy in the second half, running Spurs ragged and scoring four more without any reply but it could easily have been more. Sheridan (in only his fifth game for the club) was inspirational and was given an ovation when he was brought off after eighty-four minutes with the job all but completed.

John McGinlay (who had scored a hat-trick in the game) was gushing in praise of his colleague: "He was magnificent. He gives us that little bit extra experience and Premier League class."

After what The Bolton News described as "two sensational goals and four outstanding displays in his first five games" Sheridan had clearly done enough to persuade Colin Todd to reconsider his earlier stance and when his one-month loan came to a close the Bolton boss was keen for Sheridan to stay for a second month.

Sheridan, too, was itching to stay and although he and the Wanderers agreed on an extension, the deal again foundered on Wednesday's financial demands.

Sheridan made no secret of his displeasure at being back at Wednesday: "I am now back at Hillsborough but that doesn't suit me," he complained. "Bolton and Sheffield Wednesday are trying to sort out a deal and if it's on a permanent basis, I'll be happy to return to Burnden Park. I just hope the whole thing can be sorted out quickly. It's now dragging on and I'd like to think the deal will be done in time for Christmas."

What Wednesday wanted was a second loan payment (reportedly higher than the £20,000 "hire" fee that Bolton had been forced to cough up the previous month), and although they were apparently happy to deduct this undisclosed amount from any subsequent permanent transfer deal, the club refused to budge from its original asking price, which Bolton still regarded as too high. Despite talks between the chairmen of both clubs, no compromise figure could be agreed and Sheridan was forced to watch Bolton lose their unbeaten home record to Ipswich on 14th December from the Burnden Park stands.

This was no way for Wednesday to treat a player who had served them so well for so many years and Pleat should be ashamed of his treatment of Sheridan at this time. Surely they didn't begrudge him the right to first team football. Clearly he was not in the manager's plans and had even continued to train with Bolton.

"Pleat was messing about," Sheridan recalled with bitterness. "He wouldn't let me go. So I went back into the club and told him that I didn't want to be here anymore. I said I wasn't playing, I was wasting my time and I wanted to go to Bolton. So then he sorted it out. I was at Sheffield for eight years and it was like: "Thanks for your time, see you later.""

With Alan Thompson out injured until well into the New Year with his leg in plaster, Todd found himself short of creative options and despite having recently spent £1 million to bring in central midfielder Jamie Pollock from Osasuna, the Bolton manager now decided to bring in Sheridan on a permanent basis.

When talks resumed, Wednesday finally agreed to lower their price and the deal that took Sheridan to Burnden Park's on a permanent basis was finally concluded on 19th December. In the end Wednesday received £180,000 for the midfielder with Bolton agreeing to pay a further £25,000 if Wanderers got promoted to the Premiership, a fee the Bolton manager described as "a snip."

"There's nothing wrong with getting experienced players as long as they know their jobs," Todd explained, "and we've seen in the month he's already had with us that John knows the job well.""

"It's come at an ideal time," Todd continued. "I hope John is the one who is going to push us on in the second half of the season. In fact, with hindsight, we could probably have done with him on Saturday."

Having agreed personal terms, the move was completed in time for Sheridan to face Swindon on 22nd December. Again the result was a draw, their sixth in their last eight games. Bolton now had now failed to win in eight League matches, and were no longer top of the League.

Sheridan issued a rallying cry to his team-mates to get their campaign back on track: "We've drawn a lot of games and that's not good enough. We've got to make sure we get up there," Sheridan stressed. "That's where we all want to play; it's where all the best players are and it's where all the top clubs are. It's the only place to play. I just hope I can help Bolton get back up there."

With Sheridan back in the side Bolton picked up sixteen points out of a possible eighteen from their next six games and although he would appear mainly as a substitute once Alan Thompson returned from injury on 29th January, Bolton would lose only one more game in the League that season (although they would exit the League Cup at the Quarter-Final stage, losing 2-0 to Wimbledon and bowed out of the FA Cup in the Fourth Round, losing 3-2 to Chesterfield) to pick up the First Division title and its iconic old trophy.

They had scored exactly one hundred goals and were only denied the chance to become the first team to finish on one hundred points when they conceded an injury time equaliser at Tranmere in their last game of the season to restrict them to ninety-eight. It was, nevertheless, still eighteen points more than second placed Barnsley.

Having played twenty games for Bolton (eight as sub) Sheridan naturally qualified for a medal – only the second winner's medal of his professional career.

It had been a great season for Bolton and a great way to bid a fond farewell to Burnden Park, their home of one hundred and two years as they prepared to move to their new all-seater Reebok Stadium.

Manager Colin Todd spent the pre-season reinforcing his squad by bringing in full back Neil Cox (from Middlesbrough for £1.2million), Robbie Elliott (from Newcastle United for £2.25 million), Peter Beardsley (from Newcastle for £450,000) and Arnar Gunnlaugsson from I.A Akranes for £100,000.

Sheridan was thrilled to be back in the big time and was looking forward to pitting his wits against the best when disaster struck him down yet again. It was while playing the second half of a pre-season friendly against Crewe on 16th July that Sheridan picked up another knee injury and instead of facing the likes of Liverpool, Manchester United and Arsenal, Sheridan instead found himself facing two minor operations, a long period of rest and a spell on the sidelines that would ultimately last six months.

Consequently Sheridan had to watch from the sidelines as his Bolton colleagues could win only one of their first ten League games, and that on the opening day of the season at Southampton.

This dismal run of results forced Todd back into the transfer market: bringing in Mark Whitlow from Leicester City for £500,000 and South African international central defender Mark Fish from Lazio in September for £1 million in September, and then splashing out £3.5 million to lure Dean Holdsworth from Wimbledon in October.

Unfortunately these investments did little to significantly improve the Trotters' fortunes and by the time Sheridan was ready to return to first team action, Bolton were sitting second from bottom in the League, and had been dumped out of both the League Cup (in the Fourth Round by Middlesbrough) and FA Cup (in a Third Round tie against Barnsley, whose line-up, incidentally, featured Sheridan's younger brother Darren).

Sheridan had to wait until December before he could even start training and it wasn't until January that he was fit enough to make himself available for selection. "John would have been a big help to us, if he'd been available," Colin Todd acknowledged in January. "We've virtually had to discount him up to now but he's starting to train again and could be just two or three weeks away."

In the end Sheridan would not make his comeback until 31st January against Coventry. It turned out to be a game too soon for Sheridan who, by his own admission, had a game to forget as Bolton slumped to a 5-1 spanking and Sheridan was relegated to the bench for the next three games.

By the time he returned to the starting line-up due to Scott Sellars' absence against Liverpool on 7th March the real John Sheridan finally emerged, although he was powerless to prevent another defeat as the Trotters went down 2-1, despite being a goal up at half-time through Alan Thompson. "For a player who spent the first six months of the season sidelined with a knee injury," wrote the Bolton News, "Sheridan held his own in illustrious midfield company at Anfield, fully deserving of the pat on the back from his manager."

But another defeat meant that Bolton now hadn't won a match since 1st December.

"We've had no luck," Sheridan asserted, "typical of teams when they are down at the bottom. The first half at Liverpool was an example - Thommo scored that great goal and we were looking comfortable. Then he hit the bar. If we'd have been at the top, that would have gone in. In the second half Arnar's [Gunnlaugsson] gone through and, if he'd been playing with a bit of confidence, he'd have scored."

Sheridan kept his place for the next game, a home encounter with Sheffield Wednesday (who had beaten Bolton 5-0 at Hillsborough the previous November), now with Ron Atkinson back in charge after the club had finally kicked Pleat to the kerb in October after a disastrous series of results.

Sheridan was understandably fired up for this encounter, desperate to prove that he could cut it at the top level, not only to the travelling fans who had once worshipped him but also, with Bolton seemingly unlikely to offer him a new contract at the end of the season, to any potential employers.

"I'm getting on now," the thirty-three year-old Sheridan acknowledged, "and I don't know whether I'll be here next season. I don't even know whether I'll be playing tomorrow but hopefully I can help in some of the remaining games. I'm determined to keep Bolton in the Premiership because they deserve to be there and, if I'm not going to be offered a new contract here, I need to prove to other people that I still have something to offer."

Ahead of the Wednesday game, Sheridan believed they needed to take two wins from their next three fixtures – against the Owls, Arsenal and Leicester – if his side were to have any chance of staying in the top flight: "We'd like to win all three. That's not impossible but it's going to be difficult. The lads certainly don't think it's all over though. They haven't been playing badly and they only need to get that first win that would make all the difference...and the sooner the better. When we had fifteen or sixteen games to go we thought we had time on our side but now, with ten, we're desperate. When I was at Sheffield Wednesday we got relegated and we only needed four points from seven games! Teams can think they are safe and they aren't. It will probably go to the last couple of games but I certainly think we can catch Tottenham and Everton."

One man who did not need convincing that Sheridan "still had something to offer," was Ron Atkinson, who, upon hearing of Sheridan's possible inclusion in Bolton's starting line-up, described him as "the best player I have ever worked with" and warned his Wednesday midfield of the threat he would pose if he played at the Reebok.

Sheridan, naturally had no time for sentiment: "I had a lot of happy years with Wednesday and enjoyed playing for Big Ron, who was a good manager and always got his teams playing good football. I was fortunate to score that winning goal at Wembley. But all I'll be interested in, if I play, will be getting the three points, which we need badly at the moment."

Despite the fact that Bolton hadn't won since 1st December the footballing fates ensured that there could only be one result and Sheridan duly inspired his team to twice come from behind to win 3-2 win.

Although it was Alan Thompson who grabbed the headlines for knocking in the winner from the spot, the youngster was quick to praise his midfield partner for his contribution to the long-awaited win. "He's helped a lot since he came back into the side," Thompson said. "He tells you what to do, where to go, when you can go and when you can't. He's been a magnificent help to me."

With Sheridan in the side (he would keep his place for the remainder of Bolton's fixtures), Bolton then lost only one of their next four games (at home to eventual Double winners Arsenal), beating Leicester, drawing with Wimbledon and beating Blackburn Rovers.

But just when it seemed like Todd's side had turned a corner they succumbed to two successive defeats at Derby County and at home to Leeds.

With only three games remaining Bolton found themselves five points adrift of their main relegation rivals Everton and with a much inferior goal difference. It looked all over.

But while Everton were losing 3-1 at home to Wednesday and 4-0 to Arsenal, Bolton won 3-1 at Villa and thrashed Crystal Palace 5-2, the latter result taking them out of the relegation places for the first time since December.

Bolton went into their final game of the season one point ahead of Everton. A win against Chelsea would keep them up. A draw would be good enough if Everton failed to beat Coventry.

Tragically, although Everton drew with Coventry, Bolton went down 2-0 at Stamford Bridge. Bolton and Everton both therefore finished on forty points, having won nine, drawn thirteen and lost sixteen. Both sides had scored forty-one goals but, unfortunately for Todd's side, the Toffeemen had conceded five fewer and so by the thinnest of margins it was Bolton that went down.

What made their demotion more difficult to swallow was the fact that when Bolton had played Everton in just their fourth game of the season a Bolton shot had hit the underside of the crossbar and bounced a foot over the line. Unfortunately the referee did not allow the goal and the match had finished goalless.

In addition, things might also have been different if Todd had been able to call upon Sheridan's experience and class throughout the season. The statistics spoke volumes: Bolton had won only four games from the twenty-six they'd played without Sheridan in the side and won five from twelve with him in it.

Nevertheless, as Sheridan had himself predicted earlier in the season, Bolton declined to extend his contract. It was understandable really. Not only was Sheridan now thirty-three, but his spell at Bolton had been plagued by injuries. In addition the Lancashire club wanted to build for the future.

For the first time since being released by Manchester City as a teenager Sheridan now found himself without a club.

John in his Bolton Wanderers playing days

Chapter Ten

Although Sheridan later revealed that he considered retiring after being released by Bolton because of the state of his right knee, his love for the game made it impossible for him to walk away and he remained convinced he still had something to offer.

Incredibly there were no League clubs within the pyramid prepared to offer him a deal. Sheridan did have a trial with Huddersfield Town but when that didn't work out he was invited to train and keep fit with Conference club Doncaster Rovers who were now being managed by his former Leeds team-mate Ian Snodin.

The previous season Donny had won only four of their forty-six League games (losing a record thirty-four times) and had finished fifteen points adrift at the bottom of the table and relegated to the Conference and, if that wasn't forbidding enough, when Snodin had taken charge on 1st August he arrived at the Belle Vue to find he had a squad of only five players.

It was therefore quite an achievement just to be able to field a side for their first match of the season, a 1-0 defeat at Dover Athletic.

Snodin decided to plug the gaps in his squad by picking himself and making a few phone calls to some friends and former team-mates: Neville Southall, Tommy Wright, Steve Nicol and John Sheridan, all of whom found themselves without a League club.

Southall (one of the finest goalkeepers of his generation, arguably the greatest goalkeeper in the world at one time) probably echoed the sentiments of the others when he said: "If I came from Denmark, I would probably have got a job with a Football League club."

Sheridan would make his Doncaster debut in Rovers' fifth game of the season against Kingstonian Rovers on Saturday 29th August 1998.

In front of a scant 1,942 at the Kingsmeadow Stadium it was not an auspicious occasion. Despite lining up with Southall, Snodin, Wright and Sheridan in their team Doncaster lost 2-1 to record their third defeat of the season (although Sheridan had almost opened the scoring when he rattled the bar with one of his trademark free-kicks).

Sheridan kept his place in Snodin's side for Rovers' next three games: a 1-1 draw with Kettering and the defeats to Forest Green Rovers and Hayes (Steve Nicol making his Doncaster debut in the latter).

Although Sheridan missed Doncaster's next game (a 3-2 defeat to Southport) he returned for their next four fixtures: a 1-1 draw with Rushden and Diamonds, a 2-1 win against Morecambe (the only time Sheridan ended up on the winning side during his time at the Belle Vue), a 2-2 draw with Yeovil and a 2-1 defeat against Farnborough.

Sheridan's Doncaster sojourn was only ever meant to be a short-team arrangement and after these eight games he duly left the Belle Vue, although, since there were still no offers from a League club on the table, his destination seemed uncertain.

Salvation arrived in the shape of Andy Ritchie, who was then manager of League Two outfit Oldham Athletic, having taken over from Neil Warnock at the end of 1997-98 season.

Ritchie had considered making a move for Sheridan after his former team-mate had been released by Bolton but had been deterred by Oldham's parlous financial position. In fact Ritchie was operating on such a small budget he had been forced to staff his first team with youth players. Perhaps inevitably this had not been a success and with his team struggling and in the relegation places by October something clearly had to be done to stop the rot. An experienced head in the middle of the park was needed desperately and, as far as Ritchie was concerned, John Sheridan was precisely the man to fit the bill.

Again Ritchie avoided making Sheridan an offer simply because at that time he thought his old friend was fixed up with Doncaster and it was only a chance encounter with Chris Waddle at an Oldham reserve game that prompted Ritchie to finally make his move. As the two men discussed Sheridan's move to Doncaster it was clear that Ritchie did not know that the player had in fact left the Conference side, so when Waddle set him straight Ritchie was on the phone to his old team mate that very night to offer him a trial.

Although he had initially only been invited to train with the Latics, Sheridan was instantly pitched into Ritchie's team against Wycombe on 24th October 1998. He had such a superb game in the goalless draw that he was ushered straight into the board room after the match and offered an eighteen-month contract. He signed and his League playing career was not only prolonged but he would end up spending over a decade at Boundary Park.

"I had known Andy for years because we played together at Leeds," Sheridan explained, "so I was only too willing to join him at Oldham. He wanted me to add experience to the team he had just taken over, which was something I enjoyed doing. It was good to be out there every week because the love of playing competitive football never really goes away. I was trying to make the most of the time I had left. My knee had been a problem for a while and I thought I had two years, maybe three at the most, left in my career."

Sheridan would reward Ritchie's faith by playing in all but two of Oldham's remaining thirty-two League fixtures that season. Sheridan, who quickly formed an effective central midfield partnership with the tenacious Lee Duxbury, was, inevitably, an immediate hit with the Boundary Park faithful. Age and his troublesome knee might have dimmed his mobility but not his appetite for the game or for that matter his eye for an incisive, defence-splitting pass (although his new, less gifted team-mates, perhaps understandably, weren't always on the same wavelength). Even at thirty-four Sheridan could still ooze class and a player of his quality hadn't been seen at Boundary Park for many a long year.

Even Sheridan couldn't perform miracles, however, and Oldham could only win two of his first ten games for the club and the Latics ended 1998 in twenty-second position in League Two.

Although the new year brought four wins from five to climb up to seventeenth, they would win only one of their subsequent eleven (the sole exception being a sweet away victory against eventual play-off winners Manchester City) and slipped ominously back into the bottom four.

Fortunately three wins from their penultimate five games was enough to give them hope but still they remained in the drop zone as the season headed to its final weekend. With so many teams involved in the dog fight it was possible that Oldham could even win their last game and still go down. As it was while York City were losing 4-0 at Manchester City, Oldham beat Reading 2-0 in front of a crowd of 7,724 to stay in League Two by a single point, thus avoiding the prospect of being the first founder members of the Premier League to be relegated to the bottom division.

It had been a dreadful season for Oldham and despite cheating relegation by the skin of their teeth it was clear they needed a massive influx of new players if they were ever going to mount a serious promotion challenge. Sheridan though had impressed throughout the season and was voted Oldham's Player of the Year.

The Latics remained favourites for the drop the following season and their start to their season did nothing to dispel such predictions. In fact the Latics lost their first five League games (during which they scored only one goal) and seven of their first nine. Sheridan had been moved to sweeper at the start of the season but since he was clearly still Athletic's most creative player the experiment was ditched after just one game.

It wasn't until 11th September that Oldham were finally able to record a League win when they beat Bury 2-0, and although they were beaten by Bristol Rovers seven days later (despite Sheridan opening the scoring after three minutes with a remarkable free-kick that was officially measured at 44.9 yards!) the Latics lost only three of the following fourteen League and Cup games between 25th September and 27th November to inch their way to lower-mid-table obscurity and progress to the Third Round of the FA Cup (having seen off Chelmsford and Swansea City).

Although Oldham would then crash to two consecutive defeats at Preston North End, 2-0 in the League and 2-1 in the FA Cup, Ritchie's side responded with four wins and two draws in their next six – including a particularly sweet 1-0 win against high-flying North West rivals Wigan (for whom John's brother Darren now played his trade, albeit as an unused sub that day).

Thereafter the Latics were consistently inconsistent. Although Ritchie's side put together another six match unbeaten run between 4th March and 1st April, for example, they then lost four of their following five games (with Sheridan absent for three of these defeats), the sole exception being another win against Wigan on 11th April. With Darren Sheridan in the Wigan starting line-up this time the game, which ended 2-1 to the Latics, marked the first time the Sheridan brothers had lined up against each other.

Oldham concluded their campaign with a win against Notts County and 1-1 draws with Blackpool and Luton to finish in fourteenth place (with Sheridan again absent for all but the last half-hour of the Luton game).

Sheridan had taken some part in all but ten of Oldham's 52 League and Cup fixtures in the 1999-00 season (starting 39 and coming on as sub 3 times) scoring twice and was once again voted Oldham's player of the year and his contract was extended for a further twelve months.

Sensing that his playing career could not go indefinitely Sheridan revealed plans to start taking his coaching badges. "I'm going to see if coaching is for me," he said. "And if it isn't, I'll buy an ice cream van."

Like the previous season, Oldham started the 2000-01 campaign poorly recording only one win in their first eleven League games, the opening fixture: a 4-1 win against Port Vale. Incidentally this was the only game in which Sheridan featured before he was forced to undergo yet more surgery on his game knee.

The injury would sideline him until 16th December and when he returned to the side Oldham were nineteenth in the League and facing yet another season battling against relegation.

In addition to the impressive form of new signings of David Eyres and Tony Carss (both of whom had joined the club in Sheridan's absence), Sheridan's return seemed to inspire his team-mates as Oldham lost only twice in the twelve games that followed.

Sheridan also returned to goal scoring form in the eighth and ninth game of this sequence with a brace of twenty-yard free kicks against Wigan Athletic (with brother Darren again in their line-up) and Luton Town (scoring in consecutive games for the first time since November 1996).

By the time the Latics had thumped Wrexham 5-1 on 10th February Ritchie's side had clawed their way up to eleventh in the table and a position of safety. Indeed it was really only down to defeats in their final two fixtures (including a 5-0 walloping from Millwall on the final day of the season) that Oldham dropped to a disappointing fifteenth in the final reckoning.

Following his return, Sheridan missed only three League games (all of which were lost) throughout the remainder of the season and contributed four goals. Although another player, Tony Carss, had the gall to snatch Oldham's player of the year award, Sheridan had done enough to earn another twelve-month deal (a contract that would take him through to June 2003) as well as promotion to player-coach. "John has tremendous experience within the game," Oldham's chief executive Alan Hardy said, "and he will be a great asset to the club."

In the summer of 2001, Oldham was taken over by Oxford-based businessman Chris Moore who vowed to take the club back to Premier League football within five years. He put his money where his mouth was and bankrolled a large influx of new signings throughout the season, including Darren Sheridan, who was signed in August after the being surprisingly released on a free transfer by Wigan. When Darren and John Sheridan turned out for Oldham in the opening game of the season at Wrexham, it was the first time the two brothers had played on the same side.

For the younger Sheridan it had been a circuitous route to reach this point. Although he had been signed as a schoolboy by Leeds prior to John's arrival at Elland Road, Darren would never make a first team appearance for Leeds. One of his jobs as an apprentice, interestingly, was to clean his big brother's boots but Billy Bremner decided that he wasn't good enough to lace them and he was shown the door. For a while Darren drifted out of the game and into odd jobs. Fortunately he was spotted whilst playing Sunday League football by a scout for Non-League Winsford, where he was in turn spotted by a Barnsley scout who invited him to Oakwell for trials. Darren did enough to impress and eventually made almost two-hundred League appearances for the South Yorkshire side before moving on to Wigan in 1999.

With the Sheridan brothers in tandem, Oldham started the 2001-02 season well. Despite a pre-season vow by Ritchie to use John Sheridan sparingly the midfielder was ever present throughout the first eight games of the season, scoring once (with

Darren ever present for the first ten games, scoring twice). In fact the Latics lost only one of their first eleven games (winning six) and briefly topped the table in mid-September. It had been Oldham's best start for eleven seasons. But just when it seemed Oldham had finally turned a corner, following that promising eleven game sequence Oldham promptly lost each of their next four games. To underline their importance to the side the Sheridan brothers were both sidelined by injury for three of these defeats.

Although Oldham rallied to draw with QPR in the League on 27th October and then beat Tranmere in the LDV Vans Trophy four days later it was not enough to save Ritchie's job and just hours after the Tranmere game he was relieved of his managerial duties.

Strangely the dismissal was dressed up as the result of a decision by Moore to restructure the coaching set-up. With the club apparently keen to create a new position of head coach, the idea was that Ritchie would "move upstairs" to become technical director with responsibility for all footballing matters. Ritchie turned the offer down.

"Our supporters deserve promotion," Moore pronounced, "and having monitored the situation carefully over the past six months, I have decided to undertake a restructuring programme at the club. Andy was offered the promotion which he regrettably declined, leaving us no option but to terminate his contract. Andy is a popular character and has been an excellent servant to Oldham Athletic. During my time at the club he has worked tirelessly to achieve our objective. However, our target is promotion and I feel we need a head coach that will bring fresh ideas and deliver success. It is regrettable that he has not taken our offer but we wish him well in his future."

Sheridan, who took training with Assistant Manager Billy Urmson following Ritchie's departure, was sad to see his former team-mate go: "Andy is a great lad and he was unfortunate to get the sack, especially as he could have done a lot of good things for the club."

Although there were rumours that Chris Waddle was in the frame to replace Ritchie, in the end the job of head coach went to highly thought of Mick Wadsworth who was appointed on 7th November.

Under Wadsworth, with whom Sheridan also got on well, Oldham gradually started moving in the right direction and five wins from six games either side of New Year pushed the Latics to the verge of the play-off places. Although this run was followed by a defeat at Port Vale and a draw with Bournemouth, a win against Notts County on 2nd February pushed Oldham up to sixth. Although Oldham also won their next match against Brighton, a further injury to his knee meant this would be the last game of Sheridan's season.

Without Sheridan, Oldham could win only four of their last fourteen games and slipped to ninth in the League. It is significant that brother Darren, too, was injured throughout this period and would only start three of these games.

Ninth was disappointing after a season that had promised so much more and Wadsworth quit as manager at the end of May 2002 due to differences with the board over the direction of the club. In his place came former Northern Ireland international Iain Dowie, whose arrival seemed to spell the end of Sheridan's playing career.

Following a revamp of the backroom staff Sheridan became player/assistant youth coach, working under Bill Urmson, and he kicked off the season in his usual position in central midfield. Although Sheridan started the first three games of the season (a home loss to Cardiff, a win at Peterborough and a goalless draw with Brentford), he would miss the home win against Tranmere and would only appear as a substitute in both the goalless draw at Blackpool and the home defeat to Wycombe that followed. In fact Sheridan would not play again in the League that season and would make only one further first team appearance that season in the 3-2 League Cup win against Notts County on 10th September.

To make Oldham successful, Dowie had decided he needed to build a younger, fitter team and introduced a harsh, military style training regime often involving double sessions, boxing and seven a.m. swims. As Sheridan was now approaching thirty-seven (and still nursing a bad knee) there was no way he could even attempt to take a full and active part in the new manager's training programme and it was with great reluctance that he had to face up to the fact that his playing career was now, effectively over.

"I did not play much after that because Iain Dowie took over as manager with another new approach," Sheridan explained. "Iain had us working extremely hard in training and, because of my knee, the way he did things was beyond me. It reached the stage where I would play on Saturday and do very little during the week, so the time seemed right to pack in. Nobody wants to retire, but I decided it would be better to concentrate on the coaching."

In April, Sheridan confirmed his retirement, admitting: "It has come sooner than I wanted, but I can't grumble too much. I've had some great experiences."

Greatest of all, he reflected, was his involvement in the 1990 and 1994 World Cups and named Ruud Gullit, Marco van Basten, Chris Waddle, Paul McGrath, Roy Keane and Paul Gascoigne as the best players he ever played with or against.

*****

Iain Dowie's arrival at Boundary Park might have ended Sheridan's playing career (or at least, as it turned out, placed it on pause) but his methods seemed to transform Oldham's fortunes as they made their first serious challenge for promotion since Sheridan joined the club. In fact, after the thrashing of 6-1 Mansfield on 14th September, the Latics were never lower than fifth and indeed topped the table briefly in October.

Although Dowie's side eventually finished the season in fifth place this did guarantee the club a place in the play-offs (where they would meet QPR), something which neither Ritchie nor Wadsworth had achieved. Unfortunately it would be the West Londoners who would advance to the Final after holding the Latics to a 1-1 draw at Boundary Park, and winning the second leg 1-0 at Loftus Road.

It was at this point Chris Moore decided to end his interest in the club (selling his ninety-five per cent shareholding) and since he had been bankrolling its weekly losses of £50,000 he left Oldham facing some rather large debts that forced the club to sell half a dozen of their better players – at a fraction of their true value.

With the Latics now operating on a week-to-week basis there looked a very real possibility that they would go out of business and on 1st August the Inland Revenue issued a winding up order, "in view of unpaid national insurance and PAYE."

On 19th August 2003 the club went into administration and were informed that they had to find £1.2million by the end of September or face the prospect of folding. "The club have got sufficient funds to take them through to the end of September," Paul Ashworth, spokesman for administrators PKF intoned, "by which time we will know whether the club has a viable future. Whether they survive will depend on new investors coming forward, either individuals or on a consortium basis. The club is looking for £1.2m to take them from the beginning of October through to the end of May next year. Someone needs to come in within four weeks really and show the colour of their money because it would take a further two weeks to put various things in place. A large chunk of that money is required immediately and the rest over the course of the next six to seven months."

"It's early days yet and we're hopeful," Ashworth continued, "but as well as the £1.2million to take the club through to the end of the season, there will be a further requirement for the following season. The largest expense for the club is the players' monthly salaries. The club simply cannot afford to pay the players wages at the level they have been doing. And that is why - to a large extent - they find themselves in this position today."

Having seen his squad depleted by the harsh realities of Oldham's financial situation and having lost the opening game of the season 3-1 at home to Brighton & Hove

Albion Dowie had no alternative but to call upon the services of virtually the one class player left on his staff – John Sheridan.

In August Sheridan therefore signed non-contract forms to re-register as a player, even though it was almost twelve months since his last appearance and about five months since he'd even trained. Sheridan, however, admitted he couldn't pull his boots on quick enough!

"The gaffer asked me to sign non-contract forms so I decided it was time to put my boots back on," the player told The Manchester Evening News. "It was just one of those things I had to do. My knee can't stand up to the physical demands of a long season and I can't train every day and keep up with the rest of the lads. But I will play as long as the gaffer needs me. I love the game and always felt I could play in one-off matches, there was no question that I was going to say no. I was right up for it."

After a brief appearance as a substitute in Oldham's 2-1 defeat against Scunthorpe in the Carling Cup, Sheridan would make his post-retirement League comeback against Sheffield Wednesday who had sunk like a stone since he had left the club. Following Sheridan's departure David Pleat had continued his hare-brained policy of signing far too many mediocre foreign mercenaries whose wages all but bled the club bone dry. After his inevitable but overdue sacking, Dave Richards and his fellow board members had then proceeded to appoint a parade of managers who were either not given enough financial backing or should never have been appointed in the first place. After Pleat's departure came Danny Wilson, Ron Atkinson, Paul Jewell, Terry Yorath and Peter Shreeves. Of these only Atkinson had done well (though he too was jettisoned, some said out of petty revenge for the way he had left them in the lurch in 1991). Now it was the club's former goalkeeper Chris Turner that was in the hot seat.

Sheridan's return to Hillsborough on 16th August would prove to be an emotional day as he was greeted by a standing ovation from all sides of the ground: "It was a dream come true because I'd never been back as a player," Sheridan recalled. "The reception was one of the highlights of my career."

And the dream got better after only three minutes when Graeme Lee brought down Oldham's French striker Mickael Antoine-Curier in the box. Referee Roger Beeby pointed to the spot and it was Sheridan who stepped up to put away the penalty in front of Hillsborough's Spion Kop. Out of respect for the home fans, Sheridan refused to celebrate, he just turned and expressionlessly walked back to the halfway line. Quite remarkably, even though they had just seen their side go a goal down, the home supporters also applauded Sheridan's goal.

"I scored from the penalty spot but I didn't celebrate when it went in only because I was playing for Oldham Athletic and I was concentrating on getting three points,"

Sheridan elaborated. "If David Eyres had been playing I wouldn't have taken it, but I have been a penalty taker over the years and I felt it was my responsibility. I would have made the same decision had we been playing at Hartlepool."

Although Wednesday hit back with two goals from Finnish striker Shefki Kuqi Oldham refused to capitulate and were justly rewarded when Antoine-Curier conjured up an equaliser, volleying low into the bottom corner after a knock down from John Eyre and Sheridan's Hillsborough return ended honours even. When Sheridan left the field at the end of the match he did so to a another standing ovation from both sets of fans. His eyes were quite understandably filled with tears.

"If this was John Sheridan's last league game at Hillsborough," reported the Oldham Advertiser, "then he will have left an abiding memory for the fans who voted him Sheffield Wednesday's best-ever player. What a swansong. This was vintage Sheri ... and the performance in an exciting and entertaining 2-2 draw could not have been better timed. He had wondered what reception he would get on his first time back since leaving the steel city seven years ago. He needn't have bothered, it was more like the hero's return. They say fans are fickle, but the Wednesday supporters showed nothing but admiration and appreciation for a talent that made him a legend. Their legend. Sheridan, at thirty-eight, may not have the legs but the vision is still there and he was often applauded by the home fans for his silky skills."

It had been a truly memorable day for Sheridan. "Going back to Hillsborough was probably the proudest moment of my career," Sheridan reflected. "I couldn't believe the reception I had from the Wednesday fans; it was something that money simply couldn't buy."

"Playing at Hillsborough was always going to be special because I hadn't been back since I left," Sheridan reflected. "It is something I thought would never happen and I certainly didn't need asking twice. We had a good team and I played my best football during very happy times there. I know the fans hold me in high regard and I have always appreciated that. It turned out to be a good team performance which was just as well because I wasn't going to run all around the pitch. The Wednesday fans certainly made me feel welcome and they gave me a terrific send-off at the end of the game. It could all have backfired. I could have had a nightmare but it became an afternoon I will never forget. Talk about being stiff the day after, though. I was aching all over my body. When everyone is fit I will sit back and concentrate on coaching, which is something I am really enjoying. The gaffer is an excellent coach and I am learning all the time."

Although Oldham then lost both of the games that followed the Wednesday fixture, they then embarked on a nine match unbeaten run (that included five wins) that saw them leapfrog from twenty-first place to ninth in the League. Inevitably the key to Oldham's revival had been the form of John Sheridan. By early October Sheridan was incredibly Oldham's top scorer with five goals (all penalties) and he had also contributed several assists with his defence-splitting passes.

Naturally manager Dowie (who was continually being linked with other jobs around this time) was keen to pay tribute to his veteran midfielder, whom, he also revealed, was not even getting paid for his efforts: "He's doing a great job," Dowie remarked, "and the disappointing thing is he's not being paid for it. I've asked the club to give him appearance money and they haven't. John is on a very low salary and should be getting a little something."

Indeed it was scandalous that he wasn't being properly remunerated, particularly since every game left him in severe pain.

"John's knee is that arthritic now it's almost solid," Dowie quipped. "I'm not sure how it even moves anymore. If he could have my knees, I would give them to him but he's a quality player and a terrific lad who's also enjoying his coaching role. What I won't do is cripple John, so there'll come a time when the likes of Darren [Sheridan] or Ernie [Cooksey] will have to slot in for him. We realise times will come when his knee is just too sore to play."

Despite this Sheridan would stay in the side for the fifteen League games that followed his Hillsborough return and would only lose his place after getting himself sent off against Plymouth on 1st November for an off the ball confrontation with Argyle's French midfielder David Friio. Friio also received his marching orders for his part in the incident and was chased by an irate Sheridan down the tunnel!

With Sheridan suspended Oldham lost three of their next four League games (drawing the other) and also bowed out of the FA Cup following a humiliating 5-2 home defeat to Blackpool. The club now found themselves in nineteenth place and seemingly in freefall once again.

Dowie decided that he'd had enough and left to take up the manager's job at Crystal Palace. Many Oldham fans would be bitter about the manner of his departure. After repeatedly denying any interest in the Palace job he secretly met with their chairman Simon Jordan and then announced on 19th December, after taking training and picking Oldham's side for the following day's game, that he was accepting the job after all and flew down to London to finalise the details of his contract.

On Dowie's recommendation Sheridan and fellow-veteran David Eyres were placed in temporary charge as joint caretaker managers and their interregnum began on 20th December, 2003 with a 2-1 home win against League leaders QPR, thanks to a late winner from John Eyre.

Since Oldham would not be in a position to appoint a new manager (or, for that matter, bring in any new players) until they finally came out of administration in January the following year, Sheridan therefore had several games to stake his claim to get the job on a permanent basis and made no secret of his ambition.

"Do I want it? Of course I do," Sheridan admitted candidly. "Management is something I have long wanted to do and the opportunity is there. It is a chance I am hoping to take. I believe in my own ability and I am going to give it a full go. You never know what can happen."

Sheridan was soon relishing these first steps in management: "It's my first chance at this level," he said, "but I'll give it everything I've got. I would definitely be interested. I believe in my own ability and I'm confident I could do the job. Results speak, so it was great to get the win against QPR and I'll try to take my chance over the next few weeks. Obviously it isn't my decision, but it would be nice to be in a strong position whenever the new manager is appointed. I can't really comment on Iain's choice to join Crystal Palace, but he thinks he has gone on to better things and we all wish him luck. He has been good to me and I think he will coach at the highest level. Everybody is disappointed, but these things happen in football and you just have to get on with life."

Initial results were encouraging as the Latics lost only one of their first seven games under Sheridan, the sixth of which saw Oldham beat Sheffield Wednesday 1-0 at Boundary Park on 17th January. The manager selected himself for the Wednesday match and when he brought himself off towards the end of match he received another ovation from all four sides of the ground.

By the end of January Oldham had finally come out of administration, after the Football Association and Football League eventually approved a takeover bid by a trio of New York-based English mobile phone magnates - Simon Blitz, Simon Corney and Danny Gazal – who promised to bring financial stability back to the club.

"We are pleased today to start a new era at Boundary Park," Blitz announced. "We do have a clear vision for the future. But the difficulties the club has gone through over the past twelve months means we have a period of consolidation and the implementation of a rebuilding strategy."

The new owners, however, seemed in no mood to make appointing a new manager their priority, and although Oldham lost the eighth match of Sheridan's caretaker reign, going down 4-1 away at Rushden and Diamonds, the new owners decided to give Sheridan an extra five matches to prove that he was the right men for the job.

"There have been interviews," Simon Corney revealed, "but John is doing a fantastic job in a difficult situation. We felt he deserved a chance to continue and he is doing so well that we do not need to rush our decision. There's still a possibility we could extend his period in charge until the end of the season."

By now of course, Sheridan had been well and truly bitten by the management bug. "Being the manager wasn't something I was actively pursuing at the time and making that transition from being one of the lads to boss has had its difficult moments," he admitted. "But I've caught the bug, there's no doubt about that. I won't make any bones about it. I want to be this club's full-time manager and the people in charge at Boundary Park know that. The players have given me everything and I know I've got the backing of our supporters but, of course, the decision about whether I become the permanent manager is out of my hands. But I do believe that I can do the job - and do it well. I see myself now as the manager of a soccer club. Hopefully it will be here at Boundary Park, but if not here, somewhere else. Sometimes you don't know that a job will suit you until you are actually doing it, but I know now that being a manager suits me right down to the ground. All I can do is to hope that the people running this club feel the same way."

Having sat out the draw with Blackpool and the defeat at Rushden that followed the win over Wednesday, Sheridan recalled himself to the team and enjoyed one last late career highlight when he starred, playing in front of the defence, in Oldham's 6-0 thrashing of Grimsby Town on 8th February.

"To be able to run a game from midfield on one working leg and with your 40th birthday peeping over the horizon," wrote Paul Hince of the Manchester Evening News after the game with the Mariners, "you need one of two things - talent beyond the normal, or determination by the bucketful. John Sheridan is blessed with both of those qualities. The first - his wonderful natural talent - has given him a magnificent playing career which now stretches back over two decades. The second - his sheer, bloody-minded determination - could yet see his soccer career extended still further... as the full-time manager of Oldham Athletic. The 13,000 non-paying customers who marvelled at Sheridan's midfield mastery in last Sunday's 6-0 trouncing of Grimsby Town at Boundary Park will take great exception to me referring to the 39-year-old Latics caretaker player-manager as a cripple. But in soccer terms, that's exactly what Sheridan is. In non-medical parlance, his right knee is knackered. The problems in his knee which began while he was a Bolton player in the 1990s, have worsened to the extent that he now needs replacement surgery. He can't train and, probably, shouldn't even be walking, let alone playing."

"Oh, I'll get myself a new knee sooner or later," Sheridan told Hince as though he was talking about replacing a beat-up pair of Hush Puppies. "We are a bit short of players at the moment so I have to keep picking myself. Anyway my game has always been about passing. I've never been one who liked to gallop about all over the pitch so playing with only one good knee hasn't been too much of a disadvantage. I've only ever used my left leg to stand on, anyhow."

"I've been struggling with a knee injury for about eight years now and but for that I reckon I could have gone on playing at the age of forty-five. But I'm going to have to call it a day soon. To be honest I've only been picking myself because I've got a very young team which needs an old head, a bit of experience, in its midst. You know, I'd love David Batty to come and play at Oldham. He'd fit the bill perfectly."

The reality of the situation was however that Sheridan really shouldn't have been playing and thirteen days after the Grimsby match, on 21st February 2004, Sheridan would play his last ever game as a professional footballer in Oldham's 1-1 draw with Tranmere.

Still Oldham remained without a manager and by the end of February Sheridan felt it was getting beyond a joke and called for a new man to be appointed sooner rather than later.

"It's unfair on the players," he beseeched after the 1-0 defeat at Bournemouth on 28th February. "Someone might come in soon, but it would be better if the lads knew what's going on. Hopefully it'll be soon as we need to get out of this dogfight. I'm still keen to have the job but we desperately need to bring some players in to strengthen the team."

Sheridan's pleas, however, went unheeded. Although the new owners confirmed that they were close to securing the services of the manager they wished to appoint full-time, a delay in finalising the nuts and bolts of this agreement meant that Sheridan's caretaker-ship would extend for one more game - the Latics trip to play League Two high fliers QPR (and eventual runners-up) on 6th March (which ended in a creditable 1-1 draw).

Sheridan's record in his three months in charge was three wins, six draws and four defeats. Not disastrous but not enough to make his claims to get the job full-time unanswerable. Nevertheless Oldham's new owners were keen to ensure that the appointment of a new man in charge would not bring to an end Sheridan's involvement with the club.

"John Sheridan has done a very good job and we're very happy with him," director Simon Blitz said. "Although we feel that this is probably not the right time for him, we will be looking to keep him involved."

Following the QPR game the Oldham board finally unveiled the club's new boss: ex-England international and former Rushden and Diamonds chief Brian Talbot who had man marked the precocious Sheridan in the 1983 Arsenal versus Leeds FA Cup tie. Sheridan's consolation prize was to be Talbot's right-hand man.

Talbot took charge of his first game on 13th March against Colchester and under his stewardship Oldham picked up nineteen points from a possible thirty-six, losing only once in their last twelve games to avert relegation and finish in fifteenth place.

On 30th March Sheridan confirmed his retirement for a second time, a decision he vowed to stick to this time.

"That's it. I won't play again," Sheridan insisted. "It had to come sometime and I have had a long and successful career. I have many, many happy memories and I enjoyed every minute of it. I have also been fortunate to line up alongside some very good players both at league and international levels. In the past I have always made myself available, but not again. I only have to look at videos of me playing to realise that I shouldn't be out there. My knee just can't stand up to it any more. You think you can play forever but, if I am honest to myself, I should probably have packed it in three or four years ago."

And Oldham's new manager confirmed that he would not be asking Sheridan to come out of retirement again, no matter what the emergency. "John is on this side now and he has been excellent and very helpful," Talbot confirmed. "He can't train and does not really want to play. He now has a new future to concentrate on."

True to his word, there would be no more comebacks and the 1-1 draw with Tranmere Rovers on 21st February 2004, would remain Sheridan's last ever game as a professional footballer.

When Sheridan signed for Oldham in October 1998 on a short-term basis, few would have predicted he would still have been playing for the club six years later. Instead, remarkably, Sheridan had ended up playing one hundred and thirty-two League games for the Latics plus a further thirteen from the bench, scoring fourteen goals. He also made fifteen appearances in the FA Cup (including one as a sub) scoring twice, four in the League Cup (including two as a sub) and made one start in the Football League Trophy.

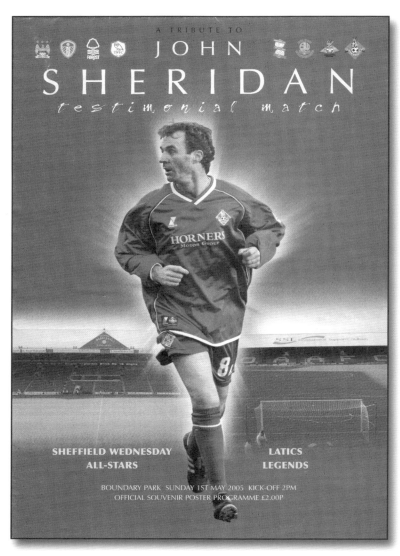

John Sheridan testimonial match - Oldham programme

Chapter Eleven

In what was becoming an annual event, Oldham once again made an indifferent start to the new season, winning only three of their first fifteen League games (losing eight) and crashing out of the League Cup after a 6-0 mauling by Tottenham Hotspur. It was this sequence of results that prompted Brian Talbot to reshuffle his coaching staff, demoting Sheridan from Assistant Manager to Youth-Team coach with Tony Philliskirk moving the other way.

Whether this had anything to do with anything is moot but certainly Talbot was able to slowly turn things around. Indeed between 30th October and mid-December his side put together an impressive sequence of nine wins in ten games!

In early January there was yet more good news for Talbot when Oldham beat Manchester City in the Third Round of the FA Cup (after seeing off Thurrock and Leyton Orient in the earlier rounds). Unfortunately following their defeat by Bolton Wanderers in the Fourth Round Oldham slumped to seven consecutive defeats. The last of these was a 5-1 thrashing by Bristol City on 22nd February which proved to be Talbot's final match in charge. Seven consecutive defeats would probably spell the end for any manager but Talbot had also latterly riled the Latics faithful by suggesting it would have been better for the club if he had taken them down the previous season, as that would have enabled him to build a new team! By mutual agreement Talbot was duly shown the door.

"It was a genuinely mutual agreement between ourselves and Brian," club owner Simon Blitz maintained. "We had a long discussion yesterday and everybody put their cards on the table. Brian was very much a gentleman about it all and said he believed it to be in the best interests of the club. It was a combination of views from both sides, but the writing was on the wall.

"We have had a very rocky season. We had one run in mid-season that made us think we were better than we actually were, but for some reason the players could not perform to the standard they actually are. Brian himself said that the players were good enough but it just wasn't happening out on the pitch for us. You can not blame him entirely for that and we didn't have very much luck with injuries."

As Talbot's assistant the post of caretaker this time went to Tony Philliskirk, who took charge for Oldham's visit to Huddersfield where a 3-1 loss extended Oldham's run of defeats to eight - the club's longest sequence of consecutive defeats since 1934-35 - plunging them deep into the relegation mire.

Clearly Oldham needed a new man in charge and quickly and although Sheridan was among the fifty applicants for the post, once again his claims were ignored.

It looked as though Sheridan would forever pay the price for Oldham's continued mediocrity. Every time they got in a pickle, it seemed, the board were forced to appoint someone with enough experience to keep the club in League One (the division having been renamed at the start of the 2004-05 season), but, ultimately, not enough nous to prevent them landing right back at square one the following season.

As a result, on 3rd March, the club appointed former Rotherham boss Ronnie Moore, initially on a short term contract until the end of the season with a view to a new deal being agreed in the summer. Moore brought with him his own right hand man John Breckin (who had been with him at Millmoor) but Philliskirk and Sheridan were both retained.

Moore arrived in bullish mood and at his first meeting with the players he confidently told them, "We can stay up."

"I reckon we need five wins from our last twelve games," Moore predicted, "and, although that's a tough task, it's something we can achieve. We've lost eight on the belt, which can't be good for confidence, but I guarantee the fans that these lads will show a great attitude."

"Avoiding relegation is absolutely the main concern," Moore continued, "but I see this as a long-term job because I want us to be pushing for the Championship next season. My contract is fairly short at the moment, but I don't feel on trial here, the contract was something agreed by both parties. We can discuss it again in the summer. The most important thing was to just get in here, start working and start picking up points."

Moore's reign in the Latics hot seat began in encouraging fashion as fellow-strugglers Port Vale were comprehensively beaten 3-0 at Boundary Park with notable improvements in all departments.

And although Oldham were unable to deliver the five wins from twelve that Moore had requested, they did manage four (including the win against Vale) as well as four draws which was just enough to escape relegation. The Latics did leave it late again, however, and had to rely on a final day victory against Bradford City at Boundary Park to beat the drop by single point and finish nineteenth.

Sheridan's Youth Team meanwhile had no such worries as they romped to another Football League Youth Alliance Merit (North) title, earning their boss a twelve-month contract renewal in May. Sheridan enjoyed working with these youngsters, several of whom would graduate to and flourish in the Oldham first team for several years to come.

"They are a talented bunch of lads and there is no doubt that some of them will have what it takes to go all the way," Sheridan asserted proudly. "We have lads at sixteen playing for the under-19s and in that age group and some have even played for the first team this season [such as Neil Eardley, Chris Taylor and Matt Wolfenden]. They have shown they are capable of winning things and, in many ways; that makes my job easier. But they are also a good bunch and I really enjoy working with them."

For Sheridan there was another reason to celebrate when on 1st May his services to Oldham Athletic were recognised as Boundary Park played host to a benefit match between a team of Wednesday All-Stars and Latics Legends.

As a mark of how well thought of he was in the game, dozens of former team mates and footballing legends were only too happy to turn out for his big day.

Among the Wednesday stars turning out were Chris Woods, Peter Shirtliff, Chris Waddle, Nigel Jemson, Carlton Palmer, David Hirst, Viv Anderson, Mark Bright, Richie Humphries; while the likes of Gary Kelly, Denis Irwin, Andy Ritchie, Frankie Bunn, Neil Redfearn, Shaun Garnett, Mike Milligan, Lee Duxbury, Rick Holden, Tommy Wright, Richard Jobson, Neil Adams and Iain Dowie would all appear for the Latics. In addition Ian Snodin, John Barnes, Peter Beardsley, Kevin Moran, Scott Sellars, Paul Gascoigne and Bryan Robson would all turn out to pay their respects.

In front of almost three thousand fans (including around 800 travelling Owls fans) Sheridan would make an appearance for both sides as the Wednesday Legends beat their Latics counterparts 3-2 thanks to a David Hirst hat-trick.

Following the benefit match (from which some of the proceeds went towards the reconstructive knee surgery he had continually postponed during his playing days) Sheridan spent the summer completing his UEFA A Coaching Badge (to give himself a better chance of getting into management, he said) and looked ahead to the following season.

With Moore in charge there was once again hope that Oldham could finally climb out of League One. Moore and his assistant Breckin had won admirers during their eight-year spell at Rotherham, winning successive promotions and establishing the South Yorkshire club in the second tier of English football on the thinnest of shoestrings. There was therefore hope and expectation that they could cast the same spell at Boundary Park.

To make a pleasant change the Latics did start the new season promisingly, winning three of their first four League games, but then won only three of the next sixteen League and Cup fixtures.

Fortunately their home form was sufficient to keep them out of too much trouble and even allowed them a brief, albeit unconsummated, flirtation with the play-off positions. Between 16th November and 25th March, Oldham would lose only one of their thirteen League and Cup games played at Boundary Park (winning nine). Unfortunately, while Oldham's supporters may have appreciated the results, the manner in which they had been obtained had left many disenchanted and Oldham's failure to win in any of their final seven games ended the season on a sour note (taking only one point from their last six). The Latics finished tenth, six points adrift of the play-offs.

Ultimately this was not enough to keep Moore in his job. Moore had never really enjoyed the whole-hearted backing of the Boundary Park faithful, who had never warmed to the style of football his team had served up and indicative of this disaffection was the fact that season ticket sales were down by a third in pre-season. The Oldham board therefore felt it was time to dispense with his and John Breckin's services and bring in someone new.

Having overlooked him twice before, the club at last turned to John Sheridan who cancelled a family holiday to Florida (with his wife Jeanette's permission) to make himself available to accept the job. Sheridan was duly appointed on an initial twelve-month deal.

Within days he had made his first signing, making his good friend and former team mate Tommy Wright his assistant manager, promoting him from his job as coach of the Oldham Under-16s. "I always said that if I went into management I would take him with me," Sheridan told the club website. "Tommy has a terrific record at bringing young players through this club and, like myself, is very excited about the future." In another popular move Sheridan also appointed his former midfield partner and loyal club servant Lee Duxbury to replace him as reserve team coach and retained Tony Philliskirk as Youth Team Coach.

"The coaching staff are all young, like myself," Sheridan remarked, "and that might be a plus point. The lads I have brought in know the club and which way it wants to go, and what type of football the fans need."

After making the step up to management permanently Sheridan announced that he was keen to draw on his experiences of playing under Wilkinson, Clough and Atkinson, particularly the latter whose style he most closely wished to emulate: "Those three are all different, but Ron Atkinson has to be the best manager I have worked under because of his man-management, which was his real strength. He knew how to get the best out of players, which is something I feel I am capable of doing. Howard Wilkinson was very well-organised, knew his set-pieces, knew what he wanted from his players and drilled it into them. And Cloughie just played off the cuff. He concentrated on how his team were going to play, and never worried about the opposition. He just created great football teams and went out and entertained. They were all different, but hopefully, I have taken bits on board from all of them to help me in the long run. I didn't play much under Clough or Wilkinson, but really enjoyed playing under Ron. The other two were very good managers in their own right, but I liked the way Ron encouraged his players and seemed to get more out of them."

Nevertheless Sheridan was intent on being his own man and couldn't wait to introduce his own ideas, foremost among them would be to get his players playing with smiles on their faces. Although he had inherited the makings of a good squad (with several of the youngsters he'd coached in the past few seasons ready and waiting in the wings) he knew he would need to add a few new faces to play the passing game he so passionately believed in.

"The budget is going to be tight and I know what I have got to work with," Sheridan acknowledged. "But I will be looking for players who can take us that little extra step further," he announced. "I would like to sign three or four players if I can. There is a lot of hard work ahead but I am looking forward to it. I know the way I want to play. I want players to have smiles on their faces with confidence all round the club."

Money was in fact so tight at Boundary Park that all of Sheridan's summer imports would be free transfers. His first signing was midfielder Gary McDonald (from Kilmarnock) and he followed this up by bringing former Latics keeper Les Pogliacomi back to the club from Blackpool, as well as Craig Rocastle (from Sheffield Wednesday) and Neil Wood (also from Blackpool).

Sheridan was, however, all too aware of the realities that governed life in the third tier of English football and asked Oldham's fans to show a little understanding and patience while his new signings bedded in and his players got accustomed to the way he wanted them to play: "I was fortunate enough to play with some world-class players in the Premiership," he explained, "which helps when you like to get the ball down and play. I'd like to say I will get it down, and I will try and pass it, but people have to understand that is sometimes difficult in this division. We will come up against sides with a physical presence, so you might have to vary the way you play."

Within weeks of taking up the post Sheridan had already placed two pieces of silverware into the Boundary Park trophy cabinet: the Lancashire Senior Cup and the Rose Bowl, winning both on penalties against Preston North End and Rochdale respectively.

"Everything has gone well since I took over and I have had to learn pretty quickly. I am sure I will pick up a lot more as the campaign moves on. I am not making any predictions or setting targets, but the players know what I want. They have to be hungry - and winners. There is no better way than winning games, even if it is only five-a-side, and I will be going into every fixture feeling that is what we can do. I had every confidence in my ability as a player and I don't feel any different now that I have moved into management. One thing is for certain, I will be doing things my way. I have a good backroom staff who I can trust and that will be important. Home form and consistency are going to be the key... We have been dealt a tough start in our opening four games, but that is the way I like it. If we get the right results then it will be as tremendous boost to our confidence. We have picked up two trophies in pre-season and that's not a bad way to start. Promotion? I shouldn't have to say anything about it because that's what the lads should want. We have the players who can do well, now they have to go out and believe in themselves. We will take it one game at a time but I expect them to perform in every one."

Winning the two regional pots was nice but what really mattered was a good start to the League campaign and in another of those wonderfully capricious twists of footballing fate Oldham would face their old boss Ronnie Moore, now at Tranmere, in the season curtain-raiser at Prenton Park.

Sheridan couldn't wait to put one over on the man he'd replaced at Boundary Park, in the nicest possible way. "Ronnie is a great bloke and I got on very well with him while he was in charge," Sheridan said. "No disrespect to him, but I want us to play a bit more football this season - that's the way I was brought up. I am ready for the challenge and I am hoping the lads are just as excited as me."

For the match against Tranmere Sheridan handed starts to all his four summer signings as Oldham kicked off the season playing a slightly experimental 4-3-1-2 formation.

Unfortunately it was Moore who had the last laugh as the home side won a tense encounter 1-0 and to add to Sheridan's woes Oldham had two men sent off – youth team products Chris Taylor and Neil Eardley – in the dying minutes.

Things if anything got worse in Sheridan's second game in charge against Port Vale as his side succumbed to another 1-0 defeat, a reverse which was compounded by a nasty injury to his first choice keeper, Les Pogliacomi.

Despite being goalless and pointless after two games, Sheridan refused either to panic or abandon his footballing principles, although, after remembering something Wigan boss Paul Jewell had said to him during a summer coaching seminar, he did decide to abandon his 4-3-1-2 formation. "We tried it in the first couple of games and, though we played some good football attacking-wise, we weren't quite right," Sheridan noted. "Then I remembered that little bit of advice Paul had given me over the summer, and how he had done well in this division with 4-4-2."

The change appeared to work as Oldham registered their first win of the season against Swansea. Unfortunately Oldham could only pick up one more point from their next three games (which left them third from bottom in the League) and also crashed out of the Carling Cup (3-1 to Rotherham).

As far as Sheridan was concerned his team were playing well and all they needed was his goal shy strikers to start firing (his team had only mustered two goals in their first six fixtures) and a bit of luck to turn it around. Unfortunately luck was in short supply during the first few weeks of the season particularly in the goalkeeping department.

After Pogliacomi had been injured in the second game he was replaced by Chris Howarth (who Sheridan had signed on loan from Bolton Wanderers only a couple of days earlier) who was then himself injured in the fifth game and replaced by young reserve Terry Smith, then in the following match on-loan Middlesbrough stopper David Knight was sent off for handling the ball outside the area just thirty-eight minutes into his debut.

But just when Oldham fans might have been forgiven for thinking "here we go again" Sheridan's side turned the corner in fine style, registering back-to-back wins at home to Scunthorpe and away at table-topping Nottingham Forest. The latter win was particularly morale-boosting and it evidently ignited Oldham's season as Sheridan's side went unbeaten in eight and started climbing up the League.

It was as a result of this unbeaten run that Sheridan was awarded the Manchester Evening News Sport/BBC Radio Manchester Sports Personality of the Month award for September (ahead of Manchester United's Cristiano Ronaldo, Manchester City's Micah Richards, Bolton veteran Gary Speed and Salford's British light-middleweight champion Jamie Moore), much to the manager's bemusement who saw little difference between the Oldham side that had been seriously shot down in August and the one that was riding high in September, and put the change in fortune down to the maintenance of self-belief in his dressing room.

"In the first four games we were beaten 1-0 three times and won 1-0 in the other, and played well in all of them," Sheridan said. "There was never a suggestion that heads might drop. I have a good dressing room, and the players stayed positive even though they were as disappointed as I was. The old maxim of finding out more about your players in defeat held good at that time. You could see the lads were not at all happy about getting beaten, and I was telling them to stay positive. The only thing we lacked in those games was someone to put the ball in the net, because we were making chances. We lost three of the first four games but still had the most crosses and corners of anyone in the division."

Although Oldham suffered defeats against Yeovil and Chesterfield they then won their next six games to earn Sheridan the League One Manager of the Month award for November, which wasn't bad going for someone so new to the profession.

By 27th November Oldham were fourth from top and were fast gaining a reputation for playing some of the best football in League One, which in turn saw those fans who had slipped away during Moore's reign returning to Boundary Park.

Oldham won all four of their games over the Christmas period beating Northampton (3-2), Rotherham (3-2), Gillingham (3-0) and then, sweetest of all, trouncing Forest 5-0 at the City Ground on New Year's Day to give Sheridan's side their twenty-eighth point out of a possible thirty-three from their last eleven games.

Although Oldham crashed out of the FA Cup when Wolves beat them 2-0 in a Third Round replay at Boundary Park on 16th January (with a goal from future Sheridan signing Craig Davies, who had also scored in the initial 2-2 draw at Molineux) promotion remained the priority and when they beat Northampton 3-2 on 28th January the Latics went second in the table.

A week later they were top thanks to a last-gasp winner against Tranmere and stayed there when they beat Swansea 1-0 the following Saturday. It had been the first time the Latics had reached the summit since October 2002.

Despite going top of the League Sheridan did his best to keep his players' feet firmly on the ground and urged them to take one game at a time.

"We haven't won anything just yet," Sheridan cautioned. "I am not getting carried away and it is important the players keep their feet on the ground. There is still a long way to go and in a division where every team is capable of beating each other, a lot can still happen. The job isn't done yet."

True to Sheridan's warnings, Oldham's form then faltered drastically as they slumped to four consecutive defeats (against Millwall, Port Vale, Bournemouth and Blackpool) in eleven days, conceding eight and scoring just two goals to tumble down to fifth place.

To add to Sheridan's woes, both Stefan Stam and Craig Rocastle had limped out of the Port Vale game, a bad tempered clash which also saw Les Pogliacomi red-carded, then on the 24th February it was confirmed that striker Chris Hall had broken his leg and would miss the rest of the season (joining midfielder Neil Wood who had been similarly sidelined with cruciate ligament damage) and then defender Ben Turner, on a month's loan from Coventry, was sent off in his debut in the Blackpool match which meant that he too would miss three games.

Having been top of the table a little over a fortnight ago, Oldham now seemed in danger of slipping out of the promotion picture altogether.

"We haven't been playing with the confidence we should be after taking over as League leaders," Sheridan admitted. "We should have been thinking we could win every game, but it just hasn't happened and I don't know why. The goals we are conceding are a bit of a joke and it is costing us. We have to start winning again or we will find ourselves slipping right down the table. We are on our worst run of the season and it is important we stick together to turn it round. Things aren't going our way and there is no way we can keep performing like this. We have got to roll up our sleeves."

Fortunately the Latics were able to arrest the slide, following their four game wobble with another unbeaten streak that would eventually stretch to seven games.

By April Oldham's millionaire backers had seen enough and offered Sheridan a three-year contract extension that would tie him to the club until June 2010. "I'm happy with the way things are going this season," Sheridan told the club's website, "and now this is sorted out we can push on."

Although Sheridan's men would lose only twice more after their February blip they were unable to push on sufficiently to achieve automatic promotion and had to settle for sixth place and a berth in the play-offs where they were drawn against League One top scorers, Blackpool, who, ominously for the Latics, had finished the season with seven successive wins.

The first leg was staged at Boundary Park and although Oldham edged the goalless first half, in the second half it was one-way traffic as the Tangerines laid siege to their hosts' goal and went ahead seven minutes after the break through Shaun Barker.

Against the run of play Oldham equalised when Andy Liddell scored from the spot but with three minutes to go Wes Hoolahan took advantage of a defensive lapse to earn the visitors a deserved winner.

Blackpool had created a whole host of chances that on another day could have settled the tie there and then but as it was, with the aggregate score at 2-1, Sheridan believed the tie was still delicately poised: "We find ourselves still in the game, it's only halfway and we've still got a great chance of getting through the tie. We know we have to go there, score and try to win the game. We'll be trying to get a goal and the earlier we get it, the better. We've got to be cautious, we don't want to go there, take the game to them and leave gaps because it'll be difficult if they score. It's going to be a very tight game. I don't see any difference if we were going there 2-1 up, we know what we've got to do there. I know they're on a great run, they're the favourites and everyone expects them to win but we've got nothing to lose - they possibly should have had the game won. They know they should have won the game - not down to their good play, we were sloppy - but it's definitely a game we can go there and win."

Unfortunately the Latics were unable to turn it around at Bloomfield Road. Cheered on by 1,800 travelling fans Oldham took the game to their opponents, but struggled to create clear cut chances and when Keith Southern put Blackpool ahead after twenty-eight minutes Oldham had a mountain to climb, particularly since Sheridan's side had never come from behind to win a game all season.

Sheridan's men however did make a game of it and had the referee not waved away two worthy penalty appeals (both for handball) and had Andy Liddell not had a perfectly good "goal" ruled out for offside in the fifty-eighth minute they might have turned the tie around completely.

Instead it was Blackpool who scored next when Andy Morell made it 4-1 on aggregate with just fifteen minutes to go and although Oldham youth team product Matt Wolfenden did head home a consolation in the with seven minutes remaining Blackpool sealed their ninth successive win three minutes into injury time when Keigan Parker struck to book their place in the Play-Off Final against Yeovil.

Despite the play-off disappointment Sheridan could reflect on his first season in charge with a measure of satisfaction. After an indifferent start Oldham had completely turned their season around, embarking on several lengthy unbeaten runs and had played the style of football that Sheridan had promised to bring back to Boundary Park.

Ultimately transforming a side that had spent several seasons of either battling against relegation or settling for mid-table mediocrity into one capable of challenging for promotion in his first season was a considerable achievement for the rookie boss.

Having come so close to promotion in his first season, Sheridan might have been forgiven for merely tweaking his squad, instead the pre-season saw a mass exodus from Boundary Park and a large influx of fresh blood. Indeed Sheridan spent virtually the entire summer wheeling and dealing.

Out went Richie Wellens (to Doncaster), Paul Edwards and Craig Rocastle (to Port Vale), Will Haining (to St. Mirren), Chris Hall (to Stalybridge), Paul Warne (to Yeovil), the previous season's top scorer Chris Porter (to Motherwell), Simon Charlton (released) and in came experienced keeper Mark Crossley (from Fulham), JP Kalala (from Yeovil), John Thompson (from Nottingham Forest), ex-England international Michael Ricketts (from Preston), former Latic Mark Allott (who returned to Boundary Park from Chesterfield), pacy 21-year old striker Craig Davies (from Italian Serie B side Hellas Verona for an undisclosed fee), and Lee Hughes.

The latter acquisition was, without a shadow of a doubt, the most controversial. Hughes had been jailed in August 2004 for six years after colliding with an oncoming car, killing its driver, father of four Douglas Graham and leaving the scene of the accident. Having served half of his six-year sentence, Hughes had been freed on parole and was now able to resume his career.

Hughes' signing was nevertheless widely condemned, so much so that club director Barry Owen was forced to make the following statement: "While looking forward to Lee's arrival, we have no intention to glorify matters. Whilst not wanting to patronise anyone, as a family club we are very aware of the victims of the incident involving Lee and will always be mindful of their feelings and suffering."

It was a tough call but Hughes was a proven and prolific scorer, certainly at lower League levels and, without wishing to sound insensitive, Oldham were in no position to look such a gift horse in the mouth.

Sheridan wisely decided to keep out of the controversy. "I haven't had a lot of involvement, I've let other people get on with it," he demurred. "Obviously there's going to be a lot of interest and people will have opinions, but at the end of the day, I'm not getting involved in anything - he's come here as a footballer and hopefully he can do well for us. He's got to get on the training pitch and we'll take it from there. If he's available to be picked I'll have a look at him. I was excited we had a chance of getting him - on a football basis, if he's the player he was, he will do very well for us. He's got to get his sharpness at this level but I think he's going to be a massive player for us. I've spoken to him briefly and he can't wait. Obviously he's been out of the game for a few years but he's excited about coming and hopefully we can help him settle in quickly."

Ahead of the season Sheridan was convinced that he had assembled a stronger squad than the one that had taken them to the play-offs the previous season and was particularly excited about the strikers he had brought in, believing that Davies, Hughes and Ricketts were all capable of contributing scoring twenty goals apiece.

"The last campaign was a learning curve for me," Sheridan admitted, "but up until Christmas I thought we were the best team in the division. Expectations are higher than ever and I want fans to believe, I don't mind that. I want my players to believe it and I want to go higher, I honestly feel we can do that. I have three of the best strikers in League One who have the experience and ability to get quite a few goals between them. We have players in other areas who can also score and I don't see any problems on that count, but we have still to do a lot of work defensively as a team and stop giving away sloppy goals. If we can keep some clean sheets I am sure we will win lots of games."

Despite the optimism around Boundary Park, Sheridan's side had an awful start to the League season. After beating 2-1 Swansea on the opening day of the season (thanks to a last minute winner from debutant Craig Davies) Sheridan's side slumped to four consecutive League defeats and also bowed out of the Carling Cup (losing 3-0 to Burnley) during which their much vaunted new look strike force had scored only once.

After five games the Latics thus found themselves bottom of the League. Having also started the previous season poorly Sheridan might have been experiencing a sense of déjà vu but whereas in the 2006-07 campaign he had refused to panic, convinced that his team had been playing well, this time he didn't seem so sure. It was without doubt the biggest crisis Sheridan had faced in his short managerial career to date and he decided that what the players needed was a kick up the proverbial, warning his under-performing charges to get their act together or face being left out of the side.

"If they don't start listening to what I have to say they will be out of the team," he threatened. "No one is playing well enough to say they will be in the side next week. Everyone in the squad, no matter who or how old they are, now know they all have a chance of playing. Believe me, places are up for grabs and I won't be frightened of making changes because if we don't start winning games we are going to be in a very dangerous position. I have been there before as a player and you have to work hard and hope your luck changes. We are in a slump and the important thing is that we all stick together."

The rollicking appeared to have the desired effect, at least temporarily, as Oldham chalked up back to back victories at Walsall (3-0) and Crewe (coming from two goals behind in the latter to win 3-2), before Sheridan's men again went six games without a win.

But just when it looked like the Latics would have to endure another season-long relegation battle, Sheridan's men again turned it around in some style, suffering only one defeat in their next seventeen League and Cup fixtures and eventually chalking up a staggering seven consecutive away wins – a club record!

Particularly pleasing during this run was a 3-2 win away at Millwall in December, in which Oldham ended a five year winless London hoodoo thanks to a Lee Hughes hat-trick and a 3-1 win away at Leeds United on New Year's Day, which Sheridan described as his "best win as manager."

A week later Sheridan had revised his opinion. Having seen off Doncaster (after a replay) and Crewe in the first two rounds of the FA Cup the Latics were drawn against Premiership form side Everton in the Third Round at Goodison Park.

Upsetting the odds seemed like a tall order. In addition to home advantage Everton had won thirteen of their previous seventeen games while Oldham were in the middle of an injury crisis that had left Sheridan struggling to field a full squad. Nevertheless Sheridan went into the game with the confidence of a man whose side had just won six away games in succession.

"We will be giving it real go, no worries" he promised. "Everton have class throughout their side and there would be no point going to Goodison to defend and hope to hang on. We have won our last seven away games by attacking and scoring, so if we go a goal up who knows what can happen? We will be well under strength and that's a shame, but there will be a shock somewhere in the competition - let's hope it is our game. It is going to be tough because Everton are one of the form teams in the Premier League. They will have that winning mentality. The important thing is that we don't let ourselves down."

Far from letting themselves down, Sheridan's men produced the shock of the round to knock the 1995 winners out of the competition, thanks to a superb twenty-five-yard strike by Gary McDonald at the end of the first half, and some courageous backs-to-the-wall defending throughout the second.

Sheridan was naturally delighted with his side's memorable win: "To come to a Premier League ground against a team who are really flying at the moment was a great performance," he beamed. "I told the players to really enjoy the occasion, because things like this might not happen to them again. I was so pleased and proud of them. I believed we could get something from the game, we have won seven on the trot away now, so we are doing something right. I can't praise them enough. The togetherness was outstanding, kids and experienced players."

It should have been the result that pushed Sheridan's side on to greater things but it was not to be as they drew each of their next three games and then crashed out of the Cup at the hands of Huddersfield Town, ironically then managed by former Oldham boss Andy Ritchie.

To Oldham's credit they put that disappointment immediately behind them when they beat Carlisle 2-0 three days after their Fourth Round defeat. Of greater significance was the fact that this was the first time the Latics had won in the League at Boundary Park since their 3-2 victory against Crewe on 29th September.

Having broken their barren home spell, the Latics then won their next two at Boundary Park against Gilligham and Yeovil to take them within six points of the play-off places and when they beat Huddersfield 4-1 on 29th March Oldham had reduced the deficit to just four with five games remaining. Although time was running out Sheridan still believed his men were in with a chance and urged his side to take maximum points from their run-in.

"If we are to go on our longest winning run, this is the time to do it," he stipulated. "We have shown this season that when we are on song we are as good as anybody in our division. If we are to have any chance at all of a top-six finish we need to pick up all the fifteen points on offer and see if it is good enough. We will be giving it our best shot."

Although Sheridan's men delivered three of these wins, the other two games were lost and in the end Oldham finished their season a fairly emphatic nine points short of the play-off places in eighth place.

Sheridan's team had shown throughout an up and down season that, at their best, they were a match for anyone but injuries had robbed him of big players at crucial times. Inspirational skipper Sean Gregan spent six months out following surgery on his damaged Achilles and Sheridan had been denied the services of Lee Hughes throughout large chunks of the season due to a niggling groin injury which eventually required surgery in March. On the plus side the season had seen the true blossoming of several the youngsters that Sheridan had nurtured during his time as Youth Team coach. Neil Eardley, played forty-two League games during the season, skippered the side in the absence of Sean Gregan and won his first handful of caps for Wales, while Deane Smalley played thirty-seven, Matt Wolfenden played twenty-five, Kelvin Lomax (who Sheridan had brought back to the club the previous season after he had been released by Ronnie Moore at the end of the 2005-06 campaign) played twenty-one and Lewis Alessandra played fifteen times. Local lad Chris Taylor meanwhile appeared fifty times during the 2007-08 season and in so doing reached the one-hundred appearance mark for the club he had supported as a boy despite being still only twenty-one.

In addition, the manager could take particular pride from their run of seven consecutive away victories that included that famous win at Goodison. All in all, Sheridan could be reasonably satisfied with the progress his side was making.

Chapter Twelve

Sheridan now had a good blend of youth and experienced campaigners (such as Mark Allott, Andy Liddell, Sean Gregan, Mark Crossley and fit again Lee Hughes) and there seemed every chance that 2008-09 could finally be Oldham's year and the manager heaped pressure on himself by predicting his side would have a good season.

Sheridan knew that after two seasons in charge it was time to deliver. "I'm not daft," he acknowledged. "This is my third season as manager and I've got to win promotion this time, otherwise I'm in trouble."

"I've been here two years," he added. "Not many managers stay in a job more than two years."

Having made poor starts in his first two seasons in charge Sheridan demanded his players get off to a flier and his team responded in blistering fashion, winning their first three games against Millwall (twice coming from behind to win 4-3), Leeds (winning 2-0 thanks to two goals from Chris Taylor) and Cheltenham (winning 4-0 thanks to a seventeen-minute Lee Hughes hat-trick and a goal from new signing Danny Whitaker) to storm to the top of the table.

After the Cheltenham game a delighted Sheridan beamed, "Some of our football in the second half was absolutely brilliant, the best since I took charge. Our performance was spot on and we might have scored a couple more goals in the first half. The way we passed the ball was top-drawer stuff and Lee Hughes showed what he is all about. He is a poacher and a very good one. He is very clever in the penalty area, he knows where to be at the right time and when the ball falls to him he usually puts them away. Hughesy is a big player for us and the trick will be to keep him fit. But we have several players playing really well and if they can maintain that week in, week out we will win mo re games than we will lose. But I will keep their feet on the ground and none of them will get carried away, I will make sure of that. I have told them there is a long way to go and, for the moment, to enjoy being top of the table. I said before the season that we will score goals and no one can argue with ten in three games. We have got the start we wanted and we now have to keep it going for as long as we can."

In fact Oldham collected sixteen points from their opening six games to record their best start to a season since 1991 and eventually stretched their unbeaten run to eight games.

Prior to the season however Sheridan had suspected that his defence was not the strongest in the division and without the suspended skipper Sean Gregan, Oldham were dismantled by local rivals Stockport County on 4th October to register their first defeat of the season.

Oldham quickly got their promotion push back on track with a 4-0 demolition of Hereford but after drawing 1-1 with Leicester on 18th October (which marked Sheridan's ten year anniversary with the club) the Latics would lose three out of their next four games, with all three defeats coming away from home against Bristol Rovers, Swindon and Yeovil Town.

Sheridan was particularly scathing about his side's display at Swindon: "It was like watching schoolboy football with some of the decisions we made on the pitch," he blasted. "We were poor from one to eleven and it was our worst performance of the season. I am a very angry man and I can only apologise to the travelling fans. The goals we conceded were a joke and I won't stand for it. We looked a poor team and some players must think they are in the comfort zone with a guaranteed place week in, week out. Well, they are not - there are no automatic choices and there are other players waiting to come in. I will sort it out and we will be working long hours in extra training to put it right."

Despite four defeats in seven games, Sheridan's side responded in impressive fashion as they embarked on a ten-game unbeaten run that would stretch from 15th November to 12th January.

But just when it looked like Oldham had built a solid foundation platform from which a tilt at promotion could be sustained results and performances slumped wretchedly which led to a calamitous sequence of events that would lead to the end of Sheridan's time as Oldham's manager.

Perhaps the beginning of the end of Sheridan's reign came when Oldham visited strugglers Hereford on 17th January. It was a game they were expected to win comfortably, having beaten their opponents 4-0 earlier in the season at Boundary Park. Instead Hereford gained their revenge in ruthless fashion, annihilating Sheridan's side 5-0. Sheridan couldn't believe what he had witnessed after his side's abject display. Hereford made it look simple on an afternoon when nothing went right for the visitors who found themselves four down by half time. It was a dire display from Oldham and their biggest defeat under Sheridan.

A fuming Sheridan offered no excuses and said, "We ran away, got bullied and then battered. It won't happen again, believe me. That was the lowest point in my short time as a manager. We were abysmal and I can only apologise to the fans. It was not on and they have every right to moan and groan. Let's hope it was a kick up the backside we needed because we can't afford any repeats. There were no positives, nothing. Some of the players turned up and thought it was going to be easy but we got what we deserved - a real kick in the teeth. We were shocking and I won't stand for it. It is my job to put it right and I will. I won't stand for anything like that. It was an embarrassment and the players had better be hurting as much as I am."

The manager duly called his squad in for extra training on the Sunday and told them there would be no days off the following week and this appeared to do the trick as Stockport were beaten 3-1 the following Saturday. Unfortunately Oldham could not build on their derby win and could only win twice more (at home to Northampton on Valentine's Day and away at Millwall on 28th February) in the eight games that followed.

Oldham's season reached a new nadir during this period with a scrappy 2-2 draw against Yeovil on 21st February. The Latics came away with a point but it was a truly inept, error strewn performance that was described by Sheridan as the worst of the season. Sheridan's men were guilty of static, nervous defending, missed sitters (and a missed penalty), sloppy back passes and were barely able to muster an attack of any description for long periods of the game.

"We couldn't control the ball and it was a shocking game from both sides," Sheridan lambasted. "Considering the manner of the performance, I have to be pleased with a point but there was very little to get excited about."

Two wins in eight was hardly promotion form and Sheridan knew it and after his side's 1-1 draw with Leeds United on 2nd March (Oldham's second game in three days) he decided what was needed was couple of days off and a spot of team bonding.

The day after the Leeds game Sheridan had decided to take his squad out for the day before they headed to the Belle Vue Greyhound Stadium in Manchester for an official club function. The night had been advertised as an opportunity to meet the players in an "informal environment," and the event was a sell-out with around two-hundred fans in attendance, each paying £15.

It turned out to be a debacle of tabloid headline grabbing proportions.

The function was covered by Channel M's The Great Manchester Football Show and from the interviews and clips that were screened everyone appeared to be full of the joys of spring, with Sheridan and Lee Hughes sharing a drink and a laugh at the bar.

"We'll let our hair down, enjoy it and get our minds away from football," Sheridan informed the show. "We've had two hard games and are in a decent position in the league so we'll have a few drinks and enjoy ourselves."

"All the boys can have a few beers, let their hair down and have a get together," Chris Taylor added. "Hopefully we'll have a good night, boost spirit and togetherness. If we have a good night then we can come together even more for the last part of the season."

"You get a few who are a bit merrier than others," keeper Mark Crossley quipped on Channel M, "but it's all good for morale.

What was no so good for morale was the decision at some point in the evening for the manager, his staff and his players to discuss between themselves the reasons behind the team's slump in form. Alcohol and candour are rarely a good mix and it was inevitable that there would be some frank exchanges of views. Matters then escalated and eventually, allegedly, threatened to spill out into violence. First club captain Sean Gregan (who was also alleged to have exposed himself at some point during the evening) was alleged to have lunged at young winger Chris Taylor and then Lee Hughes allegedly scuffled with his manager before grabbing him in a headlock, at which point big goalie Mark Crossley allegedly jumped in to break up the altercation before matters combusted into a full-scale brawl. It was also alleged that Sheridan and his players rowed with staff at the Belle Vue which, if true, was a bit rich given that the Belle Vue not only sponsored their club but were also footing the bill for their evening out. That the whole embarrassing scene was played out in front of the fans who had paid good money to meet their "heroes" only added to the black comedy of it all.

The next day Sheridan and his players' boozy antics were splashed all over the national newspapers and to make matters worse the whole thing had been captured by the Belle Vue's CCTV which was going to make talking oneself out of trouble very difficult for those who taken things that step too far. To say Sheridan's employers were spitting feathers about the incident is an understatement and when they learned the players had also been given two days off training they were incensed yet further.

"What has gone on is incredible," a club source stated. "We should be working together to get promotion and instead everyone is fighting each other."

"I am aware that there were some incidents during the night which are now the subject of a full investigation," Oldham chief executive Alan Hardy stated. "We are reviewing some CCTV footage and if any member of staff, including players, are found to have acted inappropriately then we will take the strongest possible action."

As part of his investigation Hardy visited the dog track twice to speak to staff who witnessed the alleged drunken and lewd behaviour (and to apologise on behalf of those involved, naturally) and was even reported to have sought legal advice to determine what action the club could and could not take in terms of punishment. "If anyone is found to have been acting inappropriately," Hardy forewarned, "thus bringing the club into disrepute, I would expect the strongest possible action to be taken. We have to look carefully at all the evidence, but cannot discount sackings on the ground of gross misconduct."

On 11th March the board of directors held an emergency meeting and decided upon their course of action. In the event one player was fined two weeks' wages (believed to have been Sean Gregan, the club did not name names) while two others (believed to have been Sheridan and Hughes) were severely censured and warned as to their future conduct.

"Investigations into the reported incidents at Belle Vue dog track on Tuesday, 3rd March have now been concluded," the club's statement intoned. "Latics' directors have viewed CCTV coverage of the night, taken statements from staff at Belle Vue and spoken with club staff and players who were in attendance at the event. From the evidence that the club has gathered it is apparent that reports carried in the media have been exaggerated. There is no evidence to suggest that any player or staff member was involved in fighting, however the directors were disappointed with some of the behaviour during what was an official club function. The outcome of the investigation, after taking legal advice, is that one player has been fined the maximum amount of two weeks' wages and two others have been severely censured and warned as to their future conduct. The directors now consider this matter closed and hope everyone - fans, players and management - can move forward in our quest for promotion."

Sheridan, too, wanted to put the matter behind him and the following day refuted suggestions that there was unrest among his players and reiterated his determination to guide the club to promotion.

What Sheridan and his players therefore badly needed off the back of this debacle was a winning sequence of results. Sadly they were not forthcoming as Oldham (with Hughes and Gregan both playing the full ninety minutes) slumped to a 1-0 home defeat at the hands of Colchester (who went ahead after only ninety seconds, dominated the first half and soaked up everything Oldham could throw at them in the second half). The result meant that Sheridan's side had now collected just one point at home from a possible nine and had slipped to fifth in the League.

Once again Sheridan was left struggling to explain why his team hadn't performed. "First-half I thought we were shocking," he said, "the worst performance since I've been here and I won't accept it. We had a good opportunity to get back in the game in the second half but it's very disappointing, we just keep letting ourselves down. It's happened too many times. In the first half I didn't know who I was watching. They are the same players who pulled out performances against Millwall and Leeds, and yet, again, I'm stuck for words. I am learning very fast, it's my first job, and I'm going to go with my instinct from now on. I think some of the players knew they were going to be playing and that's not on. They have spoiled my weekend and I hope they take a good look at themselves. We are running out of games and I don't want to leave it late."

Ahead of the game against third placed MK Dons on 14th March Sheridan finally broke his silence about the Belle Vue fracas, and defended the way he had handled matters, and stressed his anger at the way the whole matter had been reported: "Whatever went on prior to the Colchester game, in my eyes, has been dealt with. I was there and I've heard and read lots of things. One or two's behaviour wasn't right, and although people want to say I didn't deal with it, I think I dealt with it in the right way. I know what happened. A lot of things were made out about Lee Hughes and myself but he didn't fall out with me, it was jovial. As far as I'm concerned it's gone. In my eyes I've been getting too much bad press and I don't think I deserve it. I haven't said anything, I've sat in the background and read things about me that I disagree with, but that's other people's opinions. They don't know what went on. I wasn't happy with a couple of players' behaviour but I dealt with it the way I wanted to deal with it at that moment in time. The most important thing as a manager is having a good dressing room. I've got a great dressing room and people outside can't tell me any different."

"My job is about winning games," he continued, "and if I don't do that and take the club where they want to go, I will get the sack. I'm not stupid or naive. All I want is to get the team out of this division and to do well. If I make mistakes along the way then so be it."

In addition, Sheridan remained convinced that his team could yet turn it around, starting with their visit to MK Dons.

"We have been in the top six all season so we must be doing something right," Sheridan added defiantly. "There is an opportunity for us to get out of this division. And I just ask the fans to get behind us even though I understand some of our performances haven't helped."

Unfortunately Oldham's players could not match their manager's defiance. Despite taking the lead on two separate occasions through Kevin Maher and Lee Hughes during the match, some atrocious defending meant that the Latics ended the game on the wrong end of a comprehensive 6-2 stuffing.

Oldham were still in eighth position and only a point away from the play-off positions, but in the opinion of the club's directors the parabola of Oldham's season was heading downward. The next day, on Sunday 15th March, following talks between Sheridan and Simon Corney, the club announced that they and their manager had parted company. In Sheridan's stead it was announced that former boss Joe Royle would return to the club for the remaining nine games of the season.

Perhaps Oldham regretted their hasty decision or maybe they didn't, but certainly only one of their remaining ten games of the season was won (away at Walsall on the final day of the season) and Oldham finished the season in a desultory tenth place. Joe Royle, probably wisely, decided against taking the job permanently and in the pre-season he was replaced by Dave Penney. Oldham Athletic remain to this day in League One.

For Sheridan it was Oldham's poor results that had cost him his job and was keen to underline the fact that his exit from Boundary Park had absolutely nothing to do with the notorious night at the dogs.

"Lee Hughes did have me in a headlock, but in a jovial way. It was results that cost me the job," Sheridan told BBC Radio 5 Live. "Lee Hughes did nothing whatsoever. There was no aggressive nature in Lee's actions. People have made things up. One or two of the players did have too much drink. Their behaviour was not right and I dealt with it on the night. I know for a fact that it was nothing to do with me losing my job. The results over probably the last ten games were not what we wanted. We were in a good position but we have let ourselves down. It is always about results and the people in charge felt they were not good enough."

Shortly after his departure from Boundary Park, Sheridan agreed to sit for an interview with his former Sheffield Wednesday team-mate Lawrie Madden who was now working as a journalist. When asked how he viewed his time at Oldham Sheridan replied, "I have left the club on good terms and hope they do well... I enjoyed the job and wanted to see it through and get promotion. I know that the budget is a lot less than many clubs and we have probably over-achieved. I have spent about £50,000 over the three years I have been in charge and have brought on some very good and talented young players so I am proud of what I achieved."

Madden also asked what Sheridan planned to do next, to which he responded, "Well it's strange not going into work but I want to get back into management sooner rather than later and hopefully people will look at what I achieved at Oldham and consider me if an opportunity comes up."

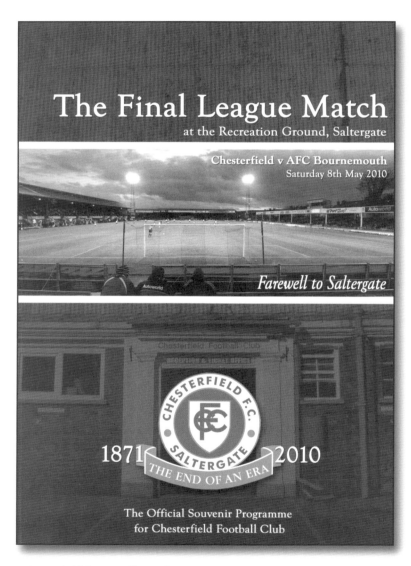

The Final League Match
at the Recreation Ground, Saltergate

Chesterfield v AFC Bournemouth
Saturday 8th May 2010

Farewell to Saltergate

1871 CHESTERFIELD F.C. SALTERGATE THE END OF AN ERA 2010

The Official Souvenir Programme
for Chesterfield Football Club

Chesterfields' Farewell to Saltergate programme

Chapter Thirteen

Having stated his desire to return to football management as quickly as possible, Sheridan did not have too long to wait and on 9th June he was appointed manager of League Two side Chesterfield. Sheridan signed on a three-year contract after reportedly having beaten off forty-nine other applicants for the vacant manager's job (including his old chum Andy Ritchie), the Derbyshire club having parted company with Lee Richardson at the end of the 2008-09 season.

Bringing Tommy Wright and Mark Crossley with him from Oldham, as his assistant manager and player-coach, Sheridan declared himself excited by the challenge: "Chesterfield FC is a very ambitious club and that appeals to me because I'm a young and ambitious manager. Within four or five years we would like to get into the Championship. It will be a very hard job but I am confident that I can do it. It is a job that will take a lot of doing because the Championship is a hard league to get into but I am looking forward to it and I am glad to be here."

He also vowed to continue to pursue the same brand of exciting and attacking football that he had believed in throughout his entire professional career: "I like football to be played in the right way and we will try to do that but it is most important to have a winning mentality and to play winning football."

These were exciting times for the Derbyshire club. With former Wednesday chairman Dave Allen having joined the club as its new major shareholder, money was not only available to strengthen the squad but at the end of the 2009-10 season the Spireites would move into a brand new £13million stadium in Whittington Moor on the north side of the town, funded by grants, the sale of Saltergate and Allen's munificence.

Sheridan moved quickly into the transfer market, bringing two former Chesterfield captains back to Saltergate. First classy centre-half Ian Breckin (who had made two-hundred appearances for the club in his earlier spell and had captained the Spireites to promotion to the third tier in 2000-01) was snapped up after being released from Nottingham Forest and he was soon followed by Mark Allott (who had played with and under Sheridan at Oldham) after the player had been released by Tranmere. In addition twenty-three year-old former Sheffield Wednesday winger/striker Drew Talbot (who had been on loan at Saltergate the previous season) was brought in from cash-strapped Luton Town.

The capture of Ian Breckin was widely seen as a particular coup, with Sheridan beating a host of rival clubs to the former Forest captain's signature. "There was a lot of interest but it was Chesterfield that caught my eye," Breckin explained, "and it was a combination of factors that attracted me. I'd been here before and enjoyed success and they had a new manager in John Sheridan who impressed me. Next season will be the final year at Saltergate before a move to a new ground and they offered me a two-year contract. The new ground will give the club a fantastic start and I wanted to be part of that. I'm very glad to be back at Saltergate. The fans have had a bit of an up and down time but the future looks really positive. The future looks bright."

And the Sheridan era at Saltergate got off to a great start. In his first public game in charge goals from Rob Page and Scott Boden saw Chesterfield come from behind to beat Derby County 2-1 to lift the Derbyshire FA Centenary Cup for first time since 2001.

Although the first two competitive games of Sheridan's reign were both lost – away at Torquay and away at Scunthorpe in the Carling Cup – Sheridan won his first two competitive games at Saltergate against Northampton and Notts County (with one Lee Hughes in the opponent's starting eleven) and then followed this up with draws away at Shrewsbury and at home to Morecambe and an impressive 5-1 win away at Burton Albion in the Johnstone's Paint Trophy.

Although Chesterfield lost three of their next four, Sheridan's men bounced back in some style to win seven of their next eight League games (and only lost the other - 1-0 at Hereford, a game the visitors had dominated – largely due to poor refereeing decisions), to climb into the play-off places.

Having won four of the five games they'd played in October, Sheridan was duly awarded the League Two Manager of the Month. "Chesterfield won more matches in the month than any other team," Alan Curbishley, Chairman of the Awards panel adjudicated, "and John Sheridan fashioned great wins against top of the table Bournemouth, Barnet and a 5-2 mauling of Burton Albion who have also been doing very well."

Unfortunately the curse of the Manager of the Month award struck as Chesterfield were dumped out of the FA Cup by Bournemouth on 7th November, going down 3-1 at Saltergate. In an intriguing statistic, this now meant that Chesterfield had failed to beat a fellow League side in the competition since their Quarter-Final win against Wrexham during their memorable run to the last four in 2001.

Despite the fact that the Bournemouth match had been the first time Chesterfield had lost at home all season, this clearly wasn't enough for some fans, with one bonehead telling the manager to "go back to Sheffield."

Rather than let the matter drop Sheridan instead decided to confront the hecklers, and advised them to "stay at home" if they could not back his team.

"I don't understand one or two people who are moaning and shouting for me to go back to Sheffield," a baffled Sheridan responded after the match, and reminded the supporters that, yes, his team had played poorly but he and the players were just as frustrated as the fans. "I have only been here three or four months. I just don't understand them, so if they want to carry on like that, please stay home."

Although Sheridan's men silenced the critics by returning to winning ways away at Rochdale the following Saturday and again at Darlington seven days later, Chesterfield endured a disappointing end to the year, losing five of their next six fixtures between 24th November and 2nd January.

Sheridan's men stopped the rot with a win at home to Torquay on 16th January and a clean sheet and a point at Northampton a week later. But another home defeat at Rotherham on 26th January made it three defeats from five at Saltergate. Having dropped only two points from their first nine League matches at Saltergate this was a worrying development.

Sheridan however refused to compromise his footballing principles (although he did admit to being sick of people telling him how well his side had played in defeat) and this stance was rewarded as his side embarked on a run of six consecutive wins between 26th January and 24th February - beating Morecambe away (1-0), Lincoln at home (2-1), Port Vale away (2-1), Bury at home (1-0), Darlington away (3-2) and Crewe away (1-0) - to put them firmly back among the promotion-chasing pack and earn Sheridan his second Manager of the Month award of the season.

"John Sheridan's kept up the heat on the League Two leaders with a string of impressive performances in February," Awards Panel chairman Alan Curbishley declared. "Their win over Bury was a tremendous result and helped to underline their credentials as serious promotion contenders this season."

The run of good form had come at a cost, however, with knee injuries to three key players: central defender Aaron Downes (who would miss the rest of the season), full-back Phil Picken and top scorer Jack Lester whose cartilage tear (that had already limited his appearances in recent weeks) required surgery that would keep him out of action until 5th April.

Although their winning streak came to an end at home to Aldershot on 27th February, when they beat Cheltenham Town 1-0 on 6th March it marked the first time that Chesterfield had won five consecutive away games in over seventy-six years! At this stage of the season a play-off position at least seemed virtually guaranteed.

Although Sheridan's men could not stretch their run of away wins further when they lost at Notts County on 9th March (after which Sheridan was found guilty of misconduct for abusing match officials and slapped with a £500 fine and a two-match suspension from the dugout) when Chesterfield faced Sheridan's Port Vale at Saltergate four days later they did so in the knowledge that a win would take them into second place.

Instead Vale romped home 5-0 winners - Chesterfield heaviest at home since 1976 – plunging Sheridan's men back into the play-off lottery. It was their third defeat in four games and Sheridan was so ashamed of his side's abject display (which had been greeted by chants of "what a load of rubbish" from sections of the home crowd) he felt duty bound to issue a public apology: "'I would like to apologise on behalf of the players," he doffed. "We were not good enough and a performance like that will not get you anywhere. We just did not get going. We were not at the races, simple as."

Although the manager ordered his players into work on the Sunday following the Port Vale humiliation to replay the unedifying spectacle on video, the punishment did little to affect Chesterfield's stuttering form when they visited Burton Albion the following Saturday. Having beaten the Brewers 5-1 in the Johnstone's Paint Trophy and 5-2 in the League in September, this was a game that the Blues had every right to expect to win and although Chesterfield led twice through debutant winger Ishmel Demontagnac (who had arrived on loan from Blackpool to become, incredibly, the fortieth name on a Spireites team sheet that season) and Scott Boden, Burton were able to pull it back on both occasions, their second goal coming in the 95th minute, to steal a point.

Incensed by the award of a highly dubious penalty in the eighty-ninth minute, the length of the added time and the appalling overall standard of the refereeing he'd witnessed from the director's box (where he had been serving the first of his two-match ban), Sheridan again incurred the wrath of the FA by remonstrating angrily with the match officials at the end of the game. The FA promptly found him guilty of breaching their codes of conduct and handed him a £750 fine and another three-match suspension from the dug-out. Ultimately this would mean that Sheridan would be banned from the touchline for five games in a row!

As a result, Sheridan sat in the stands as the Spireites could only muster four points from the remaining four games of his ban – losing 2-1 at home to strugglers Hereford (their third defeat at Saltergate in a row), beating Rochdale 2-0 to stop the home rot, losing 3-1 away at Barnet and drawing 2-2 at home to Dagenham and Redbridge.

This run of poor form had come at the worse possible time and Sheridan was at a loss to explain it and believed his side were "playing like a team that is in the relegation zone."

Chesterfield then drew their next game (2-2 with Grimsby) but when they slumped to a 2-0 defeat at Macclesfield Town on 17th April Sheridan's men dropped out of the play-off positions for the first time since January. Chesterfield were now in eighth place in League Two with sixty-six points, level with both Aldershot and Dagenham and Redbridge, but behind on goal difference. Only three games remained of Chesterfield's season, against Bradford City, Accrington Stanley and Bournemouth, and Sheridan desperately needed points.

"Dropping out of the top seven for the first time since last January is a stark reminder that we need to start winning games," Sheridan urged. "With just three games left it's time for the players to stand up and be counted. Although we are still in a very good position of reaching the play-offs we will only succeed if we all stay together and battle for the results we need, starting this weekend against Bradford City. It now looks as though there are nine teams all competing for one of the four play-off positions and we want to ensure we are one of them."

Chesterfield had now won only two from their last eleven games and after drawing with Bradford and losing to Accrington Stanley, Sheridan accepted that this was not going to be their year and blamed both the players and his own performance.

"We haven't been good enough," he acknowledged. "We've let ourselves and the fans down badly. The way we're playing at the moment, we don't deserve to be in the play-offs, we're not winning football matches. I look at myself and I look at the players and I've used too many players this season, which I don't like doing. It won't happen again because next season I'll hopefully have players in who are consistent. I've changed the team this season because players haven't been consistent in their performances. We should have got out of this division, play-offs at the least and we've let the fans down in the last ten or a dozen games. I'd like some of the players to stand up and be accounted for and tell me why they've all performed well at times but not over a consistent period and I'm very angry."

As they went into their final fixture – and their final ever League game at Saltergate – there was still a faint hope that the Spireites could yet qualify for the play-offs in seventh place. All they had to do was beat already promoted Bournemouth and hope that Rotherham could beat Dagenham and Redbridge (who, ominously, had won five of their last seven), and cross their fingers that Bury and Port Vale also failed to win.

The game against Bournemouth was a game Chesterfield simply had to win. Not only was there still a slim chance of making the play-offs but a victory was the only fitting way to give their dilapidated but still much loved home of one-hundred and thirty-nine years a fitting send off. In front of a capacity crowd of almost 8,000 (about 1,000 of whom had taken part in a colourful parade through the town prior to kick-off) it looked, for the majority of the match, like the occasion would end in anti-climax. Bournemouth took the lead in the forty-second minute and held on to it until the eightieth minute when Jack Lester equalised with a brilliant right-footed finish from the edge of the area. It was Lester's twelfth of the season which meant that despite being absent for a large chunk of the season, he had topped the Spireites goal scoring charts for the third successive season.

The scores remained deadlocked as the ninetieth minute came and went and Bournemouth almost ruined the parade in injury time when Brett Pitman rattled the Chesterfield bar.

Fortunately the footballing Gods were not going to let Chesterfield mark the end of an era without one last win and six minutes into injury time Derek Niven hit what would prove to be the winner with a powerful twenty-five-yard strike which prompted a mass pitch invasion which included the curious sight of a disabled man rolling his wheelchair into the Bournemouth half.

It was fitting that Chesterfield should win and it was equally fitting that Niven should treasure the honour of scoring that last ever goal. Not only was he the longest serving player on Chesterfield's books but the player had also recently battled back to fitness after overcoming testicular cancer.

The game did briefly restart and when the final whistle blew thousands swarmed back onto the pitch to salute both the old ground and Sheridan's players who waved their own appreciation from the director's box.

Amid these emotional scenes the news had inevitably filtered through that Dagenham and Redbridge had secured a 3-2 win against Rotherham to clinch the last play-off place. Chesterfield thus finished in eighth spot with seventy points; two shy of the top seven and within three of all four teams above them. But the day had been as much about the occasion as the result, and nothing could take away the fact Chesterfield's supporters and players had given Saltergate a wonderful send-off.

Chapter Fourteen

When the tears had dried and the bunting had come down after the Saltergate farewell, Sheridan admitted he had some "difficult decisions" to make as he moved to shape his squad for the following season.

"I want to thank all the players because they have been quality and shown a great attitude and not one of them caused me a problem," Sheridan affirmed. "But we haven't done enough and eighth isn't good enough."

With this in mind, twelve out of contract members of Sheridan's squad were allowed to leave: Kevin Austin, Danny Boshell, Adam Rundle, Barry Conlon, Alan Goodall, Danny Hall, Phil Picken, Paul Harsley, Lloyd Kerry, Terrell Lewis, Matt Malak, and Simon Whaley.

Sheridan also quickly settled on the players he wanted to retain. Midfielder Dan Gray and strikers Scott Boden and Jordan Bowery had already signed new two-year contracts, and Sheridan also offered new deals to midfielder Wade Small and defenders Jamie Lowry and Gregor Robertson. In addition nine players were still under contract: Mark Allott, Ian Breckin, Aaron Downes, Martin Gritton, keeper Tommy Lee, Jack Lester, Derek Niven, Rob Page and Drew Talbot. Rounding off his squad ahead of the new season Sheridan also offered professional contracts to five of the Chesterfield Youth team who had reached the Quarter-Finals of the Midlands Cup the previous season: midfielder Craig Clay, striker Tendayi Darwikwa, left midfielder Jimmy Adcock and full-backs Chris Tingay and Ryan Granger.

That this was a record number of new professional contracts offered to and signed by Chesterfield's scholars delighted youth team manager Dave Bentley who paid tribute to Sheridan's decision to keep one eye on the future. "Since manager John Sheridan joined us last summer the words were, "If they're good enough I'll put them in,"" Bentley genuflected, "and credit to the manager he's done just that. He's got them involved in training and they've had good experiences throughout the season."

During the summer Sheridan quickly bolstered his squad with four exciting new recruits: experienced former Republic of Ireland Under-21 midfielder Dwayne Mattis was acquired in May after he had been released by Walsall, and he was joined a fortnight later by attacking midfielder Danny Whitaker (who had played for Sheridan at Oldham). Having persuaded these two to drop down a division Sheridan then pulled off another coup by bringing in Jamaican international Simon Ford from Scottish Premier League club Kilmarnock in June in a bid to beef up his leaky back line that had conceded 62 goals (one more than the Spireites had scored) the previous season.

By the start of July, Sheridan had also brought in twenty-four year-old Welsh International Craig Davies (another who had played under Sheridan at Oldham) on a free from Brighton and right-back Jack Hunt on loan from Huddersfield.

On 5th July Chesterfield FC were handed the keys to their brand spanking new 10,500-capacity all-seater ground, the B2Net Stadium. Built by GB Building Solutions Chesterfield's new home was pretty as a picture with two magnificent curved main stands and without a single load bearing pillar to block the view in any part of the ground. And the new venue certainly captured the public's imagination with Chesterfield selling a record 2,750 season tickets ahead of the new season.

The pressure was well and truly on, then, to make the 2010-11 season one to remember.

Chesterfield would kick off the campaign at the B2Net against Barnet and Sheridan's side (including five debutants in the starting line-up: Danny Whitaker, Dwayne Mattis, Davies, Simon Ford and Jack Hunt) duly christened their new home with a 2-1 win.

The curtain raiser was not without its nervy moments for the Spireites, however. Although Dwayne Mattis and Jack Lester put the hosts 2-0 ahead, Barnet pulled a goal back on seventy minutes and then Craig Davies was sent off for a challenge on Barnet's Steve Kabba in the eighty-second minute. Indeed Barnet also had the ball in the net with only two minutes remaining but Mark Byrne's effort was judged to be offside.

Although Chesterfield lost their second game of the season 2-1 at home to Middlesbrough in the Carling Cup, League form was the priority even at that early stage and Chesterfield won each of their next three games at the B2Net: Hereford (4-0 in which Danny Whitaker bagged a hat-trick), Lincoln City (2-1) and Cheltenham (3-0).

The Spireites also remained unbeaten on their travels during this period (with draws against Port Vale, Macclesfield and Morecambe) and in fact did not lose in the League until 25th September when they lost 1-0 at Rotherham who foiled Chesterfield's bid to set a new club record of eight games unbeaten from the start of a season.

The Spireites bounced back to win their ninth game of the season, coming from a goal behind to beat Northampton 2-1 away (with second-half strikes from Dean Morgan and Craig Davies) to go second in the League but then came dangerously close to losing their unbeaten home record in the following game.

Crewe Alexandra were the visitors and after only thirteen minutes Chesterfield found themselves three goals down. Although Jack Lester pulled one back after twenty-three minutes, The Railwaymen restored their three goal advantage three minutes later to take a 4-1 lead with them into the break. After the fourth goal Sheridan had seen enough and replaced club captain Ian Breckin with eighteen year-old youth team product Craig Clay (making only his second senior appearance). The substitution was greeted by jeers from the crowd. "I did not like the crowd's reaction," Sheridan chided after the match. "It was a brave decision for me. He is the captain and I respect him but I could have taken anyone off. Nobody was playing well."

Remarkably, the Chesterfield boss did not say too much at the interval: "I went in there and didn't raise my voice," Sheridan revealed, "it's the first time I haven't. I just told them to get themselves together, help each other and sort themselves out. They got a grip and just went for it."

After the break, roared on by a six-thousand-plus crowd Chesterfield dominated but were unable to find a way past a resolute Crewe defence.

Eventually Lester pulled one back with a close range far post header and shortly afterwards Whitaker netted from the spot to make it 4-3. Within a minute however Alex had scored again and with only two minutes of normal time remaining Chesterfield looked dead and buried.

With just two minutes to go the Spireites were offered a lifeline when they were awarded a second penalty, won by Clay, and once again Whitaker made no mistake. When the fourth official held up the board announcing four minutes of added time the crowd sensed that Sheridan's men were destined to steal an unlikely point and those who had heckled the manager's decision to introduce Craig Clay were left eating humble pie when the youngster hammered in a low twenty-yard equaliser at the death.

Despite the frustration of conceding five goals at home Sheridan acknowledged that the match had been something special: "It was one of the best games I have been part of, as a player or a manager. It was enjoyable and very frustrating. The goals were gave away were dreadful but the game was a great spectacle. We could have won it. At half time I did not have to raise my voice. I told them to get themselves together and sort themselves out. I'm proud of the players for the character they demonstrated. They were determined that they would not be beaten and the fans appreciated it."

If that wasn't enough drama for one season Chesterfield's next game on 6th October saw them pitted against Sheffield Wednesday in the Johnstone's Paint Trophy and handed their manager another emotional return to Hillsborough (where he now had a lounge named after him).

Backed by around 3,500 travelling supporters Chesterfield went ahead in the tenth minute through a Dean Morgan volley and although Wednesday levelled within two minutes through Neil Mellor, it was Sheridan's men that had the better of the first half and had the ball in the net twice more through Jordan Bowery and Craig Davies, though sadly both were ruled out for offside.

Although Wednesday upped their game in the second half and hit the bar through Mellor and had a Darren Purse header cleared off the line by Jack Hunt it was Chesterfield who thought they'd stolen the spoils when Davies curled home in the eighty-fourth minute. The goal looked to have put Chesterfield in the draw for the next round – and indeed a number of Owls fans began to walk out – but the match took another twist in the eighty-eighth minute when Derek Niven was judged to have brought down the Owls' Giles Coke in the area.

Although Tommy Lee saved Marcus Tudgay's penalty the ball fell kindly for the Wednesday substitute and he tucked away the rebound to force a dramatic penalty shoot-out which eventually extended to a marathon twenty-two spot-kicks. The teams could not be separated even after every outfield player had stepped up and at 7-7 it came down to the two keepers. While Wednesday's keeper Nicky Weaver (who had already made saves to deny Danny Whitaker, Dwayne Mattis and Simon Ford) kept his cool Chesterfield's keeper Tommy Lee blasted the decisive kick wide, and it was Wednesday who advanced to the Northern Section Quarter-Final.

Although Sheridan was disappointed with the result he was nevertheless delighted with the way his players had performed. "I'm very pleased we approached the game and we matched them in all areas," Sheridan told BBC Radio Sheffield. "We should have won the game. I thought we'd see the game out and win the game. I can take lots of positives from this. I thought we played really well and it's just a shame we didn't get the reward."

Sheridan's men shrugged off this setback by winning five of their next six games – beating Southend 2-1 at home, Wycombe 2-1 away (after which Chesterfield went top of the League), Shrewsbury 4-3 at home (a game in which Sheridan's men had at one stage led 4-0), drawing 0-0 away at Stevenage, beating Accrington 5-2 at home and beating Harrow Borough 2-0 away in the FA Cup.

Chesterfield then suffered a bit of a wobble, finally losing their unbeaten home record to Burton Albion on 13th November and although they beat Aldershot away the following Saturday, Sheridan's men then lost again at the B2Net (going down 2-1 to Oxford to slip back to second in the League table) and then lost in the FA Cup to Burton Albion to register their first back-to-back defeats of the season.

174

Sheridan was less than impressed with the nature of the FA Cup defeat (which extended for at least one more year Chesterfield's embarrassing record of not having beaten a League side in the competition since 1997) and he apologised to Chesterfield supporters who had made the trip: "We had a brilliant following and our display didn't warrant any credit from anyone and I apologise to the fans for that. We started all right for the first five or ten minutes and the two goals we conceded were shocking. We were just not switched on for the first one. One of their lads had gone down injured so we had time to organise. I'm sick of it happening. I keep telling them but with most of them it's going in one ear and out of the other. I'm going to have to react, sort it out and make tough decisions. The second goal, we're on the attack and people just make the wrong decisions. It's people not doing their jobs."

Although the Spireites would play only one game in December due to the atrocious weather (a 1-0 win over Torquay), Sheridan's men started the New Year in swashbuckling fashion - beating Stockport (4-1, thanks to a Jack Lester hat-trick), drawing 2-2 with Accrington Stanley, beating Southend away (3-2), beating Stevenage (1-0), drawing with Shrewsbury, beating Gillingham (2-0, thanks to a brace from 22-year-old Deane Smalley, whom Sheridan had signed on loan from Oldham) and then sharing four goals with Bradford – to reclaim, maintain and ultimately stretch their lead at the top of the table and also earn for their manager a League Two Manager of the Month nomination for January.

Although Chesterfield would eventually extend their unbeaten run to ten games with draws against Stockport and Aldershot, this meant the Spireites had now drawn three in a row, prompting Tommy Wright, who had been particularly unimpressed with the team's display against Aldershot (which had required a late equaliser from Deane Smalley, his seventh goal in eight games, to rescue a point), to issue some harsh words: "We were very fortunate to get a point. In the second-half our performance was poor. We had no tempo, no rhythm. You can't just turn up and win football matches. If you get in a comfort zone, you get your backsides kicked. It is not acceptable. Aldershot were better than us in the second half. Far better. We were bitterly disappointed with that performance."

Things then got worse as Chesterfield's unbeaten run came to an end on 11th February with a 1-0 defeat away at bogey side Burton Albion (then in one of the two relegation spots). It was the third time the Brewers had beaten the Spireites that season.

Chesterfield responded with an away point at promotion rivals Bury and two successive wins at Lincoln and Bradford, and although they lost 2-0 at home to Morecambe, Sheridan's men quickly re-established their nine-point lead at the top of the table thanks to a comprehensive 4-1 victory over second-placed Wycombe on 1st March (a game which Chesterfield had dominated from start to finish). Five days later they'd stretched this lead to eleven points when they visited Cheltenham Town and outclassed the home side to win 3-0 and then made it three wins in eight days when they beat Northampton 2-1 at the B2Net.

Sheridan was particularly delighted with the victory against Cheltenham (which had made it ten points from twelve on their travels) and said: "I thought we played really well, a very good performance by a team that looked as though they were at the top of the table. An excellent performance, a clean sheet and again we could have scored a few more goals."

Although they lost at Crewe four days later Chesterfield again proved their class in front of a record crowd of 10,089 at the B2net and Sky Television's cameras by walloping Rotherham 5-0 with goals from Craig Davies and Dean Holden (another former Oldham man who had been brought in on loan until the end of the season in February) and three from Jack Lester. Lester's hat-trick not only took his goal tally to fourteen for the season but also elevated him to seventh place on the all-time Chesterfield scoring list.

"Jack has energy around him," Sheridan congratulated. "I do not expect him to run around all the match but he is very clever. When he gets in there, he can find half a yard. He's the best in the division at that. I would love him to be twenty-seven or twenty-eight – I could get a lot of money for him! I try to look after him. He's a good pro and he trains very well. I've told him to come to me if he needs a rest. He's top drawer for us, a massive player."

The win against Rotherham took Chesterfield thirteen points clear at the head of the table (and cost Sheridan's opposite number Ronnie Moore his job) and the Spireites edged ever closer to promotion with a 2-2 draw with Barnet (with goals from Deane Smalley and Craig Davies) and a 2-0 win against Port Vale on 4th April thanks to second-half goals from Jack Lester and Deane Smalley.

Smalley's opener against Barnet was notable because it made him the fourth member of Sheridan's squad (alongside Craig Davies, Jack Lester and Danny Whitaker) to break the ten-goal barrier for the season – a statistic that hadn't been achieved by Chesterfield since 1979/80.

With automatic promotion tantalisingly within their grasp Sheridan's men then lost 3-0 at Hereford, a performance Sheridan described as "shocking."

"People keep saying this, that and the other, and we've been playing well and we're ten points clear," Sheridan seethed. "That performance won't get you anywhere."

Nevertheless with five games to go Chesterfield (on seventy-eight points) were still nine points clear of second placed Wycombe and ten points ahead of third placed Bury (who had played one game less).

Chesterfield again bounced back, coming from behind to win 2-1 against Macclesfield on 16th April (with goals from Davies and Whitaker) which put them within one point of automatic promotion which was all but confirmed six days later when Wycombe Wanderers could only draw with Torquay.

Wycombe's draw meant Chesterfield could not realistically be overhauled and their return to League One was rubber stamped the following day when Sheridan's men earned a hard-fought goalless draw against Oxford United.

"It's been a long season and we've been in a position where everyone thought we were going to get promotion," Sheridan stated proudly. "I didn't mention it too much myself, but in the back of my mind I thought we were in a good, healthy position to do it. I'm just pleased for the players ... [they] are the ones who need patting on the back."

"If you've got players who are comfortable [on the ball] and get in dangerous positions and score we might as well play to our strengths and I think we've done that. I think we've been very entertaining, especially at home [where] we've got at teams and had some quality performances."

"You've got to stay positive and you've got to keep everyone on their toes and not get carried away and that's what we've done. We've been professional about it. We haven't spoken too much about what we're going to do, we've just taken one game at a time, the staff, the fans and the players all just kept concentrating on the next game and luckily for us once or twice when we've had a bad result teams haven't been able to get positive results to try and catch us up. And when we've lost we've always usually bounced back and that shows good character from the side."

Now all that remained to be settled was the issue of the title. The draw with Oxford United had nudged Chesterfield to eighty-two points but second placed Bury had fast gained ground having won five on the spin and by the time of their visit to the B2Net on 25th April they had reduced the deficit to just five points. Nevertheless a win for Chesterfield would see Sheridan's men crowned Champions.

In what would prove to be a topsy-turvy game, Bury twice went ahead and twice the Spireites pulled it back through Craig Davies (his twenty-fifth of the season) and Jack Lester. With only three minutes remaining Bury scored what would prove to be the winner. Not only did this guarantee Bury automatic promotion but it also reduced Chesterfield's lead at the top of the table to just two points with two games remaining.

Four days later on Friday, 28th April Chesterfield visited Torquay where they ultimately had to settle for a hard-fought but unsatisfactory goalless draw.

This rather handed the initiative to Bury who knew that a home win against promotion chasing Wycombe Wanderers the following day would see them leapfrog Sheridan's men at the top of the table on goal difference. Fortunately Wycombe Wanderers then did Chesterfield a massive favour by beating Bury 3-1 which left Sheridan's side needing just a point from their last game on 7th May to secure the title.

Their opponents would be Gillingham who themselves were still in the running for a play-off place. To make matters even less foregone, Andy Hessenthaler's side had not been beaten on their travels for four months.

To some extent history was also against Sheridan's men. Not since 1936 had a Chesterfield team wrapped up any Championship at home.

Nevertheless having been top of every League table published in 2011, Sheridan's men were in no mood to have the title wrestled from their grasp on the final weekend of the season. Although they needed only a point Sheridan told his men to go for the win.

When the game kicked off amid a barrage of noise from the sell-out, 10,000 strong crowd, the Spireites started brightly and enjoyed the bulk of the possession. Unfortunately aside from a long range effort from Danny Whitaker they struggled to create too many chances and the first half would end goalless. Nevertheless with Bury drawing 2-2 at Stevenage, Chesterfield were still in pole position.

Although Gillingham forced three corners in quick succession at the start of the second half, they could find no way past Tommy Lee (who had been ever-present throughout the season). In the fifty-fourth minute the home side finally went ahead when Danny Whitaker latched onto a loose ball on the edge of the opposition's box, rounded the Gills' keeper and slotted home from an tight angle for his thirteenth of the season.

Although chants of "Champions" started to resound around the B2Net the home supporters' nerves were soon rattled when Gillingham equalised in the sixty-seventh minute through Cody McDonald and then moments later the news filtered through that Bury had taken the lead at Stevenage. This meant that if Gillingham scored again and the scores at Stevenage remained the same the title would head to Gigg Lane.

Fortunately Chesterfield's fans only needed to keep their fingers crossed for six minutes. Within three minutes Stevenage had equalised (their game with Bury would finish 3-3) and three minutes later Chesterfield restored their lead when a cross from Scott Griffiths found Jack Lester who helped himself to his seventeenth League goal of the season (all of them scored at the B2Net, incidentally).

The issue of the League Two title was then settled beyond doubt in the eighty-second minute when Deane Smalley added a third (his twelfth of the season) from close range after another fine run and cross from Griffiths.

Ten minutes later it was all over and amidst joyous scenes Chesterfield were finally crowned Champions of League Two. They had won twenty four, drawn fourteen and had lost only eight, scoring eighty-five and conceding fifty-one to finish on eighty-six points, five ahead of second placed Bury and six ahead of third placed Wycombe. It had been a fantastic season and the perfect way to mark their first at the B2Net.

"It's been a long time coming," a delighted Sheridan told BBC Radio Sheffield after the game. "We've been in a very healthy position for a long time and I'm just so pleased and proud of the players, how they've responded and reacted to the things we've tried to put to them all season and it's just great for everyone involved in the club. The support was brilliant again today and I'm just so pleased we've got a trophy to put in the cabinet and [the players have] got a winner's medal."

"I think we've played the type of football that would attract the fans and we've got results and we just had that winning mentality and we started off early in the season doing it and it just breeds confidence and lucky for us it's taken us all the way through."

It remains to be seen how far this Chesterfield team can go but the portents seem to be decidedly in their favour. They've got a sound squad of players (which Sheridan will undoubtedly look to strengthen over the summer), a wonderful stadium and the support to fill it, the financial backing, the incentive of renewing local rivalries with both Sheffield clubs (following United's relegation from the Championship), the winning habit and last, but not least, in John Sheridan (who was offered a five-year contract two days after the title had been secured) a highly ambitious and determined young manager.

"We're a club who is hopefully going to go forward," Sheridan stated after the title had been secured, "and we're going into a very difficult division next year but we're going there believing we can compete and that's what we're going to do."

Fingers crossed the League Two Championship is only the beginning for both Chesterfield and Sheridan.

The future undoubtedly looks bright.

Career Statistics

LEEDS UNITED

	League		FA Cup		League Cup		Others (Full Members /Play-Offs)	
	Games	Goals	Games	Goals	Games	Goals	Games	Goals
1982-83	27	2	2	1	-	-	-	-
1983-84	11	1	-	-	-	-	-	-
1984-85	42	6	1	-	3	-	-	-
1985-86	31 (1)	4	- (1)	-	3	-	1	-
1986-87	40	15	5	-	2	-	6	1
1987-88	36 (2)	12	1	-	4	2	1	-
1988-89	38 (2)	7	2	-	2	1	2	-
TOTAL	**225 (5)**	**47**	**11 (1)**	**1**	**14**	**3**	**10**	**1**

NOTTINGHAM FOREST

	League		FA Cup		League Cup	
	Games	Goals	Games	Goals	Games	Goals
1989-90	-	-	-	-	1	-
TOTAL	**0**	**0**	**0**	**0**	**1**	**0**

SHEFFIELD WEDNESDAY

	League		FA Cup		League Cup		Others (Full Members /Europe*)	
	Games	Goals	Games	Goals	Games	Goals	Games	Goals
1989-90	27	2	2	-	-	-	2	1
1990-91	45 (1)	10	4	1	9	1	1	-
1991-92	24	6	1	1	2	-	-	-
1992-93	25	3	8	1	7	2	1*	1*
1993-94	19 (1)	3	-	-	2	-	-	-
1994-95	34 (2)	1	2 (1)	-	4	-	-	-
1995-96	13 (4)	-	-	-	-	-	-	-
1996-97	- (2)	-	-	-	-	-	-	-
TOTAL	**187 (10)**	**25**	**17 (1)**	**3**	**24**	**3**	**4**	**2**

BIRMINGHAM CITY (on loan)

	League		FA Cup		League Cup		Others (Full Members)	
	Games	Goals	Games	Goals	Games	Goals	Games	Goals
1995-96	1 (1)	0	-	-	2	-	-	-
TOTAL	1 (1)	0	-	-	2	-	-	-

BOLTON WANDERERS

	League		FA Cup		League Cup	
	Games	Goals	Games	Goals	Games	Goals
1996-97	12 (8)	2	2	-	2	-
1997-98	12	-	-	-	-	-
TOTAL	24 (8)	2	2	-	2	-

DONCASTER ROVERS

	Conference League		FA Cup	
	Games	Goals	Games	Goals
	8	-	-	-
TOTAL	8	-	-	-

OLDHAM ATHLETIC

	League		FA Cup		League Cup		Other (FA Trophy)	
	Games	Goals	Games	Goals	Games	Goals	Games	Goals
1998-99	30	2	4	-	-	-	-	-
1999-00	34 (2)	1	3	1	1 (1)	-	1	-
2000-01	22 (3)	4	1 (1)	-	-	-	-	-
2001-02	24 (3)	2	4	1	-	-	-	-
2002-03	3 (2)	-	-	-	1	-	-	-
2003-04	19 (3)	5	2	-	- (1)	-	-	-
TOTALS	132 (13)	14	14 (1)	2	2 (2)	-	1	-

OVERALL

TOTAL	League		FA Cup		League Cup		Others	
	569 (37)	88	44 (2)	6	45 (2)	6	17	4

TOTAL APPEARANCES
(NOT INCLUDING DONCASTER ROVERS)

676 (+ 41 as Sub)

TOTAL GOALS 104

INTERNATIONAL RECORD:
34 Republic of Ireland Caps, 5 Goals*

Date		Opposition
23/03/88	v Romania	(H) W 2-0 (Friendly)
27/04/88	v Yugoslavia	(H) W 2-0 (Friendly)
22/05/88	v Poland	(H) W 3-1 (Friendly)*
01/06/88	v Norway	(A) D 0-0 (Friendly) sub
16/11/88	v Spain	(A) L 2-0 (World Cup Qualifier)
28/03/90	v Wales	(H) W 1-0 (Friendly)
27/05/90	v Turkey	(A) D 0-0 (Friendly) sub
02/06/90	v Malta	(A) W 3-0 (Friendly)
30/06/90	v Italy	(A) L 1-0 (World Cup Finals) sub
12/09/90	v Morocco	(H) W 1-0 (Friendly) sub
17/10/90	v Turkey	(H) W 5-0 (European Championship Qualifier)
22/05/91	v Chile	(H) D 1-1 (Friendly) *
01/06/91	v USA	(A) D 1-1 (Friendly) sub
11/09/91	v Hungary	(A) W 2-1 (Friendly)
09/06/93	v Latvia	(A) W 2-0 (World Cup Qualifier) sub
13/10/93	v Spain	(H) L 3-1 (World Cup Qualifier) sub*
20/04/94	v Netherlands	(A) W 1-0 (Friendly)
24/05/94	v Bolivia	(H) W 1-0 (Friendly)*
29/05/94	v Germany	(A) W 2-0 (Friendly)
05/06/94	v Czech Republic	(H) L 3-1 (Friendly)
18/06/94	v Italy	(N) W 1-0 (World Cup Finals)
24/06/94	v Mexico	(N) L 2-1 (World Cup Finals)
28/06/94	v Norway	(N) D 0-0 (World Cup Finals)
04/07/94	v Netherlands	(N) L 2-0 (World Cup Finals)
07/09/94	v Latvia	(A) W 3-0 (European Championship Qualifier)

12/10/94	v Liechtenstein	(H) W 4-0 (European Championship Qualifier)
16/11/94	v N. Ireland	(A) W 4-0 (European Championship Qualifier)*
15/02/95	v England	(H) Match Abandoned (Friendly)
29/03/95	v N. Ireland	(A) D 1-1 (European Championship Qualifier)
26/04/95	v Portugal	(H) W 1-0 (European Championship Qualifier)
03/06/95	v Liechtenstein	(A) D 0-0 (European Championship Qualifier)
11/06/95	v Austria	(H) L 3-1 (European Championship Qualifier)
16/09/95	v Austria	(A) L 3-1 (European Championship Qualifier)
13/12/95	v Netherlands	(N) L 2-0 (European Championship Play-Off)

International Record:
Played 34, Won 17, Drawn 7, Lost 9, Abandoned 1